Pedagogies of Collapse

ALSO AVAILABLE FROM BLOOMSBURY

Education, Equality and Justice in the New Normal, edited by Inny Accioly and Donaldo Macedo
Storying our Relationship with Nature, Amanda Fiore and Jing Lin
Freire and Environmentalism, Greg William Misiaszek
Rethinking Education for Sustainable Development, edited by Radhika Iyengar and Ozge Karadag Caman
Ecopedagogy, Greg William Misiaszek
Leadership for Sustainability in Higher Education, Janet Haddock-Fraser, Peter Rands and Stephen Scoffham
Educational Leadership for a More Sustainable World, Mike Bottery

Pedagogies of Collapse

A Hopeful Education for the End of the World as We Know It

GINIE SERVANT-MIKLOS

BLOOMSBURY ACADEMIC
LONDON • NEW YORK • OXFORD • NEW DELHI • SYDNEY

BLOOMSBURY ACADEMIC

Bloomsbury Publishing Plc, 50 Bedford Square, London, WC1B 3DP, UK
Bloomsbury Publishing Inc, 1359 Broadway, New York, NY 10018, USA
Bloomsbury Publishing Ireland, 29 Earlsfort Terrace, Dublin 2, D02 AY28, Ireland

BLOOMSBURY, BLOOMSBURY ACADEMIC and the Diana logo are trademarks of Bloomsbury Publishing Plc

First published in Great Britain 2024
Reprinted 2026

Copyright © Virginie Servant-Miklos, 2024

Virginie Servant-Miklos has asserted her right under the Copyright, Designs and Patents Act, 1988, to be identified as Author of this work.

Cover design by Holly Capper

This work is published open access subject to a Creative Commons Attribution-NonCommercial-NoDerivatives 4.0 International licence (CC BY-NC-ND 4.0, https://creativecommons.org/licenses/by-nc-nd/4.0/). You may re-use, distribute, and reproduce this work in any medium for non-commercial purposes, provided you give attribution to the copyright holder and the publisher and provide a link to the Creative Commons licence.

Bloomsbury Publishing Plc does not have any control over, or responsibility for, any third-party websites referred to or in this book. All internet addresses given in this book were correct at the time of going to press. The author and publisher regret any inconvenience caused if addresses have changed or sites have ceased to exist, but can accept no responsibility for any such changes.

A catalogue record for this book is available from the British Library.

Library of Congress Cataloging-in-Publication Data

Names: Servant, Ginie, author.
Title: Pedagogies of collapse: a hopeful education for the end of the world as we know it / Ginie Servant-Miklos.
Description: London; New York, NY: Bloomsbury Academic, 2024. | Includes bibliographical references and index.
Identifiers: LCCN 2024010989 (print) | LCCN 2024010990 (ebook) | ISBN 9781350400498 (hardback) | ISBN 9781350400481 (paperback) | ISBN 9781350400511 (epub) | ISBN 9781350400504 (ebook)
Subjects: LCSH: Critical pedagogy. | Education–Philosophy. | Environmental degradation. | Psychic trauma in adolescence.
Classification: LCC LC196 .S47 2024 (print) | LCC LC196 (ebook) | DDC 370.11/5–dc23/eng/20240417
LC record available at https://lccn.loc.gov/2024010989
LC ebook record available at https://lccn.loc.gov/2024010990

ISBN: HB: 978-1-3504-0049-8
PB: 978-1-3504-0048-1
ePDF: 978-1-3504-0050-4
eBook: 978-1-3504-0051-1

Typeset by Deanta Global Publishing Services, Chennai, India
Printed and bound in Great Britain

For product safety related questions contact productsafety@bloomsbury.com.

To find out more about our authors and books visit www.bloomsbury.com and sign up for our newsletters.

For Ariane and Tinashe
With gratitude
For the World we knew.
If tomorrow it's gone
At least I shared it with you.

Contents

List of Figures and Tables viii
Preface ix
Foreword xii

Introduction 1

1 Collapse, Climate and Capitalism 11
2 Education in Catastrophic Times 47
3 Reflecting on Collapse 85
4 Experimental Pedagogics 127
5 Imperfect Solidarities 159
6 Learning, Loving, Living in Times of Collapse 197

Notes 229
Index 268

Figure and Tables

Figure

1	Global energy consumption since 1800	38

Tables

1	The XP Project Matrix	145
2	XP Matrix for Course Coordinators Adapted for *The Climate Crisis*	151

Preface

Writing *Pedagogies of Collapse* has been an arduous and emotional journey. After a decade of scientific writing, I was used to the soulless endeavour of journal manuscripts that masks human warmth behind bland professional language. When penning this book for the future of humankind, a plea for the education we deserve in times of collapse, there was nowhere to hide, no choice but to write with passion and etch words from the heart. *Pedagogies of Collapse* is part scientific analysis, part philosophy, part poetic writing and part autobiography, bringing together a decade and a half of experiences as an activist and educator, in the field and in the classroom. I attempted to weave together my lives as a human rights activist, political economy lecturer, psychology researcher and educator into a coherent narrative. In reflecting on my complex journey with education, I revealed myself as inescapably human, fallible, often mistaken, and still searching for answers. I refused easy solutions, binary thinking, fundamentalisms and ideologies of all kinds. I realize that in a polarized world, this puts me in a rather delicate position. I accept that what I have to say will inevitably be disagreeable to some. I hope the words on these pages are seen as an invitation to imperfect dialogues rather than an opening of hostilities.

Writing *Pedagogies of Collapse* was so different from anything else I had done before that I needed the gentle support, constructive critique and encouragement of my colleagues to persevere and see this project through. I am particularly grateful to my critical readers, in no particular order: Prof Hanne Leth Andersen, Prof Diana Dolmans, Dr Daniel Kontowski, Ollie Bream Mackintosh, Prof Derk Loorbach, Prof Rutger Engels, Lene Rachel Andersen, Tim Logan and Jelle Hatenboer. I am honoured and grateful for the foreword gifted to this book by the inimitable Prof Stephen Chan – for this and the encouragement, support and invariably reasonable advice he has given me throughout the years.

PREFACE

I have two women to thank for giving me the courage to abandon the traditional research-focused academic pathway and jump into an impact-first career where books like this are possible: Prof Liesbeth Noordegraaf-Eelens and Prof Semiha Denktas. From the moment we met over a decade ago, they saw me through difficult personal and professional moments and gave me the space and resources to grow and shine.

I'll never forget the people who offered me the chance to work in education when my plans for a career in human rights fell apart: Prof Gordon Redding, who supported my first educational projects, and Prof Henk Schmidt, my erstwhile doctoral supervisor. I was a difficult and unruly student, but I hope I made them proud.

Today, I'm blessed to work in an environment filled with people who care: my undergraduate and graduate students, my colleagues at the *Behavioural Resilience in Action* group at the Erasmus School of Social and Behavioural Sciences and the *Design Impact, Transitions Platform* at Erasmus University Rotterdam; my fellow volunteers at the *FairFight Foundation*; the inspiring educators in the *Global Bildung Network*; you're the reason I look forward to my day, even when it's cold, wet, windy and dark outside (welcome to winter in Holland in times of climate breakdown).

I can only express my gratitude to those whose love saw me through hard times: my long-suffering husband, Zoltan Miklos, my girls, Ariane and Tinashe, my brother Yannick Servant, my soul-sister Tung Tung Chan, and my wonderful friends and colleagues in the Netherlands, UK, France, Denmark, Zimbabwe, Zambia, India and the other four corners of the world where we lived the adventures that inspired this book.

I am grateful for the financial support of the Erasmus Trust Fund, the Erasmus University Open Access Fund and the NRO Comenius Senior Fellowship, which all supported the publication of this book.

Finally, I want to express my gratitude for the existence of Simone de Beauvoir, for the paths she forged, for the revolutionary writing and activism that showed us the way towards imperfect solidarities and for the courage to be queer in a time where this was taboo. She died one month before I was born, so I never got to share a planet with her, but the novels and essays she left behind gave me the courage to write authentically.

In this book, I mention several organizations with which I work or have worked. It is important to clarify that the opinions and perspectives in this volume are strictly my own and do not represent the opinions, perspectives or policies of any of the organizations mentioned.

Foreword

Confronting Collapse

It's perhaps not quite the end of the world if we can all mobilize the learning and passion of Ginie Servant-Miklos. The passion is both a relief and a release from the world of academic writing and its soulless professionalism. But the learning is that of a scholar deeply steeped in philosophy. An admirer of Simone de Beauvoir, Dr Servant-Miklos has produced a book that refuses the formation of women as helpless – the formation of all of us as helpless – in the face of disaster, both social and environmental.

It is an important book, in many ways a new kind of book – deeply personal, deeply learned and deeply committed to going forward on behalf of all equal human beings.

In my Paris retreats, I lived next to de Beauvoir's final apartment in Montparnasse and also next to the cemetery where she is buried. Every morning, a new, long-stemmed rose is laid on the grave. If my own respect for de Beauvoir comes by way of pilgrimage, my paths (plural) have crossed with those of Dr Servant-Miklos in more ways than one. Firstly, as an academic, with a shared history at the University of Kent, then in the world of martial arts, which is simultaneously arcane and a means of fighting back. Back against what? The romantic ancient ethos was against injustice, catastrophe and the collapse of innocent lives.

Dr Servant-Miklos sees lives as agency-bearing and self-agency-directed. She made her academic name with a series of papers scientifically setting out the desirability, and efficacy, of self-directed agential pedagogies. What Paulo Friere located in communities, Servant-Miklos located also in each individual. The search for a just template for all in the world was also the quest for a terrain where there could be a fair fight – where each could go forward, even with struggle, on a terrain which accorded equality to all. Equality and the freedom of the individual agent were expressed scientifically but clearly derived from her burning passion for a just world.

This passion was there even though it recognized that the world in which justice was sought was a world in chaos, not least because that world's biosphere is in danger of great damage, if not collapse. But even to dream in a world of chaos was a revolutionary step. And a very difficult step. Anxiety about both the challenge and the overarching absurdity of the human condition led her to an existential breakdown, from which she emerged by embracing the conditions of love, learning and the taking of large risks. In short, as with de Beauvoir, in agreeing with herself to live in *praxis*. And this meant also living beyond herself in her role as an educator. The classroom was a site of praxis and a site for inculcating praxis.

Race, gender and class, however, pervaded the classroom as determining forces. The struggle to learn was often a struggle against structural forces. Learning had to continue, be forced through, even if it was a learning in despair. But the work of Freire, to an extent also the Frankfurt School of Critical Pedagogy, helped. It led to a practice and praxis of learning in dialogue in which each voice was valued. And even teachers had a praxiological duty to revolt and to rise up. This book, which Servant-Miklos has written, is part of that rising up.

It's hard to rise up. And so is commitment to continuing action in coherent programmes. Pain binds us in doing so. But love binds us too. So does hope.

Dr Servant-Miklos's work in a philanthropic organization she founded in 2015, and of which she is still the Chair, the FairFight Foundation, does not feature as much in this book as I myself would have hoped. In Rotterdam, her home base, but also in Zimbabwe, Zambia and India, the Foundation empowers vulnerable young women, including those without families, literally to fight for themselves. This is where her karate training comes in and, to this cause, she has enlisted international champions who travel with her and her close colleagues to far-off places to support girls and young women for whom the world so often fails to care.

The case in India is instructive for its challenges and its contradictions. Varanasi, where the charity's Indian programme is located, was once called Banaras, an ancient city through which the holy river Ganges flows. It is the site of a very old university where de Beauvoir's old philosophical sparring partner, Andre Malraux, once hoped that East and West might meet in shared learning – Malraux also being the archetypical praxiological person, fighting in revolutions and rebellions on many fronts: China, Spain and in the French Resistance. But Varanasi is also the most violent city in India – quite an achievement – when it comes to women's rights. Female abuse and modern slavery are writ large, a gendered venality beside the river of holiness – which is also highly contaminated to the point of toxicity. In a way, Varanasi is a microcosm of the global condition Servant-Miklos challenges – with the recognition of despair but with a refusal to succumb to it. With love, learning and praxis; with passion and with philosophy; to deliver what de Beauvoir called at least an interim mercy to the world. In this book, we see a true daughter of de Beauvoir.

Stephen Chan OBE, Professor of World Politics
SOAS University of London, UK

Introduction

We are staring collapse in the face. The resurgence of large-scale warfare and pandemic disease are flickering distress signals of a global system rapidly entering a spiral of crises. In a hyper-connected world, this unravelling is live-streamed for all to see: biblical fires swallowing entire towns from Hawaii to Greece, floods tearing down buildings and bridges from Norway to China, bodies piling up in morgues during Covid-19, cities torn to shreds by Russian shelling in Ukraine and Israeli shelling in Gaza . . . we are no longer safe from history. One emergency after another steals away the promise of uninterrupted progress touted by techno-optimists and mires humanity in a repeating cycle of trauma and grief, from which people emerge numb at best and traumatized at worst, if they emerge at all. The usual patterns of oppression continue to play out: people already marginalized by socio-economic forces, gender, ethnicity, disability, among other factors, feel the brunt of the pain and have the least resources to cope. However, with the pandemic, the wars in Ukraine and the Middle East and breathtaking heatwaves baking multiple parts of the world simultaneously, summer after summer, there is finally a sense that none of us will escape unscathed as collapse gathers pace underfoot.

What a time to be young! Those born in the early noughties grew up with the promise of a bright liberal, meritocratic future, imbued with a work hard, play hard ethos. They were promised a linear trajectory from school to university, a well-paying job, a house, car, kids and a well-earned retirement. Today, the public markers of success still involve displaying a comfortable, stylish home base from which one launches into tantalizing trips in niche destinations around the world. This is not just a Global North phenomenon; from the townships of Harare to the narrow streets of Varanasi, social media globalizes the

Millennial Dream. Those who can't afford it still aspire to it and play the part for the front-facing phone camera. But now, the young come of age in a world of dissonance, still singing from the neoliberal hymn sheet but fraying at the seams. Oz-like leaders urge them on-mass into university halls, feeding them promises of eternal growth, social ascendancy and progress, chiding them not to look behind the curtain. But with every viral variant, every bomb that drops, every summer at 40°C, the dissonance rings louder in the classroom. Try as we might, educators know: we can't keep doing this forever, shouting abstract formulas over the sound of mortar fire. Fukuyama was wrong: we can't keep teaching as though history has ended.[1]

Before the storm

I taught *The Climate Crisis* for the first time in early 2020. I was given the coordinatorship of this course the year after finishing a tumultuous post-doctoral research position in sustainability education in Denmark. It was a trying time for me personally and professionally, but the chaos at home and work was compounded by a severe bout of eco-depression (Chapter 3). I knew about the climate crisis before my postdoc, but this was the first time I was confronted with the full facts. Holding my six-month-old daughter in my arms, I felt a chasm open between our willfully ignorant present and the horrific future emerging between the lines of the IPCC reports. I read far and wide, from atmospheric sciences to political economy, systems engineering to philosophy, economics to psychology. I discovered *Collapsology*, an intellectual movement in France, my home country, literally named after collapse.[2] I tried to sound the alarm around me, at home, at work and in my classes, but felt rebuffed everywhere. Students shuddered in horror, then fell back into denial within months of taking my courses. Some colleagues met my concerns with predictable claims that technology would save us, others with a philosophical shrug of the shoulders. My husband, a down-to-earth engineer who lived his early life under the Ceaușescu regime in Communist Romania and won passage into the middle class through hard work and emigration (a poster-boy for capitalism, really), chided me for obsessing over forces outside our control. Problem-solver by nature, he channelled my existential concerns into concrete steps towards resilience: we left a 29th-floor apartment in the centre of The Hague for a suburban house in a neighbourhood shared with a non-negligible population of goats, ducks and chickens. He helped me build a permaculture garden in our backyard, with a greenhouse, vegetable beds, water collectors and composting bins. We put solar panels on the roof, green roofs on every flat surface, acquired a small EV and e-bikes, insulating sun blinds on every window and a heat pump to replace the gas heating system. People around us thought it was endearingly middle class. I knew it was laughable in the context of a country almost entirely below sea level.

Then the first Dutch summer at 40°C came, shortly followed by the second. There were Covid, catastrophic floods in the Ardennes and Storm Eunice, the most powerful storm ever recorded in The Netherlands, causing 500 million euros in damages, followed within days by the Russian invasion of Ukraine, bringing the cost of a litre of petrol close to 2.30 euros. Faced with the toll of Covid and staggering energy bills, my university went from being cash-positive to being 25 million euros in the red within the space of five years. Around me, people seemed shocked, fumbling for ways to mitigate the damages and waiting for some kind of normality to return. But all this was eminently predictable – perhaps not the specific when or how, but the underlying trend towards pandemics, chaotic weather, resource scarcity and war were writ large for those who read in the right places. There will be no normal to return to. I take no satisfaction and claim no credit in having been right about this: I was channelling the warnings of better informed scientists, and I desperately wanted them to be wrong.

The storm

By the time I taught the third edition of *The Climate Crisis* in 2022, the world was a different place. Students came to class shell-shocked from two years of lockdowns. As we fumbled with hybrid learning to account for the persistently high Covid caseload, at least once a week, for the duration of the course, a student had a mental breakdown in class. Then, bombs began raining down on Ukraine.

Many students suffered from serious dissonance. My course confronted them with the reality of collapse, already engaged and yet to come. I called upon them to stare the unforgiving chaos of the world in the face. Then they walked to their next class on corporate finance and floated off into tidy abstractions. At that time, I worked at a progressive liberal arts institution; many courses openly discussed climate, coloniality and patriarchy. Most of my colleagues voted left of the Green-Left Party. If *our* students felt dissonance, what did students experience in programmes that didn't address the system's failures? I conducted a study on the subject during my postdoc, and the answer comes in different shades of denial and bargaining.[3] Students told themselves that someone, usually Elon Musk, would save them from the environmental apocalypse. They believed someone out there must have the answer; the system could not fail. Why? Because they invested years of their lives into an education system that serves the singular purpose of preparing cogs for the hungry market machine under the guise of liberal meritocracy. Accepting that this machine is broken and could fall apart at any moment asks for a painful reconsideration of the twenty-year sacrifice they just made. Most students aren't ready for that.

From all the intense moments of the course over the years, the sentence that struck my students hardest was: 'the future you were promised, it's not happening, that future is gone'. It's important to clarify this phrase because of the enormous emotional work it calls upon students to perform. I did not mean that humanity will die out within the next century. Though extinction is, frightfully, a possibility that cannot be discounted, I do not think that this is a likely scenario. I also did not mean for them to give up on their plans and dreams. Plans and dreams come in many forms, and dreaming is still possible, nay, necessary, in a world in collapse. What I will show in Chapter 1 is that the social contract has been broken. The liberal democratic system cannot fulfil its end of the linear learn-work-retire bargain under conditions of collapse. At the risk of paraphrasing Karl Marx, the welfare state, market economy and liberal democracy trifecta is doomed by its internal contradictions. These aren't abstract contradictions; rather, limits to growth are hard physical facts. How much of organized human functioning can be salvaged from the wreckage in the short and medium term is up for debate. But a future premised upon conditions of economic growth, peace and stability is, by the very physical realities of our biosphere, impossible. So dream we must, but dream in a world in chaos. Therein lies the challenge.

Riding the storm

Covid shattered the illusions of business-as-usual. It tore a hole in our collective dissonance and showed us how vulnerable we truly are: the unthinkable was not only possible but increasingly probable. Like many people, I suffered through Covid on the edge of sanity, juggling working-from-home, childcare and a total loss of support for my chronic illness, fibromyalgia. Three months without seeing a physiotherapist when you're in constant pain is a special form of unpleasantness. My husband and I finished 2021 on our knees, burnt out, battling depression, stress and isolation. When the Dutch government, cowering before the incoming wave of Omicron, announced another complete lockdown two weeks before Christmas, we gave in and took medical leave from work. I finally let go of my scientific career, a casualty of two years of mismanaged chaos in an irredeemably sick system.

Despite the hardship, I realized that in times of turmoil, there is a poetic sensuality in the moment. Stripped from artifice, in a world in collapse, the moment confronts us with what truly matters. In the urgency of the present, email battles with journal editors over minute revisions to articles lost their meaning. I am an educator, an activist, a builder and using anything less than the full capacity of those skills to meet the moment felt like a waste. My purpose is to change people's lives with words and deeds – in a present in collapse, with a future in jeopardy, nothing short of complete commitment can meet the moment.

In this book, I explain how I built Experimental Pedagogics (XP), an educational meta-framework to guide young people through learning in times of collapse. I piloted the first XP programme in Russia, of all places, in a bastion of liberal education ensconced in a stiff post-soviet state university. I soon followed up with a pilot programme in Holland, taught entirely online in lockdown with a shaky Wi-fi connection from a neighbour's garage at unhealthy hours of the evening. I remember walking home in the dark just before the Covid-curfew time, buoyed by the sensation of doing something that mattered. I also describe how the pandemic moved me to lean into my commitments with the *FairFight Foundation*, a charity that I founded in 2015 to support vulnerable girls and women in Africa and Asia through martial arts and educational support, such that we doubled in size since 2020. Premised on the book's core concept of 'imperfect solidarities', these deeds gave me the will to fight on.

I admit, the fight takes its toll. I'm often tired and in pain, and I still don't feel like it's enough. But as the threat of nuclear annihilation looms over us once again and climate chaos engulfs the planet, concrete acts of solidarity, imperfect as they may be, bind me to the moment, shake me from the funk of despair, call me into the thick of life. Holding on to the living in times of death is fundamentally an act of love, and love is a commitment to the present when the future is at stake. Love binds us to each other when the storm pulls us apart.

Love comes with a price tag. I resigned from my post in Russia on the first day of the Ukrainian war, penning words of hope and sorrow to my students on the way out. Some replied, hearts wrung tight, hopes dim, but not dead. I think of them often. Just like I think of the girls we lost to the lockdowns in India and Zimbabwe – married off or disappeared. I carry the grief of their loss with me. I want to feel it fully.

After the storm

We have left the peaceful climactic conditions of the Holocene. Given the climate system's inertia, the climate of 2024, hostile as it felt to us in the moment, is already lost. There is no technology, human genius, CO_2-sucking machine or amount of tree-planting large enough to return us to the gentle interglacial conditions within which humanity thrived. Twenty million years hence, a planet populated by foreign creatures will flourish and life will adapt, as it always does. But in this sense, the storm will not end within the timespan left to humanity on this pale blue dot. In this storm, there is no 'after' that looks anything like the 'before'.

However, the process of collapse which we have entered will end, either when there is nothing left to contract or when a sufficient outward push ends the contraction and begins a cycle of expansion anew. We have a moral obligation to push the balance of history in the latter's direction. We can lean towards an expansion not based on the pursuit of endless material growth but one which pulls us in and draws us out like breath in a regulated relationship with the biosphere. It will be an 'after' marked by loss, especially for those still around to remember the 'before'. To them, the 'after' will always have the bitter taste of squandered opportunity. With everything we had at our disposal, we could have told a story so much brighter, fairer, more plentiful.

I will be among those taking the memory of the 'before' and the sorrow for what could have been to the grave. I have seen over forty lands of this Earth, dined with millionaires and paupers, criss-crossed mountain ranges, deserts and forests in search of meaning. Blessed with solid academic capabilities, nurtured by expensive international schools and accumulating extensive amounts of cultural capital from a young age, I bought meritocratic ideology wholesale. I didn't question or seek to redress the injustice of my good fortune until my mid-twenties. By then, I had already burned more CO_2 than the lifetime consumption of an entire Zimbabwean village. If the ticket to heaven should be paid in carbon coins, I'm broke. Don't believe in neo-medieval creative carbon accounting. This isn't the Middle Ages; you can't buy your way back to righteousness with favours (or carbon compensation certificates). For those Global North dwellers of my generation, our footprint is here to stay, and we'd better learn to live with that weight on our conscience.

Our mission, as the stewards of this planet while the 'after' generation comes of age, is to face our grief and say, 'We can do better now'. Every tonne of CO_2, every square kilometre of forest and every species count. I disagree with the recent formulation of climate scientists: there is no 'end game' in matters of global heating.[4] If we lose the battle for 1.5°C, as is all but certain, then we must fight for 2°C. And if that battle is lost, as looks increasingly likely, we cannot give in until we have reined in warming to 2.5°C. Make no mistake, we will be striving for the rest of our lives. Perhaps this seems like too daunting a prospect for us to contemplate. But humans were not cut from the cloth of comfort and idleness; we are born strivers. In strife, we find our greatest selves: an ingenious, collaborative species blessed with empathy, social bonding and care.

Finally, while the 'after' with all its loss and grief stares at us from the other side of a frightening storm of collapse, perhaps it is worth pausing with gratitude for what we had and for the opportunity to rid ourselves of those things that held us down.

I am grateful for modern medicine, without which I would not have been born or survived the birth of my daughter; for the plenty this world has offered me since birth; for never having known true hunger; for the opportunity to live and love in a world more open to queerness of all kinds than at any point in history; for the chains that women before me broke so I could be free; for the vastest bounty of knowledge ever available to humanity at my fingertips; for the beauty of art, music, dance and poetry, and for the words passed on to me so I could pen my own.

I am grateful for the opportunity to rethink a society free of neoliberal capitalism, racism and patriarchy; to end selfish individualism and reforge imperfect solidarities; to find meaning in people, not things; to live a life that amounts to more than the learn-work-retire mantra.

About this book

This book is an apogee of education's power to overcome grief and trauma, a love letter to the young and their guiding lights in a chaotic future, and a think-with philosophical, psychological and pedagogical guide for overwhelmed educators. It's addressed to educators of all kinds in times of collapse: K–12 school teachers, home-schooling parents, sports coaches, university professors, teaching-college students, after-school tutors . . . anyone who has ever shared their knowledge and guided others, you're invited to this conversation, as are all students and young people with a passion for safeguarding our future, and policymakers and politicians with the power to deliver the education system we deserve. It represents fifteen years of praxis as an activist educator-scholar, a decade of scientific research, philosophical thinking and lessons learned in the fray. *Pedagogies of Collapse* is an invitation to mourn the world we are leaving behind. Healthy grieving is an inexorable part of learning in an age of crises. But they are also a call to action: the future will not build itself, willy-nilly.

Before we begin, I want to speak to my fellow educators' hope for concrete tools to address collapse in their classrooms: I will do my best to share some of the knowledge and practices developed in my own classrooms. But though I do explore relevant teaching approaches in the chapter 'Experimental Pedagogics', this book is not essentially about teaching methodologies. Rather, I wanted to offer educators a whole-system perspective on education: Where did the current system collapse come from? Why is the education system failing? How does collapse impact students, educators and their learning? Why are reform movements flailing? Where do we go from here? In the years I have been training teachers, I've always believed there was more power in giving trainees a deep interdisciplinary understanding of the history, context and systems they operate in than sticking to step-by-step methods. This is also born from my belief that I do not hold methodological answers: I am not an educational guru. However, with the right systems knowledge and framework for developing new forms of learning, educators can create methods of their own, suited to their classrooms and context.

We're going on an exciting intellectual ride together: you will dive with me into the science of planetary collapse, the history of our education system's failure, the psychology of our students' grief and existential despair and the sociology of our reform movements' incapacitation. My wish is that you come away from this book with a powerful thinking framework and a deep understanding of the moment education is living through. I hope this empowers you to build your own relevant, contextualized responses to the crises, carried by a powerful combination of rage and hope. On the other side of collapse, futures worth striving for are still possible. I hope this book provides a thinking framework through the storm.

1

Collapse, Climate and Capitalism

Before we tackle pedagogies of collapse, we should agree on a definition and a basic explanation of the mechanisms of collapse. The word 'collapse' triggers our imagination in wild ways: Are we talking about the Apocalypse, human extinction, the end of capitalism, the Third World War or all of the above? Is this a regional or global event? Will it happen quickly or slowly? It's important to outline what we're talking about if we are to find a way to teach through collapse.

A number of writers and thinkers have put their minds to the question of collapse, offering a range of angles from which to explore the problem. If you type 'collapse' into Google, you will probably come across the work of the American historian Jared Diamond, who studied the fall of ancient empires to draw conclusions about our current predicament. He linked civilizational collapse to twelve interlocking causes, from unsustainable population growth to resource strangleholds and water scarcity.[1] However, if you're looking for the heart of thinking on collapse, you will find it in France. A group of thinkers known by the *franglais* moniker 'collapsologistes' has assembled in Paris, coalescing around former environment minister Yves Cochet and his Momentum Institute.[2] This influential group of public intellectuals includes (though some would not use the label as such) astronomer Aurélien Barrau, environmentalist Cyril Dion, energy planner Jean-Marc Jancovici and agro-engineers Gauthier Chapelle, Pablo Servigne and Raphaël Stevens. In their best-seller *How Everything Could Collapse*, Servigne and Stevens use the metaphor of a car veering into a wall to dissect the biophysical, economic, political and social determinants of collapse.[3] They give a pessimistic outlook for the near-future of thermo-industrial civilization: all signs point to imminent collapse, followed by widespread hunger and energy shortages in a depleted world.

Jancovici, a darling of the French public media, focuses on the role of energy systems in determining the possibilities and limitations of humanity. He hammers home the historical link between energy supply collapse and geopolitical disasters, including the oil crises of the 1970s, the Great Recession of 2008, the Arab Spring and the Syrian civil war. He bluntly warns of a coming energy shortage, triggering a potentially fatal threat to peace, democracy and the welfare state.[4]

My own approach to collapse is inspired by my compatriots, but as a former lecturer in political economy, I also draw upon classic and modern economic thinking. In this chapter, we're going to look at collapse from the standpoints of planetary boundaries, socio-economic processes and geopolitics. Strap in: this is going to be a bumpy ride. I'm going to cite a lot of facts and numbers; all my sources are listed in the endnotes, for those interested in digging deeper.

Collapse: Planetary boundaries

Let's begin with a devastating truth: we are living through the sixth mass extinction event of planet Earth, and its primary cause is human activity. Never before in the 4.6 billion years of existence of the Earth-system has the biosphere collapsed so fast, so comprehensively. Even the dinosaurs needed a couple hundred thousand years to disappear. Humans are wiping out life on Earth more effectively than a meteorite.

Welcome to the 'Anthropocene', the *Age of Man*, a great leap off a giant cliff where we had better hope for a couple of branches along the way to break our fall.[5] We begin our investigation of global collapse with a tour of the planetary boundaries identified by the Stockholm Resilience Centre: biosphere integrity, climate change, novel entities, stratospheric ozone depletion, atmospheric aerosol loading, biochemical flows, freshwater use and land-system change, six of which we have already crossed into the 'unsafe' zone.[6] I had to update my manuscript twice while writing this chapter to reflect new scientific data from the Stockholm Resilience Centre that quantified the transgression of two planetary boundaries in 2022 and 2023: novel entities and freshwater use.

Biodiversity collapse

We begin our tour of planetary boundaries with the devastating collapse of biodiversity on Earth. Biodiversity is the foundation of the Earth-system – it holds the whole thing together. Each species in the ecosystem plays a role in maintaining the system as a whole, providing resilience against environmental shocks and softening the blow of chronic environmental degradation. By destroying biodiversity, we are cutting the parachute as we jump off the climate cliff.

Human-induced damage to plant and animal life is staggering. The World Wildlife Fund's *Living Planet* report of 2022 indicates that on average, 70 per cent of all vertebrate animals, including mammals, birds, fish, reptiles and amphibians, have died (as a percentage change of total population) since my parents were teenagers, casualties of land conversion, loss of habitat, unregulated hunting and poaching and pollution.[7] Insect populations in Europe have crashed by 70 per cent, likely victims of pesticides and habitat loss (they have likely crashed elsewhere but Europe has solid data).[8] Freshwater species populations have collapsed by 88 per cent.[9] Biodiversity hotspots in the rainforests of Central and South America are the worst affected, with staggering population drops of 94 per cent (let that sink in).[10] Of all of the mammals left on this planet, 60 per cent are livestock, 36 per cent are humans and only 4 per cent are wild, including everything from rats to blue whales. Of all the birds left on the planet, 70 per cent are domesticated poultry and only 30 per cent are wild.[11] The Intergovernmental Science-Policy Platform on Biodiversity and Ecosystems Services (IPBES) report of 2019 warned that one million species are currently facing extinction (about 13 per cent of all species), with the current extinction rate of species 200 times above the pre-industrial norm.[12]

Although climate change plays an increasing role in biodiversity loss, especially in the oceans, the bulk of the collapse of the last thirty years can be directly traced to human activity. There are now more human-built materials by mass than the entire natural biosphere – every tree, every bush, every bird and every flower in the world is now outweighed by concrete, steel and plastic.[13] Each year, we pour concrete over a surface equivalent to the size of England, accounting for 4–8 per cent of all global carbon emissions.[14] When we're not suffocating soil with cement, the agro-industrial complex is tearing down vast swathes of forests. An area equivalent to the entire surface of the Americas, North and South, is currently used for rearing livestock – one of the world's most prominent sources of methane emissions.[15] We are currently using a continent's worth of land to produce something that is largely superfluous to human needs, the overconsumption of which is actively harmful to human health, and a massive driver of climate change and biosphere destruction. Unlike energy use and transport, which are difficult to cut down, we could stop eating beef and pork overnight with no major impact on overall human well-being, yet meat production has tripled in the last fifty years and shows no sign of slowing.[16] Increased wealth generally correlates with increased demand for meat and dairy, with the bulk of recent increases coming from Asia.

Ending global meat consumption would immediately release vast amounts of land currently used for cereal production for animal feed to the wild. As of 2013, 41 per cent of all cereals produced worldwide were used for animal feed, and a further 11 per cent were used for biofuels.[17] The biggest growth in feed production over the last twenty years occurred in Brazil, where poor regulation and support from the erstwhile Bolsonaro regime enabled farmers to illegally log and burn, converting rainforest to cereal production.[18] As a result, the Amazon basin is now emitting more carbon than it stores, and scientists believe it is tipping towards savannah conditions, taking the world's richest biodiversity hotspots along with it.[19]

Climate collapse

We now move to climate change, the environmental topic which gets the most media attention because of the doomsday predictions it (rightly) triggers. Given politicians' tunnel-visioning on climate change, it may surprise you that despite warming the planet up by 1.45°C since pre-industrial times in 2023 (with a running average warming close to 1.2°C),[20] this is not one of the boundaries that we have crossed to the point of no return . . . yet. But we are well on our way to doing so. If the United Nations Environment Programme report of 2021 is anything to go by, current pledges take us into a future warmed at 2.7°C by the end of the century.[21] And these are only pledges: countries have consistently failed to stick to those ever since the Paris Climate Accord was signed in 2015. Our actual emission trajectory takes us closer to a 2.8°C increase with an upper range of 3.3°C. This is an absolutely devastating global temperature increase that could lead to 10°C of average warming at the poles, the terminal decline of glaciers, arctic and coral ecosystems, the collapse of rain forest ecosystems, the end of reliable farming seasons, stronger fires, floods, storms and heatwaves, and global sea level rises that would drown large coastal cities within our lifetimes and, given that I'm typing these words from The Hague, pretty much everything around me, including my house.[22] The consequences for humanity would be devastating: potentially 1.2 billion climate refugees by 2050,[23] the return of famine, heat waves that could literally cook people to death by breaching the limit of 35°C 'wet bulb' temperature.[24] If you want an idea of what that might look like, climate fiction author Kim Stanley Robinson gave a gruesome account of a deadly future heat wave that kills twenty million people in India in *Ministry for the Future* – at the current pace of emissions, it's not a question of if, but when and where.[25]

Current predictions, frightening as they are, represent an optimistic scenario in which we do not trigger feedback loops that send us careening towards what climate scientist Will Steffen called a 'hothouse Earth'.[26] These feedback loops include melting the permafrost, collapsing the Greenland ice-sheet, disappearing rainforests and other self-reinforcing mechanisms that, by releasing carbon dioxide and methane into the atmosphere, accelerate global heating towards a potential unliveable 'hothouse' state that could reach 6.0°C–8.0°C of warming. If that happens, it's game over for humanity and pretty much all things currently sharing the planet's surface with us. Evolution will have to start from scratch. But, as I will explain later on, there is a silver lining to our current predicament: evidence points to civilizational collapse before we trigger a total extinction event, halting us before we cross over the hothouse threshold. It's not going to be pleasant, but it beats dying in a pressure cooker.

What makes the crossing of this boundary particularly galling is that the scientific community has known what was afoot for over a century. In 1899, atmospheric scientist T. C. Chamberlin declared:

> The general results assignable to a greatly increased or a greatly reduced quantity of atmospheric carbon dioxide and water may be summarized as follows: An increase, by causing a larger absorption of the sun's radiant energy, raises the average temperature, while a reduction lowers it.[27]

Thirteen years before the sinking of the Titanic, scientists were already raising the alarm about the impact of industrial carbon production on the Earth-system. There followed 120 years of denial and dithering, copiously funded by the fossil fuel industry and right-wing lobby groups even as their own scientific calculations gave an accurate reading of the unfolding catastrophe.[28] Pitiful attempts to address the problem in the global arena resulted in much talk and little action, and twenty-eight COP conferences later, the latest of which was headed by the president of a national oil company, we are staring down CO_2 readings of 417 parts per million, and CH_4 readings of over 1900 parts per billion. The safe limit for CO_2 concentrations for a stable climate is estimated at around 350 parts per million, and since CO_2 takes tens of thousands of years to break down in the atmosphere, at the scale of human history, any extra CO_2 pumped into the atmosphere from here onwards will compound the problem. Methane comes with good news and bad news. The good news is that it breaks down within decades, so a considerable drop in methane emissions would have an impact within one generation. The bad news is that it is between twenty and eighty times more effective at trapping heat than CO_2, – so releasing vast quantities of methane all at once could tip the planet into the hothouse trajectory. The vast majority of Earth's methane is trapped under the ocean and beneath the frozen patches of the planet – those same patches that are currently melting as the

Earth warms. Methane is highly flammable – release enough of it into the air at once, and you get spontaneous combustion and super-thunder storms.

This was usually the point during my opening lecture 'The Climate Crisis', where the first breakdowns would occur. So hang in there, because we still have a long way to go, and it's not looking good.

Chemical pollution

Unlike the climate crisis, which unfolds over longer periods of time, chemical pollution presents immediate risks to human health, a visible eye-sore in the form of plastic pollution and media storms surrounding chemical poisoning scandals. Chemical pollution is a broad category comprising a range of ills, including microplastics, Polyfluoroalkyl Substances (PFAS), arsenic, lead, chromium, mercury and pesticides. Scientists determined that we crossed into the danger zone as recently as 2022, but in fairness, this is probably a quirk related to the difficulty in quantifying some of these limits. How much plastic is safe to ingest? We don't know yet, but we likely crossed the limit much earlier.

Combatting plastic pollution has been the rallying battle cry of environmental organizations since the release of shocking documentaries like *A Plastic Ocean* and *Blue Planet II*.[29] Around the time these films were released, Western consumers, including me, started bringing cotton totes on their weekly shopping trips, sipping iced Frappuccinos from reusable mugs with paper straws, and dutifully disposing of plastic containers in recycling bins. None of this made much of a difference, since 46 per cent of ocean plastic pollution comes from discarded fishing gear,[30] and a large portion of the rest is transport packaging that gets discarded before it reaches the consumer.[31] Plastics recycling is a vast pyramid scheme in which the buck gets passed until a nation too poor to turn away shiploads of Western trash dumps it onto unsuspecting rural communities. First it was China, then, when they slammed the docks shut in 2017, our soiled plastic was shipped massively to Malaysia, Turkey and Indonesia.[32] When they had enough of being our dumping ground, Western nations finally re-routed garbage ships to Laos, Bangladesh and Ethiopia and other poor nations, where much of that plastic now ends up, until storms and rains wash it into the ocean.[33] But ask any Western consumer what environmental action means to them, and they will point to their recycling container. The truth is that only 9 per cent of the plastic produced since the dawn of plastics has been recycled – or I should say, downcycled, since even when it is recycled, most plastic can only be used to make inferior quality products.[34] Ninety-one per cent of the plastic ever produced on Earth is still out there somewhere, waiting to break down into microplastics that will contaminate every remote desert, mountain summit and deepest trench of the ocean,[35] entering the human body even before birth, through the placenta,[36] leeching by the trillions of particles into babies' stomachs through contaminated bottles,[37] and so forth. We don't know the full extent of the damage caused by microplastics on the human body, but one thing is becoming abundantly clear: phthalates, a type of particle leeched into the environment by decomposing plastic, act as an endocrine inhibitor. This disrupts the human reproductive cycle, particularly in males. Male fertility in Western countries has dropped by 60 per cent in two generations (that's not to say it hasn't dropped elsewhere, but we don't have the data yet).[38] The impact of phthalates appears to be transmittable: if a male whose reproductive development has been hampered by phthalates succeeds in having male offspring (through IVF, for instance), then their phthalate concentration is passed on, only for the offspring to build up their own phthalate count on top of this.

Given all this, progress on plastics looked promising. Then the pandemic happened, and never to waste a good crisis, the petrochemical and plastic lobby saw a golden opportunity to burnish their tarnished image. Plastic is safer! Plastic is cleaner! And suddenly, the disposable plastic-coated cups, that only three years before were on the way out, were touted as the responsible, sanitary choice.[39] Billions of plastic masks made their way into the waterways.[40]

So here we are: at the current rate, the total cumulative amount of plastics produced on this planet is set to double by 2050. Don't let the Ocean Cleanup crew, laudable as their efforts are, lull you into techno-optimism: the vast majority of the Great Pacific Garbage Patch is made up of microplastics, and we are never getting it out of the water.[41] In twenty million years, the Anthropocene will be fossilized into the geological record with a layer of plastic among the rocks.

Just as we thought we were getting a grip on chemical pollution, enter PFAS, also known as 'forever chemicals'.[42] The murky history of PFAS was dramatized in *Dark Waters*, a film nominated for the Cinema for Peace Award in 2020 for its depiction of DuPont Chemical's cover-up of unregulated toxic waste dumps in their community's waterways in West Virginia.[43] PFAS are a class of chemicals used in the production of non-stick surfaces, from pots and pans to coats and industrial applications. PFAS are just about everywhere, and like their nickname suggests, they never break down, including in human blood.[44] Therefore, PFAS concentrations increase over time. By the time scientists cottoned onto the danger of PFAS contamination, they could no longer find any uncontaminated blood on Earth to use as a control.[45] They had to delve into the archives and haul out blood samples that dated from the Korean War to find clean blood.[46] This means that you, me, your kids and everyone you know are currently contaminated with PFAS. Unlike plastics, PFAS pollution is invisible, which makes it harder to address. There is also a regulatory problem: there are so many different chemicals that fall under this category that as soon as one gets regulated, companies switch to another that falls outside the legal framework but has the same effect.[47] The science is still coming in on the impact of PFAS on human health, but the data currently points to stunted growth and development, thyroid disorders, cancer, chronic inflammation and kidney and heart disease.[48] That's a hefty price to pay for non-stick pans and waterproof jackets.

Ocean collapse

The oceans and rivers are dying. The main causes of this collapse are agricultural runoff, industrial pollution, climate change and overfishing.

Agricultural runoff in rivers makes its way to the coasts, fostering algal blooms that create large estuary and coastal dead zones, where plant and animal life is choked. For instance, in 2021, the low-oxygen zone in the Gulf of Mexico was about the size of New Jersey, rendering four million acres of ocean floor uninhabitable to plant and animal species.[49] Climate change makes the problem much worse: warm water holds less oxygen than cold water, while increasing the metabolism of marine animals so that they require more oxygen. It's a lose-lose for marine life.

Chemical pollution from industrial runoff is extremely damaging to coral, coastal and freshwater ecosystems. I have seen this firsthand: having visited the Holy City of Varanasi in India several times since 2016, the state of the Ganges shocks me every time. The river, which provides water to 40 per cent of India's population, is so contaminated with runoff from tanneries, chemical plants, textile mills, slaughterhouses and vast quantities of human excrement that it is essentially an ecological dead zone.[50] Yet its special role in the Hindu religion as the place where the cycle of reincarnations can be broken by burning the bodies of the departed on the *ghats*, means that seventy million people come to bathe in the contaminated waters every year, adding food, aluminium and plastic waste from religious offerings to the waters.[51] During the Delta wave of the Covid-19 pandemic, hundreds of corpses were found floating in the river as more bodies arrived by the day than could be safely burned.[52] As bad as the situation of the Ganges is, it is hardly a unique case in aquatic ecosystem collapse. Large damming projects, agricultural overuse and drought have dried up the Aral Sea in Russia, and the Chad Lake at the border between Chad, Cameroon and Nigeria almost entirely. In both cases, over 90 per cent of the water's surface has disappeared, robbing millions of people of their livelihood.[53] In Chad, the disappearance of the lake has been linked to political unrest and violence, intertwining with the complex history of the Boko Haram terrorist group.[54] These well-known disasters are two among a litany of ecological catastrophes resulting from damming, mining, industrial activity and other facets of human industry that threaten the annihilation of freshwater systems.

The inhabitants of the oceans are under extreme threat from climate change and human activity. Corals are first in line of fire, with the death of 75 per cent of the world's corals predicted by the IPCC at 1.5°C of warming, and 99 per cent at 2°C.[55] Bleaching events occur when water heats by just 1°C for four weeks or more. Corals respond to this threat by casting out their colourful symbiotic zooanthellae, turning the coral white. Corals can recover from bleaching if water temperatures return to normal, but as the climate warms, more frequent bleaching events end up killing stressed corals entirely, at which point their structures are colonized by algae. For instance, the Great Barrier Reef in Australia suffered two mass bleaching events back-to-back in 2016 and 2017, with coral mortality of 22 per cent.[56] In April 2022, the journal *Science* published a research article evaluating the overall risk to ocean life due to climate change: we are staring down a cataclysmic extinction event comparable to 'the Great Dying', a mass extinction which occurred 250 million years ago in which 96 per cent of species on Earth disappeared.[57]

Climate change is not the only culprit; fish stocks have been declining all over the world due to overfishing, with the UN Food and Agriculture Organisation estimating that just under 35 per cent of fish stocks are overexploited; a number increasing over time.[58] In the last ten years, an alarming phenomenon has emerged: gigantic Chinese fishing fleets comprising several hundreds of vessels have been prowling the oceans, including around biodiversity hotspots like the Galápagos Islands where they logged 73,000 hours of fishing in one month, plundering everything they could find, destroying the sea bed with trawlers, then moving on to another area.[59] According to Christopher Pala, researcher for Foreign Policy, China's assault on the oceans is part of a geopolitical strategy to subdue weaker nations: its fishing practices in North Korean and West African waters deprive already malnourished populations of vital protein, thus increasing their dependence on Chinese investments.[60] This aggressive expansion is not surprising, considering that territorial Chinese fishing stocks are so depleted that one study ranked Chinese fisheries among the worst managed in the world.[61]

For all of these reasons, it is estimated that by 2050, there will be more plastic than fish in the oceans by weight.[62] The loss of ocean life is likely to cause the collapse of communities who rely on fishing and coral ecosystems for survival – mostly poorer, indigenous communities of colour around the world.

Wilderness collapse

The situation of land ecosystems is precarious. In the last two decades alone, 2.7 million square kilometres of wilderness has been lost to human activity such as mining, logging and agriculture.[63] That is 10 per cent of the total amount of wilderness left in the world. To be clear: humans have been encroaching on the wild since the dawn of civilization. The decline of megafauna, especially in the Americas, Europe and Australia, is attributed to early human migration. But the scale and pace at which the destruction is now proceeding is unprecedented. In 1700, less than 10 per cent of all habitable land on Earth was subject to human exploitation. In 2019, this was around 50 per cent.[64] In the last 100 years, we have cut down as much forest as in the last 9,000 years, with the majority lost to agriculture, especially pasture for livestock and crop fields to feed livestock.[65]

Losing wilderness is a tragedy, given the vital role that wilderness plays in balancing the planet's ecosystems, offering resilience to climate change and conserving biodiversity. But more alarmingly, human attacks on the wild are directly responsible for the worst viral outbreaks of the last decade. The emergence and frequent outbreaks of ebola since 1976, a hemorrhagic virus with a 50 per cent mortality rate, can be traced directly to human encroachment in the rainforests when the virus circulates among primate and bat populations. Outbreaks of Ebola frequently occur in areas that were recently deforested, including the 2014–16 West African Ebola epidemic, which infected over 28,000 people, of which 11,300 died.[66]

Of course, the Covid-19 pandemic is a textbook case for the dangers of wilderness encroachment. Scientists largely agree that the origin of Covid-19 is likely a wild bat, with a possible intermediary host whose body was transported to the wet market of Wuhan, China, where it infected humans.[67] Several millions of people died (it is difficult to get an accurate count given the likely undercounting in India, South America and Africa) and many millions more are suffering with long-term after-effects like long-Covid. In the months that followed the initial outbreak, many fingers pointed towards China and its unsustainable practices of poaching wildlife for sale in unhealthy and unregulated conditions. Sixty US lawmakers called for a worldwide ban on wet markets, backed by a number of animal welfare groups.[68] However, pointing fingers is a convenient way to brush over the atrocious conditions that most industrially farmed animals live in. The plight of chickens, pigs and cows dying of disease, covered in sores in cramped cage-like conditions, separated from their young at birth, and bred to grow too fast and too fat for their bodies to balance is well documented.[69] Beyond the sheer amount of suffering inflicted upon sentient creatures by these practices, this also creates a breeding ground for zoonotic diseases that can spread to humans. The dangers of mass farming were brought to light when Denmark was forced to eliminate its entire commercial minx population due to Covid-19 contamination.[70] The images of bloated, rotting minx corpses bursting through their hastily dug mass graves should have led to a worldwide reckoning on industrial farming, but this has not yet happened.

When it comes to pandemics, Covid-19 was a shot across the bow. We were 'lucky' to face a virus with a less than 1 per cent mortality rate. As the permafrost thaws, bacteria and viruses frozen beneath the surface for thousands of years will be released into animal and human populations. This is already the case with Anthrax, which was released into reindeer populations in Siberia in 2016, killing over 2,000 reindeer and one person.[71] In parallel, tropical diseases currently confined to equatorial countries will make their way northwards as temperatures increase: malaria, dengue, Zika and Chikungunya are among the likely candidates for migration.[72]

Air quality collapse

One of the rare silver linings of Covid-19 is that it brought the impact of air pollution to light. As industrial and transport activity shut down around the world, the skies cleared. The Himalaya became visible from 125 miles away for the first time in thirty years, as the smog lifted over Punjab.[73] Massive air pollution drops were recorded over China, Europe and the United States, which is just as well since research indicated a correlation between air pollution and the worse impact of Covid-19 infection.[74] However, as soon as restrictions lifted, air pollution returned to normal, unhealthy levels. The World Health Organisation (WHO) estimates that over 90 per cent of children worldwide breathe polluted air, including my daughter, since we live in the Randstad, a region with one of the most polluted airs in Europe. With climate change holding weather patterns over Europe for longer, weeks of still, sunny skies are often accompanied by pollution peaks so dire that governments clamp down on car traffic in large cities.[75] Even so, Europe's air pollution problems are still manageable. When I travel to Varanasi, black soot comes out when I blow my nose. When I lived in Singapore, we were forced indoors for days on end when the particulate matter from forest burning in Indonesia formed a dense haze around the city.[76]

The WHO links chronic exposure to air polluted with fine particulate matter to an increase in the incidence of strokes, heart disease, lung cancer, chronic and acute respiratory disease including asthma.[77] Air pollution is estimated to lead to 4.2 million premature deaths per year, mostly concentrated in Asia.[78] In addition to industrial and exhaust-fume pollution, the world will increasingly contend with fine particulate matter from forest fires, as was recently seen in the United States, Canada and Australia.

There is a paradox in tackling air pollution: particulate matter reflects sunlight back into space.[79] So decreasing air pollution actually exacerbates global heating, and we may be forced to resort to adding particulates like sulphur dioxide into the atmosphere as a last-ditch attempt to geoengineer our way out of disaster.[80] We have very little idea of the consequences of this planetary-sized experiment with no do-overs, but it is increasingly being floated as an option preferable to breaking our fossil fuel addiction. As Naomi Klein explained in *This Changes Everything*, when the political and economic right run out of road on denial, they switch to techno-fix discourses that promise business-as-usual solutions.[81] Anything but changing the system. Stratospheric Aerosol Injections (SAI) gone wrong are the plot driver for the dystopian Korean film *Snowpiercer*, and while turning the Earth into a snowball is unlikely, we have very little idea about the harms that we may unleash. What we do know is that SAI changes the composition of the stratosphere such that the sunlight reflects differently. So take some time to contemplate the extraordinary beauty of a winter sunrise, or a late summer sunset while you still can, because if the techno-optimists have their way, you'll soon be waking up to red and white skies.[82]

Biosphere collapse and socio-economic collapse

We have covered major areas of biosphere collapse. In this analysis, we have treated humanity as an undifferentiated whole, but in the next section, we will look at the impact of biosphere collapse from a socio-economic perspective. It will become quite clear that those most responsible for the breakdown of the living world are least vulnerable to the impact of collapse, while the poorest and most marginalized will suffer the most and the soonest.

Socio-economic collapse

To understand the socio-economic underpinnings of collapse, it is important to examine the tight linkage between biosphere exploitation, capitalism, energy and economic growth.

Capitalism is a 300-year-old political-economic system, first described by the Scottish moral philosopher Adam Smith in his 1776 magnum opus *The Wealth of Nations*.[83] It is characterized by the primacy of an abstract market system, in which profit-seeking firms compete for market share, supported by nation state and supranational governance that enforces property rights through the rule of law. This system emerged in the late eighteenth century as a result of several interlocking factors. While the invention of the steam engine is often hailed as the kick-off for the Industrial Revolution, the age of the machine would not have been possible without cheap, abundant human and natural resources to build it and fossil fuels to feed it. Political and social disruptions, described by Karl Polanyi in *The Great Transformation*,[84] created the social conditions for capitalism to emerge. For instance, in the eighteenth and nineteenth centuries, English landlords accelerated a movement to close off community land with hedges and fences, turning it into profitable farmland for themselves, while small tenant farmers could no longer use it to feed their family. This created a poverty crisis that forced the landless masses to move out of the countryside and into the cities, where they could be hoovered up by newly built factories as cheap labour. Ideological reforms like the rise of Protestantism changed old Christian beliefs about wealth from sinful to saintly.[85] This produced the 'superstructure' of capitalism (to borrow a Marxist term) – creating social buy-in for the system to be accepted and reproduced. But the material foundations of capitalism cannot be understood without grasping the primal role of resources and energy in making such a system possible.

Capitalism, resources and energy

The Austrian economist Joseph Schumpeter asserted that the lifeblood of capitalism is technological innovation and entrepreneurship.[86] This is only partially correct. Technological innovation and the accompanying growth of the past three centuries were not merely the result of human genius and the entrepreneurial spirit – humans have possessed roughly equivalent levels of intelligence for millennia. Innovation and growth were made possible by the immense influx of resources from colonial imperialism, and the energy burst provided by coal, then oil and gas. Breaking capitalism down to its basic fluxes of physical materials and energies demystifies the market. Once capitalism looks less like a religion and more like a species of primates moving biological and mineral materials around a precariously balanced rock in a whole lot of empty space, the reality of our predicament becomes easier to grasp.

Let's start with the material components of capitalism. If we break down what Capital really is, we're looking at physical objects that can be used to make more objects or produce services, which can be sold for money on a market. Let's take a typical means of production of the Industrial Revolution: a machine on an assembly line. This machine is an assemblage of metals and wood (later, also plastics, silicones etc.). The machine did not spring to life in the factory ex nihilo. The metals were mined, the wood was chopped and the plastics were manufactured from oil. This means that somewhere, land was converted to industrial use, trees were cut down, the ground was torn open and people performed the hard labour of extracting these materials from the ground. Where did the materials to fire up the Industrial Revolution come from? Using a Marxist analysis, historian Jason Moore built a convincing case for situating its origins in the 'primitive accumulation' of colonial plunder.[87] In the 200 years that preceded the invention of the steam engine, he argues, imperialist powers led by Spain, France, the UK and The Netherlands brutally extracted the resources they needed to get capitalism going from colonized lands. The key feature of this resource grab is that it predates the market system, the materials needed to build capitalism were not acquired using commercial exchange but brute force. No value was ever ascribed to the natural capital plundered during that time: in Moore's words, building capitalism required 'cheap' nature, available without restrictions. Crucially, 'cheap' nature included the 'cheap' labour needed to assemble the foundations of capitalism. The machine didn't build itself: women, people of colour and even some White ethnicities considered 'undesirable' (Jews, Slavs, Irish, Romani, for instance) were captured and sold by imperialist capitalists as cheap commodities. The manual labour of people of colour was appropriated through slavery, while the reproductive labour of women was appropriated through their legal status as property. For most of history, girls legally belonged to their father, who could trade them in the marriage market by means of a dowry (this is still the case in some parts of the world). Women of colour held the short end of both already-short sticks: in *Ain't I a Woman*, feminist author bell hooks offered a harrowing account of the lives of Black women forced to endure slave labour while bearing child after child that would be taken from them and sold, if they survived pregnancy, birth and early childhood on the plantation.[88]

Capitalism was therefore built upon an original internal contradiction that pre-dates the exploitation of the working class: a regime of private property and rule of law was constructed by denying personhood to large swathes of humanity, where some wealthy White men held property, and people of colour and women *were* property. Racism and sexism were therefore not incidental to capitalism, but central to its construction. French political economist Thomas Piketty chronicled the consequences of this contradiction: the abolition of slavery was conditioned upon reparations, not to former slaves, but to aggrieved slave holders who were stripped of their 'property'.[89] Thus, White men who made their fortunes on land stolen from indigenous people in the Caribbean, with labour plundered from the coasts of Africa, were generously compensated for the loss of their ill-gotten business, while newly freed countries like Haiti collapsed under the weight of reparations payments. A historical *New York Times* investigation estimated the total damage to the Haitian economy over time at 115 billion dollars.[90] It is therefore painfully obvious that the property regime and rule of law were, in their early days, not blind instruments of justice, but scaffolding for White supremacy.

While the material dimension of capitalism has been soundly analysed by critical political economists and historians, its energy dimension has been somewhat underexplored. However, the energy component and its inextricable ties to fossil fuels is crucial to understanding capitalism's growth.

What are fossil fuels? Simply put, condensed solar energy. Thanks to the solar energy stored underground by plants and animals of the carboniferous era, then compressed into a dense, energy-rich paste by geothermal forces over hundreds of thousands of years, humanity was able to multiply the amount of useful work it could produce by a factor of 200.[91] That means that, on average, every human living on this planet today commands the equivalent energy value of 200 people. Every day of our lives, every time we switch on the kettle, every time we get in our cars, we expend energy that would have required the physical labour of 200 men (global average – the average European commands the equivalent of 500–600 men). With so much labour saved in farming, then industry, time was freed up for other pursuits, giving us the thriving services sector we know today. Education as we know it is only possible because children are no longer needed in the fields or factories at a young age. Scientific endeavour is only possible because a mechanized farming and industrial system performs the invisible task of keeping scientists alive with cheap food, cheap housing and cheap heating, so that they may dedicate their productive work hours to research. In other words, innovation is only possible because we have an underlying reservoir of cheap energy that ensures the basics are covered and surplus labour hours can be dedicated to R&D work, and that is something the Austrian economist missed entirely.

I will follow Jean-Marc Jancovici in making the controversial and contentious claim that it was not the better angels of our nature that liberated women and ended slavery; it was fossil fuels.[92] When mechanical energy became cheap and abundant, slavery became much less attractive as a source of work, because machines don't rebel (yet), don't die, are easier and quicker to reproduce, and fossil fuel was cheaper than human fuel (i.e. food). This same logic is now driving the automation of most industrial processes, throwing millions of factory workers out of employment. Having built itself on the backs of people of colour, women and the working class, capitalism, in its profit-maximizing quest, is designed to discard them when they are no longer the most useful source of cheap energy.

When my mother was a child, my grandmother spent Mondays doing laundry. The whole day, every Monday, week in, week out, my grandmother pounded sheets and bloody underwear (she had four daughters) in a large soapy tub. Twelve hours of productive labour per week were assigned to the task of cleaning fabrics. When she wasn't doing that, she was slaughtering chickens, tending to the vegetable garden, preserving food in cans or sewing clothes for the family with a pedal-powered machine. When I need to clean clothes, I pop open the washing machine door, bung everything in and come back an hour later to hang it up. This has nothing to do with feminism and everything to do with energy. Only when energy-guzzling ovens, washing machines, dishwashers, fridges and freezers became available were women finally able to earn their liberation. Of course, a massive, hard-fought ideological shift had to occur alongside mechanization: places like Saudi Arabia remind us that without feminism, ovens and tumble dryers alone do not ensure gender equality, and places like the United States remind us that gains should never be taken for granted. But would feminism have succeeded without the help of coal, oil and gas? I think it is unlikely.

It is vital to understand the ways in which an abundant, cheap energy supply has shaped the globalized, liberal world, so that we may understand what is at stake when the world's energy supply collapses.

Capitalism and individualism

One of the doctrinal tenets of capitalism is that humans are, by nature, inclined to truck and barter, acting in their own economic self-interest by the means of rational, well-informed decision-making.[93] The concept of a natural 'invisible hand' of the market that coordinates selfish rational decision-making towards the greater good through the price mechanism dates back to Adam Smith.[94] But it was turned into a veritable article of faith by Ayn Rand, the libertarian Russian-American novelist whose *Altas Shrugged* sold over nine million copies and became a text of reference for the American right.[95] There is something mesmerizing about watching 1967 black-and-white footage of this sinister figure declaring in a glacial voice: 'Man's proper ethics or morality, is a morality of rational self-interest, which means that every man has a right to exist for his own sake, and he must not sacrifice himself to others, or sacrifice others to himself.'[96] It's amusing to watch the Christian Right adulate a woman who decried Christian charity as morally abhorrent. But for the purposes of understanding collapse, it's important to deconstruct two core premises of Rand's philosophy.

Her first, overarching premise is that people are rational, and should therefore use reason as the sole guide for action. Since the dawn of cognitive psychology in the 1950s, ample research has shown that humans are plagued by cognitive biases that render rational, unbiased judgement impossible.[97] Some of the best-known cognitive biases include the confirmation bias, which primes us to only consider evidence that fits with our preconceived beliefs; the misinformation effect, in which recall is distorted by leading information; the fundamental attribution error, in which the actions of others are attributed to their deliberate intentions, whereas our own actions are attributed to external factors like bad luck; and the availability heuristic, a bias that leads us to overestimate the probability of events that we are familiar with, while underestimating those we aren't. Cognitive biases affect all humans, and can at best be mitigated, not done away with entirely, even by persons who know of their existence. Therefore, the first premise of Randian libertarianism doesn't stand up to scrutiny.

The second premise, that humans have a natural propensity towards self-interest, has been examined and found wanting by numerous historians, anthropologists and social analysts. From Piotr Kropotkin's work on *Mutual Aid*[98] and Karl Polanyi's *Great Transformation*,[99] to modern works like Rutger Bregman's *Humankind: a Hopeful History*[100] and indigenous books like Kimmerer's *Braiding Sweetgrass*[101] and Simpson's *As We Have Always Done*,[102] numerous historical accounts of human development agree that reciprocity was the governing principle of human interaction until the advent of capitalism. In nature, lonesome creatures tend to have sharp claws and teeth and powerful hind legs to hunt prey. Humans have none of the above, and have survived and thrived as a species through their capacity for social learning, constructive interaction through evolved language and the transmission of knowledge from one generation to the next. Cooperation and reciprocity have guarded us in times of scarcity and ensured that tasks that were too much for one person could be done by many. Bonds of reciprocity tended to be bounded by tribal affinity, with violence and warfare often occurring between groups, but also trade and alliances. Polanyi showed that in pre-capitalist societies, trade, truck and barter were part of the fabric of social relationships, rather than self-regarding matters of interest-maximization.

What changed? Polanyi argued that an ideological shift detaching markets from society and turning land, people and money into commodities enabled individualism to take hold as the dominant mode of human interaction. This ideology was then forcefully exported by settler colonialism. I would go a level deeper and suggest that there is a biophysical rationale for this change: the release of vast quantities of concentrated energy from the soil liberated humans from needing one another. Mutual aid is not required in a civilization where almost anything can be fixed by throwing more petrol at it. The modern-day institutionalized, centralized mutual aid that has replaced tribal cooperation in the form of the welfare state, whether in its liberal (US and UK), corporatist (France and Germany) or universal (Scandinavia) variant, requires enough energy to go around so that people can contribute a part of their surplus to helping out those in need.[103] This is done in a bureaucratic, faceless manner, through paperwork and bank transfers, where no personal bonds of allegiance are formed. The modern welfare state, itself an energy-guzzling behemoth, is a machine for distributing surplus energy. But what happens to the centralized nation state and its welfare apparatus in an energy-constrained world? Jancovici doesn't think that it will hold for any great length of time.[104] The Covid crisis showed the welfare state to be more resilient than it had been given credit for, especially in Europe. But until the Ukraine war, we were still largely living in a world of plenty of energy. This is changing fast, and will challenge the way we think about individualism.

Fans of Ayn Rand are therefore invited to enjoy *Atlas Shrugged* for the fiction that it is, but should not be waylaid into thinking that a world of Dagny Taggarts and John Galts is either possible or desirable in a time of energy supply collapse. If it's any consolation, Adam Curtis' 2011 documentary on Ayn Rand, *All Watched over by Machines of Loving Grace,* reveals that Rand spectacularly failed to live up to her own rational self-interest ideals, and died alone with her cats.[105]

Capitalism and endless growth

The quest for eternal growth is a more insidious component of late modernity that needs to be carefully unpacked, because it is not grounded in biophysical processes but in performative ideology. Any mathematician or physicist worth their salt would know that what goes up has got to fall, and given the laws of nature, infinite growth is mathematically impossible on a finite planet. So how did we end up with an economic 'science' so divorced from physical reality, not only advocating eternal growth but actually *requiring* it for its models and equations to work?

Allow me to take you back to the early nineteenth century.[106] David Ricardo, an austere British political economist and the intellectual heir of Adam Smith, made two key contributions to his field: firstly, he translated Smith's insights about economic production under capitalism into a mathematical language that would form the bedrock of modern economics. Such calculations allowed him to formulate his famous *Theory of Comparative Advantages*, according to which international specialization and trade is always profitable, even where one nation appears to have all the production advantages. So powerful was this gift to the liberal cause that it remains Ricardo's best-known contribution to economics to this day. Less well known is Ricardo's realization that capitalism had to end, a phenomenon he called the 'stationary state', where population and capital growth would be choked by the restrictions of land use. Indeed, Ricardo had the common sense insight that infinite population and capital growth would necessarily collide with the bottleneck of finite land supply, particularly fertile land. Thus, a generation before Marx, Ricardo already foresaw the obvious and made it a core tenet of political economy. For Ricardo, this was an unmitigated tragedy – the end of progress, the doom march of humanity.

When Karl Marx was a rebellious youngster burning the midnight oil with Friedrich Engels to finish *The Communist Manifesto* under threat of expulsion from the Communist League, a much more serious thinker had just written *Principles of Political Economy*. Ricardo's uncontested intellectual heir was the British prodigy John Stuart Mill (he had read all contemporaneous political economy by the age of nineteen). Mill agreed with Ricardo's conclusions about capitalism: all good things must come to an end, and the stationary state is indeed the end point of economic progress. But he drew opposite conclusions to those of his predecessor:

> It is scarcely necessary to remark that a stationary condition of capital and population implies no stationary state of human improvement. There would be so much scope as ever for all kinds of mental, cultural and moral and social progress . . . Even the industrial arts might be as earnestly and successfully cultivated, with this sole difference, that instead of serving no purpose but the increase of wealth, industrial improvements would produce their legitimate effect, that of abridging labour.[107]

In Mill's stationary state, productive enterprise would make way for vast quantities of leisure time, wisely spent expanding the mind, enjoying music and arts, the awesomeness of nature, and . . . sex (Mill and his mistress-turned-wife Harriet Taylor Mill were quite ahead of their time in many respects). Mill was a gentle socialist, who cared for individual well-being and the right to eccentricity. He favoured decentralized, cooperative economic endeavours supported by a vast effort in moral education to instill values of kinship among citizens.

As Mill entered his twilight years, Marx, now in exile in London, finally got serious about political economy and read the works of his predecessors.[108] He provided meticulous, mathematical argumentation to support his view that capitalism was doomed to end, crushed by its own internal contradictions. Namely, growth tends to be accompanied by the concentration of Capital and the swelling of the working class as small business owners are routed from the market. The end point of this untenable tension is not Mill's mild socialist utopia but an outright revolution that brings about a centralized communist system. What comes after was left vague by Marx, who was more interested in his analysis of capitalism than utopian thinking. The fervour with which his earlier works on communism were seized by hot-headed revolutionaries irked him so that on his deathbed, he is said to have declared: 'I am not a Marxist'.[109]

The point of this historical detour was to demonstrate that, until the late nineteenth century, the end of economic growth was self-evident. How this end would come, and what good or ill would come of it was up for debate, but not the central premise that what grows must, according to the laws of nature, one day stop.

This all changed between 1870 and 1890, during an obscure historical event known today only to economic historians. Yet this event, dubbed the '*Marginalist Revolution*', changed the course of history and sent us careening towards collapse.[110] This rupture did not take place on battlefields but in Europe's universities. Its key actors were names you've probably not heard of, unless you happen to be ensconced in some university economics department: Stanley Jevons, Leon Walras and Alfred Marshall. The 1870s were a troubled time for the study of political economy: Mill was dead, Marx's ideas were setting Europe ablaze (again), with the Paris Commune of 1871 installing the first bona fide communist regime in history (it was crushed in blood one year later). Britain and France were busy carving up the world for themselves, while casting a wary eye towards Prussia. Under the leadership of Otto von Bismarck, the Prussians were toying with ideas that smacked of socialism to their liberal neighbours. Bismark's *Sozialepolitik*, the first genuine attempt at building a corporatist welfare state, was actually the opposite of socialism.[111] It was a clever ploy to quash revolutionary fervour by pitting different professional groups against each other to compete for social advantages granted magnanimously by the centralized state. But it sent British liberal trade groups into a cold sweat nonetheless. In response, they funded and supported the rise of young mathematicians to key posts in the field of political economy. Among them, Stanley Jevons made his mark by narrowing economic science to the calculation of rational utility maximization. Leon Walras turned the vivid, human world of trade into a series of abstract market equilibria, and Alfred Marshall adjusted this theory to take into account short-term inflexibilities and a hypothetical long-term future of infinite possibilities. All of this in an abstract, ahistorical and asocial world. By 1890, the date of publication of Marshall's seminal book on the subject, the word 'political' was dropped from the title and economics was born.[112] The Marginalist Revolution took from classical political economy what it needed to turn the world into a neat abstraction: Mill's individualism, Ricardo's mathematics and Bentham's utility maximization principle. The chimera born of this witch's brew came to be known as *homo economicus*, the economic man: a rational, self-interested utility maximizer. The marginalists knew full well that this person did not exist and was not a fair representation of reality, but they were interested in the purity of their mathematical models, not their real-world application. The marginalists weren't aiming to describe society and its physical constraints. Borrowing Jean-Baptiste Say's early nineteenth-century contention that natural resources are free and infinite (even though 100 years later it was already abundantly clear that this was not true), they excluded natural capital from their calculations and externalized all environmental and social ills from their models.[113] In effect, economics decided that nature was free – free as a source of materials and free as a dumping ground. There was nothing logical or realistic about this, it was a decision made purely for the tidiness of mathematical models that conveniently supported the economic interests of those who funded the work. Free of the constraints of accounting for natural capital depletion, capitalism looked, on paper, like an economic system capable of eternal growth. The trade liberals got what they wanted: classical political economy died as a field, Marxism became the subject of underground intellectual movements, and they now had the tools to shape the world in their image. The *homo economicus* became a performative instrument to shape markets, states and social institutions to constrain people to behave the way models demanded.

Infinite growth, meet finite planet

Although the Marginalist Revolution modelled a hypothetical world where eternal economic growth was *possible*, the shift to a very real world where eternal economic growth is *required* came a century later. French political economist Pierre-Yves Gomez traces the origins of the eternal growth *diktat* to a law passed by the US Congress in 1974.[114] It required pension funds to be independent from the companies for whom they manage employee pension investments and to diversify their assets. The reason for this change was ostensibly to protect pensions in case of corporate bankruptcy. But the consequence of the move was to turn pension funds into the worlds' largest stock market investors. As a knock-on effect, these funds require positive returns on investments year on year, meaning they require economic growth year on year just to maintain themselves, lest the entire population of the capitalist world lose their pensions. Furthermore, both private and state spending have been increasingly financed by debt in the last thirty years. As of 2022, the American government's debt stood above thirty trillion dollars.[115] This is about twelve times the value of the world's largest company, Apple Inc. There is simply no way to pay that debt within the current size of the US economy. The only hope to remain solvent is to furiously grow the economic pie so that what currently looks like a gigantic slice is proportionally reduced when the economy increases in size (in fact, US debt is currently larger than its entire annual GDP). So, according to economists and political decision-makers, we must grow – not for the sake of progress or improvement but just to stave off economic collapse.

There's only one problem: economic growth at a modest rate of 3 per cent to 4 per cent per annum will lead to the doubling of the world economy every twenty years. Translating this into the real world of materials and energy fluxes, this means doubling the quantity of cement, steel and plastics produced, of trees cut, petrol pumped, rare earths extracted, electricity produced, consumer goods on the shelves and services offered, just to avoid falling off the pensions and debt cliff.

Let's add one last inconvenient fact to this equation: the planet is finite. There's only so much petrol that can be pumped, wood that can be chopped and rare earths that can be extracted before there's none left. Even if the planet were twice the size of our current mothership, it would only take an extra twenty years (i.e. one more doubling of the economy) to use it all up! Any model that requires exponential growth just to stave off collapse is, given the laws of nature, going to collapse by definition.

This simple mathematical fact seems to elude even respected thinkers. American economist Jeremy Rifkin waxed lyrical about the power of pension funds to lead a green revolution in his book *The Green New Deal*.[116] Pension funds, he claimed, can engineer our green future by funding solar panels on every rooftop and wind turbines on every hilltop. But Rifkin did not address the scale and material dimensions of his plan: solar panels are made of *something*, and that *something* is available in finite quantities in a world in which extracting and transporting raw materials is getting increasingly complicated due to the compound effects of pandemic disruption, war and energy shortages.

We need to face the facts: renewable energy has not replaced one megawatt of fossil fuel energy on a global scale.[117] It has simply been added to the existing fossil mix. Minus the odd bump so minor it hardly shows up on the graph in Figure 1, global energy demand has risen exponentially since 1850, going from 7,791 terawatt-hours to 173,340 terawatt-hours in 2019, a 22-fold increase. New sources of energy are used to expand capacity rather than replacing old sources. Yet, despite the supposed 'explosion' of renewable energy production, all renewables put together amount to just over 17,000 terawatt-hours, or 10 per cent of the world's energy mix, of which hydro accounts for more than half. There are only so many rivers we can dam, and even that is a risky bet with rivers running dry. Meanwhile, fossil fuel consumption has increased by over 60 per cent since the first Earth Summit in Rio in 1992. Despite the outsized damage caused by coal, both in terms of CO_2 emissions and air pollution, coal use is currently fluctuating between 40,000 and 45,000 terawatt-hours. Reports of coal's death have been vastly overstated given the number of new coal power stations currently on the books in India and China. Even in the United States, where coal was supposedly in terminal decline, defunct power stations are being bought and fired up by bitcoin miners whose enormous energy needs cannot be met within the existing grid.[118] Bitcoin, touted as the future of money, is currently using more electricity than my entire country, The Netherlands; much of it is dirty, coal-fuelled electricity, without offering an ounce of the financial stability it promised.[119] The

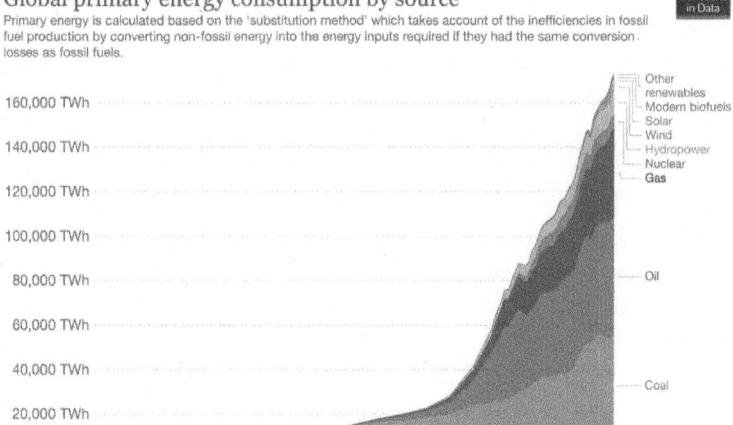

FIGURE 1. *Global energy consumption since 1800 (from Ritchie, Roser & Rosado, 2020, CC BY 4.0).*

Fukushima nuclear disaster of 2011 (in which, for reminder, nobody died of radiation poisoning) prompted Germany to shut down its CO_2-neutral nuclear power reactors early and replace them with . . . fossil fuel power![120] This severely undermined Germany's CO_2 emissions reduction targets and left it heavily dependent on Russian gas to plug the energy gap left by abandoning nuclear. The price for this decision was paid in blood by the Ukrainian people.

How about decoupling growth from environmental destruction? Politicians who can no longer deny environmental breakdown promise to solve it with 'green growth'.[121] Could this actually work? Unfortunately, decoupling has simply never happened, empirically: the very few dips in world energy consumption since 1850 are all attributable to declines in production related to war, energy shocks, recessions or other external shocks. There is no recorded instance anywhere in the world of a national economy growing without also increasing its environmental footprint – not just measured in CO_2 and methane emissions but also waste streams, chemical pollution, biodiversity loss, land conversion and freshwater contamination, among others. There is a simple explanation for the world's failure to decouple growth and environmental damage: growth isn't numbers in the sky; it is material and energy fluxes, the total number of goods and services produced in a country in a given year, minus imports, plus exports. Western countries have succeeded in reducing the carbon intensity of their GDP by exporting production to developing countries, whose carbon intensity increased proportionally, and by conveniently omitting to account for shipping in their CO_2 calculations.[122] It's easy to point the finger at China and demand CO_2 emissions reductions, but with China's production disruptions related to Covid shutdowns, we got a taster of the impact on our 'cleaner' economies in the West. Waiting twelve months for a car part will be the least of our worries if China decreases production in a manner compatible with 1.5°C of warming.

Towards a collapse of capitalism?

One way or another, the end of growth is inevitable: population growth, economic growth and resource extraction growth. Current trends closely map onto the predictions of the report to the Club of Rome of 1972, signalling that the end of growth is imminent.[123] In many ways, it is already here: the supply chain, heavily impacted by Covid, will not be restored to pre-pandemic status. Energy prices will remain volatile, the age of cheap and plenty will not return and we will never *go* back to *normal* because *normal* was not a steady state; it was always an unstable trajectory pointing towards collapse.

What comes next? There are two serious options on the table: the first is a revival of John Stuart Mill's steady state argument. Its foremost contemporary proponents include Herman Daly[124] and Tim Jackson.[125]

However, while steady state economics may have been an appealing option in the 1970s, no global economic system can reach a steady state at a level where it consumes the resource equivalent of 1.76 planets per annum.[126] That supplementary 0.76 (and counting) destroys biocapacity, meaning the sum total of the planet's usable and renewable resources diminishes with every year that consumption exceeds regeneration capacity. In other words, with every passing year, we are shrinking the maximal capacity of a steady state economy, thus decreasing the chance that we will be able to reach steady state without civilizational collapse.

This leaves us with two alternatives, in my view: deliberately dismantle thermo-industrial civilization now or let it collapse in an uncontrolled manner later. The temporal distance between the two choices is probably only a matter of one or two decades. In other words, unless you're seventy years old, you will not escape collapse by postponing action. Most environmental groups favour controlled demolition. Many advocate the end of capitalism, controlled degrowth, rewilding and intersectional solidarity to soften the blow. Environmental activists are under no illusions: this will not be pleasant. Many people will lose a lot. Those who have more will, by definition, lose more in absolute terms, which is why the rich are digging their heels in against action. But those who have less will lose more in relative terms, which is why this is a social justice issue. Many people will likely die, principally among those who are already marginalized by poverty and racism. But let that be no comfort to the Western middle classes, whose displays of NIMBYism around environmental action stem in part from their perceived immunity to the problem. Sudden death will likely also come knocking on their doors, as foreshadowed by Covid and deadly wildfires in the United States.

In sum, the world as we know it will cease to exist one way or the other: we are facing the end of cheap, reliable commodities, of food and energy abundance, of predictable, planned futures, of the generous welfare state, of travel as we know it . . . the list goes on. Everything we know about the world will change, but we still have some wiggle room to decide how. None of us in the environmental movement relishes the momentous and urgent nature of the decision-making at stake; most of us were doing quite well, all things considered, under capitalism, and if we get what we're asking for, we will be dynamiting our own lives. The reason we are advocating for controlled degrowth is because the alternatives are much, much worse.

Uncontrolled collapse could cause the deaths of millions and the misery of billions while a handful of billionaires hide out in bunkers protected by private armies.[127] Under conditions of uncontrolled socio-economic collapse, the Western middle and working classes face destitution, hunger, disease, poverty, losing their homes from random floods, fires and storms without the means to insure or fix them, loss of access to healthcare and education, and an increase in insecurity with rampant violence against women, minorities and the poor. The rule of law could be replaced by neo-feudal loyalty to cartels and armed groups, and basic human rights may no longer be protected. In other words, it would be the end of the middle class as we know it.

As drastic as this sounds, the Global South risks a fate far worse: starvation, literally cooking to death (surface temperatures topped 60°C in Central and North India on the day I wrote this),[128] entire cities wiped off the map by hurricanes, typhoons, floods and fires with no way to rebuild them, war breaking out everywhere at once, savage violence against women and children, and billions of destitute refugees massing on the borders of the Global North. Decades of efforts to vaccinate, educate, democratize and pacify could be lost in the space of a few years. It would be a tragedy of human suffering on a scale not seen since the Black Death.

There is an extra factor to consider: while the timing between controlled degrowth and uncontrolled collapse may only differ by fifteen to twenty years, those few years could make the difference between tipping towards the hothouse Earth state or not. In other words, by putting off action for twenty years, we guarantee that collapse will be worse, and might also jeopardize the possibility of organized human life on Earth.

Respectable scientists like Vaclav Smil claim that environmentalists need to 'get real' because global addiction to fossil-based industry means that a change of course is impossible.[129] Since unrealistic goals are pointless, he claims that making degrowth demands discredits the environmental movement. He states this as a matter of fact, as if there were really no choice, as if mystical forces were prying factories open against the will of decision-makers. The reality is that we could switch everything off tomorrow. Civilization as we know it would almost certainly collapse. It will collapse anyways soon enough, with or without planning, but with planning is widely preferable. Unfortunately, the kind of doomerism peddled by Smil plays into the hands of some decision-makers who, unable to deny the reality of collapse, now argue that it's too late to do anything about it, so it's best to keep the party going until the lights go off, as demonstrated by a reckless recent US Supreme Court decision to muzzle the Environmental Protection Agency and hobble federal efforts to curb greenhouse gas emissions.[130] The role of religion in this orchestrated recklessness should not be glossed over, given the role that religious fervour played in forging today's US Supreme Court. It has been suggested that Christian fundamentalists in the US welcome the climate apocalypse in the hopes of accelerating the second coming of Jesus Christ.[131] They're in for a disappointing ride when they realize that hell on Earth is something we will have to live through, not just die in.

Geopolitical collapse

Can the international order survive the end of growth, controlled or uncontrolled? Probably not.

The global international order as we know it was built from the ashes of nineteenth-century realpolitik that led to the catastrophic First and Second World Wars. Absent the Soviet Union in the early years of the United Nations, an uncontested United States set about building a world in its own image. Modern international law, with its network of treaty obligations, customary law, international courts and remedial mechanisms, are all products of the liberal theory that interdependence fosters peace.[132] So far, so good, but the key to maintaining peace, according to liberal international relations scholars, is to enforce interdependence through commercial ties. And so, the neoliberal trifecta was born: the World Bank in 1944, the International Monetary Fund in 1945, and the World Trade Organisation (formerly known as the General Agreement on Tariffs and Trade) in 1947.[133] Trade grew exponentially. For instance, US exports went from less than 200 billion dollars in 1970 to 2.44 trillion dollars in 2019.[134] In the 1970s, the bulk of the trade volume occurred between developed and developing nations, with the Global North importing cheap raw materials from the South and exporting expensive consumer goods and services back. However, in the 1990s, global trade patterns shifted, and the majority of global trade now occurs within the Global South, especially if China is counted within the South.[135] Contrarily to the warnings of critical international approaches from the 1970s, data clearly shows a correlation between increased openness to trade and GDP growth, and it is simply not true that global trade has exclusively benefited rich nations.[136] The bulk of income improvement in the last twenty years has been in developing nations, particularly in China and India, while the working and middle classes of wealthy nations have seen their purchasing power stagnate or dwindle.[137] Overall, global capitalism has been remarkably apt at making the world more stable, more peaceful and wealthier. However, the giant has clay feet.

First, global capitalism depends on cheap fossil fuels and a well-oiled shipping machine to nourish trade. Until the global supply chain crisis induced by the pandemic, few consumers around the globe paused to wonder how an object made in China with raw materials from Africa could be sold for peanuts in Europe with free shipping in record time. In 2020, containers became stranded around the world as trade routes were disrupted by Covid, and when the economy picked up again, the shortage of available shipping space multiplied the cost of hiring a container by ten.[138] We laughed when a single ship stuck in the Suez Canal in 2021 ground global trade to a halt for a few days, but the global trade system rests on critical choke-points that will become problematic in a collapsing world. Expensive shipping means more than just waiting a few months for out-of-stock consumer goods; the entire just-in-time production system risks falling apart. Cheap food, cheap goods and cheap clothes may all be things of the past: we are going to have to get used to paying more for less and simply do without a lot of things. The rich will, as usual, find ways around it, even if they have to lump what they need onto their private jets. But for the purchasing power of the middle classes of the world, this spells disaster.

Second, the global industrial system depends on having reliable access to large populations of cheap workers. We lament the fate of textile industry workers, meat plant workers, miners and other vulnerable humans doing hard labour for little pay, but our global economic system depends on the exploitation of cheap labour to function. In a world of mass climate migrations, the movement of exploitable populations will become unpredictable: how would a multinational corporation know where to build its next factory if a drought and famine displaces half of the population in the area from one year to the next? There is no option to get around this problem that would allow middle-class consumers to keep enjoying affordable prices for food and commodities. And if the American Dream disappears, then global faith in capitalism will likely collapse, and faith in the liberal international order along with it.

Couple these two points with the end of economic growth and biosphere collapse, and we face the collapse of the post-War geopolitical order. The international legal architecture, predicated on a world of abundant resources and cheap energy, would likely be the first to fall apart. What might replace it? Perhaps the global system could revert to the Westphalian order of nation states edging in and out of war in a delicate balance of power. But the nation state itself could be facing internal collapse, particularly in vulnerable areas of Africa, Central America and South and South-East Asia. We face an extremely unstable international sphere, with nuclear-armed nations such as Pakistan, India and the United States at risk of civil war, while armed groups stand ready to profit from the turmoil and assume violent control of contested regions. Unthinkable just twenty years ago, the war in Ukraine has brought the threat of global nuclear war back to the fore. Even if nation states manage to retain enough rational decision-making power to keep their fingers off the nuclear button, the climate-induced destabilization of nuclear-armed countries like Pakistan, India and North-Korea could land nuclear weapons in the hands of militias similar or worse than the Islamic State. In that case, all bets are off with regards to rational decision-making. The best we could do right now to prevent this from happening is to dismantle all existing nuclear warheads. Unfortunately, the geopolitical time for disarmament was thirty years ago. With Vladimir Putin waving around intercontinental ballistic missiles on national television, it seems unlikely that the quantity of annihilation-grade weaponry will go down in the next few decades.

Collapse is (already) here. (More) collapse is coming

A sound conclusion to draw from this opening chapter is that collapse is, to a significant extent, already here, and more collapse is inevitably coming. As Jared Diamond points out, this should hardly come as a surprise to us: collapse is the historical trajectory of all civilizations and is almost always triggered by overreaching beyond the environment's capacity to regenerate the resources required for maintaining civilization, its population and its institutions.[139] However, collapse should not be equated with the Apocalypse. Yes, human extinction is a frightful *possibility*. Even controlled demolition may *feel* like the end of the world, given the impact it would have on our lives. But there is a world of difference between a controlled collapse that keeps global temperatures below 1.5°C of warming and an uncontrolled collapse that causes warming and biodiversity loss to spiral out of control. We can take on the challenge of making our lives liveable, meaningful and even enjoyable through a controlled demolition process. The task will be a lot more difficult if we wait for an uncontrolled collapse. We have tools in hand to organize the controlled degrowth process; no miracle technology is necessary, we need to do less, buy less, build less and travel less (or at least, travel much more slowly).

The real problem, then, isn't a lack of know-how on controlled collapse. So now we get to education: if the role of education is to prepare the young for the future, and this is our future, where is the education system in all of this? What did we (not) do and are still (not) doing to prepare for a world with less and steer civilization towards the preferable option of controlled demolition? If we have known about the probability of collapse since the 1972 Meadows Report, and anyone who went through primary school after 1970 will be affected, why haven't children been taught the requisite knowledges and skills to address the crisis in the intervening years? Why are today's adults paralysed into inaction? What should we do to fix this at a systemic level? This is the subject of the next chapter.

2

Education in Catastrophic Times

Placing systems in their historical context demystifies them and allows for closer scrutiny of the realities we take for granted. To understand why the majority of the world's adult population, from farmers and factory workers to CEOs and politicians, either actively participated in or passively accepted planetary destruction, and how we can do better by today's children, we need to understand what went wrong with education. If we want to craft an education system fit for the daunting tasks ahead, the first step involves reckoning with the emergence of schooling as we know it: where did schools come from? And why have they been so bad at preparing the young for life under conditions of collapse? Perhaps this feels a little remote to educators stuck in the grinding wheels of the system, who just want practical ways to address collapse in their classrooms. But I feel I cannot achieve what I set out to do with this book unless I bring educators to question whether their mission is best served in the ruts of a dying system, or on the battlefront of a system-wide revolution. That requires the historical and systemic overview I am about to share.[1]

Learning in denial

The first step to solving a problem is admitting that it exists. In this regard, the education systems of the world are in hard denial about the reality of the world, their accountability for breeding ecocidal behaviour among the young, and their responsibility to do better. This isn't a case of bad faith among educators, although some of that definitely exists. Rather, modern mass schooling has been instrumental to the development of global capitalism, and prying the two apart may require breaking both before an educational system fit for a warmed and depleted future can emerge.

A world without schools

The modern, state-funded system of mass education has its origins in the modus operandi of industrial factories. Before the Industrial Revolution, education was largely the prerogative of the wealthy. The majority of this elite instruction was purveyed at home by a plethora of tutors, governesses and masters, who transmitted to boys the knowledge required of statesmen, officers, landlords and other upper-class pursuits, and to girls the home economy, musical and artistic skills required to run a house and adequately entertain. Schools were mostly of a religious nature, run by clergy, for clergy.

Meanwhile, children of the peasant classes were put to work as soon as they had the physical capacity to withstand the harsh conditions of outdoor labour. Children were an economic investment necessary to the survival of the small holdings managed by most of the rural population. Since around half of all children were expected to die before adulthood, education was considered at best superfluous, at worst, deprived parents of several years of productive labour before disease or accidents curtailed the child's economic contribution to the family. The peasantry found respite from hardship in religious faith, the belief in a divinely ordered class or caste system, depending on the culture and the connection between people and land. For the first 10,000 years of human history, the lot and life of the world's poor, comprising the vast majority of the human population and subsisting on small-scale agriculture, was remarkably similar and unchanging from Patagonia to the Tundra.

This changed with the enclosing of the commons and the advent of the factory system in the late eighteenth century in

Western Europe, as explained in Chapter 1. Uprooted from the land and hurled into the belly of the raging industrial machine, the alienation of factory life hit children particularly hard. The salaries of factory workers were too low to enable families to survive on the wages of parents alone, forcing children from five to seven years onwards to work in inhumane conditions for a fraction of the wage of a grown man. As cheap labour, children were prized for their small size in coal mines and factories, where they could reach into corners otherwise inaccessible to adults. Alcoholism and violence ran rife, including among children, and compounded the dumbing down of the working classes caused by brutal fifteen- to sixteen-hour shifts of repetitive, physically demanding but mentally alienating work.

Education made little sense under these conditions: working-class parents could not afford to lose the meagre income of their children, and industrialists saw no reason to curtail the mass exploitation of children, since this barely paid labour was a convenient source of profit. Decision-makers could not see a case for educating the poor: a child destined for the factory floor had little use for elementary instruction, and it was generally believed among the upper classes (perspicaciously, one might add) that educating the poor might lead them to question their lot in life, creating disruptive social unrest. As such, early laws limiting the working hours of children were roundly ignored across the industrializing world.

And yet, while such practices do continue to feed the world's hungry productions lines, with children regularly found among the work force in poorly regulated mines and factories in the Global South, 90 per cent of the world's children today are spared the horrors of child labour and attend primary school.[2] This remarkable achievement is the result of a steady increase in schooling from the nineteenth century onwards, first in Northern Europe in the 1820s, then in the rest of Europe and Japan from the 1880s onwards, with the Global South catching up after the Second World War.[3] I suggest that this global change did not happen in defiance of the logic of industrial capitalism, but as an extension of capitalist modes of production as the release of fossil energy liberated manpower for more complex tasks.

The school as a factory

The defining forces of the nineteenth century were industrialism and nationalism. Powered by ever larger quantities of fossil fuels, administrations were able to take control over bigger swathes of territory, connected physically through waterways and railways and ideologically through national identity-building programmes. For colonial powers, the material benefits of colonization doubled as fodder for nascent national identities. The pillaging of Black and Brown lands across the world fed a sense of national vitality from London to Berlin, and with it the idea that fealty to the nation and its imperial ambitions was something best bred at a young age.

In addition, two factors pushed decision-makers to re-evaluate their views on education: first, it became necessary to contain the social disorder caused by alcoholism and debauchery among the alienated working classes, and second, governments struggled to rein in regionalist sentiment and keep their young nation states in one piece. The success of national projects hinged on imparting a sense of common identity to a large mass of barely-literate folks who had up until that point identified by fief, tribe or family. In continental Europe, the majority of people spoke regional dialects as their first language. In the colonies, indigenous people spoke their own languages. Additionally, in settler-colonial lands like the USA and Australia, immigrants of different linguistic backgrounds were constantly arriving. Thus, standardizing language became an urgent priority. And for that, states needed schools. Lots of them, and fast.

The first period of expansion of mass education occurred in the early nineteenth century, in Northern Europe. In England, the British government was eager to promote schooling as a vector for shaping public mores, but was reluctant to support this scheme with public finances. For want of training and investment, early schools therefore faced a dire shortage of suitable teachers and financial means. Not to be discouraged, the British circumvented the challenge with a learning approach inspired by the hierarchical and operational functioning of factories. The prime virtues to be instilled by these schools were obedience, discipline and loyalty – not critical thinking and personal emancipation. The new system would teach the 3Rs (reading, writing and arithmetic), civics, religious and moral education to the largest number of children in the most efficient way possible: a professor delegated his authority to *pupil teachers*, who were older students acting as foremen for groups of younger pupils. The learning sequence was precisely timed, monitored with bells, whistles, hand gestures and short commands. This repetitive and mechanical method was cheap and efficient, perfect for the mass production of education on a national scale, and spread rapidly across the country.

After the fall of Napoleon in 1814, the French sent Jean-Baptiste Say (yes, the same economist who was responsible for the economic premise that nature is free and infinite) as an emissary to observe what was going on in schools across the channel. Upon his return, he set about rapidly developing this industrialized educational approach in France, and thus, the school as a factory spread across the industrialized world, including North America.

Concluding on the spread of primary education across Northern and Western Europe and the Americas in the nineteenth century, I argue that industrialists accepted the introduction of schooling not because the better angels of their nature came calling, but because on the one hand, it bred generalized acceptance of capitalism in society, and on the other, the abundance of cheap energy introduced machines that were increasingly cheaper and easier to run than children in rags. Meanwhile, in colonized countries, schooling served to destroy native culture and impose imperial rule. Indigenous children were forcibly converted to Christianity, dressed like the children of their colonial oppressors, and fed a diet of religious and civic education meant to assimilate them entirely into the colonial mindset while denying their identity and history. The mass graves of native children in the schoolyards of Canada and the United States serve as a sobering reminder that schooling has since its inception served as a tool of the oppressor to ply the oppressed into submission at their youngest and most vulnerable age.[4]

Schools for the rich, schools for the rest

Schooling has come a long way since the days of *pupil teachers* in cramped British classrooms. For a start, the first half of the twentieth century brought working-class political parties to power to build the foundations of the modern welfare state across the industrialized world, including a massive increase in educational funding, modern limitations on child labour and the lengthening of the period for compulsory schooling. This culminated in enshrining the right to free elementary education in Article 26 of the Universal Declaration of Human Rights of 1948, approved by forty-eight of the fifty-eight members of the United Nations at the time.[5] Although the declaration was not binding, it reflected a growing global consensus on the importance of primary education.

The early twentieth century also brought to the fore powerful voices for pedagogical change, including John Dewey, William Kilpatrick, Maria Montessori and Helen Parkhurst. While the philosophy and methods of these educationists varied, they shared a core belief in the centrality of childhood experiences, the capacity of children to regulate their own learning, and, particularly in the works of Dewey, the necessity of nurturing critical thinking and creativity for breeding competent citizenry in a democratic society.[6] Education's functions as a class-reproduction mechanism and an instrument for capitalism were challenged by this new conception of education as a public good for the betterment of society as a whole. The shift in mindset is evident in the Declaration of Human Rights, which stipulates that the aim of education is the 'full development of the human personality'.[7]

These changes to schooling up until 1950 undeniably made the educational experience more pleasant and less rigid. It massively increased literacy and the basic knowledge of arithmetic, building the foundations of our modern knowledge economy. However, a closer look at the make-up of school systems around the world reveals that education continued to be used for maintaining racial, gendered and class structures in service of capitalism, albeit in more subtle ways than in the nineteenth century.

Race

To begin with, the last residential schools for indigenous children closed in 1970 in Australia, 1978 in the United States and 1996 in Canada, so the racist erasure of native culture and the mass murder of indigenous children in schools is hardly the stuff of ancient history.[8] Though native Americans, Aborigines and First Nations people bore the brunt of educational imperialism, colonized children around the world were brow-beaten out of their native tongues and cultures by mission schools and state-supported education systems directly imported from colonizing powers – a legacy that lives on today. Confronting the curriculum of the scholars of my foundation in Zimbabwe always bemuses me. The girls ask for help with Jane Austen and Charles Dickens, at which point it becomes patently obvious that cultural markers I take for granted are entirely alien to them, and with good reason! Why would a fifteen-year-old girl from Zimbabwe need to understand why Harriet Smith was an unsuitable proposition for Mr Elton in Austen's *Emma*? And yet, the economic future of Zimbabwean girls depends on their ability to pass their A-level examinations. For those who choose English as one of their subjects (and many do since science education is patchy and underfunded), passing requires grasping depictions of the British class system in nineteenth-century novels. Those who fail drop out of school, and those who succeed know more about the history of the Austro-Hungarian Empire than they do about Apartheid. This is a relic of an education system built by the British to ensure the dominance of English culture and language across the Commonwealth in the early twentieth century, with no regard for the needs and aspirations of African and Asian children.

When one thinks of the deleterious instrumentalization of education in service of a racist agenda, one inevitably turns to the enduring segregation of American schools until the landmark 1954 *Brown vs. Board of Education* decision of the US Supreme Court.[9] Civil rights activist Maya Angelou narrated her childhood in the segregated South of the United States in her autobiography, *I Know Why the Caged Bird Sings*: growing up in a world where White people were never seen, existing only as alien-like others to Black children like her.[10] Yet, in Black communities, White-supremacist thinking implacably organized society from the most tender age, where school curricula in Black schools, taught by Black teachers, reinforced the perception that whiteness was the universal norm, and blackness the lesser exception. Angelou expounded the psychological impact this had on her as a child, wishing herself White and blond, hating her dark skin and hair. Though Angelou grew up in the 1930s, bell hooks showed in *Teaching Community*, that the assumption of whiteness as universal still dominated American education at the end of the twentieth century, some fifty years after official desegregation.[11]

While segregation is legally outlawed, it persists in practice in many parts of the USA, with half of the children in the country attending schools where 75 per cent of the pupils are either White or non-White.[12] It seems the trend towards *de facto* resegregation may be worsening, as conservative governance in the US spurs the development of private schools, mostly catering to White parents under the guise of 'school choice'.[13] This push for privatization, often associated with 'White flight' from public schools, comes at the expense of the latter. Public schools are left to educate non-White children with fewer financial means. Being neither American, nor Black, I find it hard to fathom the scale of systemic racism in American schooling, and therefore refer the reader to authors better placed to analyse the situation, like Ta-Nehisi Coates and Ibram X Kendi.[14]

Gender

By the middle of the last century, the education of girls lagged behind the education of boys in quantity and quality. While schools for girls had been slowly developing since the mid-nineteenth century, access to education beyond the elementary level remained highly restricted, either de jure or de facto. Most schools for girls were run by church denominations of one sort or another, with emphasis on preserving the moral purity and physical chastity of girls in preparation for marriage. The depiction of the brutality and misery of girls' schools throughout the period is well documented in literature and film, from the abysmal conditions of schooling for lower-class girls in the 1840s described in Charlotte Brontë's *Jane Eyre*,[15] to the acidic conditions of schooling for upper-class girls in the early 1900s in the Australian novel *Picnic at Hanging Rock*.[16] Girls and women who refused to conform to these strict expectations could be pulled out of school and sent instead to church-run penitentiaries to be 'reformed'. The most notorious of these were the Magdalen Asylums run by the Magdalen Sisters in England, Ireland and the USA, where 'fallen' women were held captive to work in church-run laundries for the redemption of their sins.[17] These so-called sins included sex out of wedlock, rape and sometimes even just being opinionated. Women were routinely subject to abuse and torture in these institutions, and the graves of young women found on site bear witness to their suffering. The last Magdalen laundry closed in 1996, so, again, this is hardly ancient history.[18]

Today, two-thirds of the world's countries have succeeded in achieving educational parity for girls in primary school enrollment.[19] Most of the remaining primary education gender gap is in Asia and parts of Africa. The global picture is more complex for secondary education, but a large educational gap remains in much of Africa. From rural Pakistan to the slums of Lusaka, for many economically strained families, educating girls beyond the legally mandated minimum is still regarded as a poor investment soon lost to childbearing and homemaking.

We are still failing girls, particularly Black and Brown girls, in many parts of the world. The infuriating irony of this failure is that educating girls is one of the most effective guardrails against collapse. Educated girls are better able to plan their families, to support their families economically and to make decisions that support their family's resilience. In failing girls, we fail the World.

Class

Though race and gender played an important role in defining the educational experience of youngsters in the twentieth century, I believe socio-economic class to be the defining determinant of educational opportunities. Wealthy children consistently had better access to education than their poorer peers throughout the twentieth century. Looking at the development of schooling over that period, a two-tier public-private system emerged in almost every country on the planet where rich children had access to excellent privately funded education, and poor children made do with underfunded public education (notable exceptions emerged in Scandinavia – more on that later).

Today, privately educated elites around the world share more in common with each other, even considering gender and race, than they do with their publicly educated fellow citizens. Children educated in top private schools around the world are more likely to accede to positions of power in politics, public administration, the corporate world and even academia. The UK is a case in point: twenty former British prime ministers attended Eton College, an elite London-based private school with tuition fees over 40,000 pounds (45,000 dollars) per year.[20] In most countries, the cost of quality private schooling creates an insuperable financial barrier to working and middle-class families.[21] While many private schools offer a small percentage of subsidized or free places, the conditions for acceding to these, in terms of academic performance, creates an additional barrier that excludes children from poor backgrounds.

My experience, in nearly a decade of working with struggling families from the townships of Zimbabwe to the suburbs of Rotterdam, is that the living conditions of many children below the poverty line prevent them from excelling at school, regardless of their baseline intelligence and capabilities. My fieldwork notes are replete with stories of forced migration, domestic violence, parents either incarcerated or deceased and older children acting as carers for younger siblings. Not to mention power cuts, poor internet connections, lack of access to proper technological tools and other practical impediments to studying. To add insult to injury, these children often attend underfunded public schools with large classrooms, underpaid teachers and understaffed support services, where dire social problems force teachers to act as social workers, carers and caterers. It's a wonder, under the circumstances, that many of these children finish school at all.

Even with proper financial support in place, the road to educational excellence is rocky for kids from poor families. Some educational systems, like the public school system in The Netherlands, are structurally designed to keep struggling children out the higher levels of education. Children in The Netherlands are tested at the age of eleven on a standardized instrument called the CITO test (equivalent of the 11+ in the UK). Coupled with their teachers' assessment, this forms the basis for study advice that steers the children within one of the tracks of a highly stratified secondary education system. High-scoring kids get sent to the upper echelons, with a straightforward path from high school graduation to university. In the middle echelons, kids are funnelled towards universities of applied sciences (polytechnics, as they were called in England). These lead to more applied, usually less well-paid professions than a university degree, such as design, safety management, agricultural management etc. Children at the bottom of the CITO performance ladder go to vocational secondary schools. There, they receive a short vocational or technical education leading to essential but often poorly paid professions: electricians, caretakers, nurse aids, receptionists etc. At first glance, this might seem like a fair system: evaluate children's capabilities on the basis of a standardized test at the age of eleven, then channel each according to their ability towards the most suitable educational pathway.

However, in practice, the system is relentlessly unfair. First, because there is almost no mobility between the echelons. Moving from a lower echelon to a higher one requires patience, willpower and financial support. There are a couple of complicated options for doing this, but either way, children who seek to move from the vocational pathway to university end up staying in school between three and five years longer than children who start out in the highest echelon. During my research, I interviewed a Dutch-Moroccan woman who, at twenty-six, was finally finishing her bachelor's degree, having started out in the vocational pathway at twelve. She was proud of her achievement, but somewhat baffled that correcting her poor performance as a tween had taken up so much of her life.

This brings us to the second discriminatory element of the Dutch system: eleven years of age among the poor is a very different experience to eleven years of age among the rich. The totality of the vocational school pupils I interviewed had working and lower-middle-class parents – cleaners, construction workers, truck drivers, hairdressers, nail-salon workers, primary school teachers etc. Nearly all of them had suffered traumatic personal experiences in the years leading up to their CITO test. The vast majority came from broken and reconstituted families, with large families often cohabiting in a limited space. About half came from first- or second-generation migrant backgrounds, with the challenge of learning Dutch added to their regular school work. Many faced personal traumas like the death or incarceration of a parent, bullying and mental health conditions that had been diagnosed late. And yet, these children sat the same test as children from wealthy, supportive, nurturing families. It gets worse: because teachers expect poor children to fare worse than their wealthy peers, they often give lower study advice than what the children's actual CITO test scores qualify them for. This means that even if a child studies hard, gives the CITO their all and gets a high mark, they can still be dragged down to the lower echelons if their teachers don't believe in them.[22] This happened to nearly half of the pupils I interviewed.

Unsurprisingly, few of the children I spoke to had friends or relatives that had gone to university. Most had never been to a university campus and had very little idea of what a university is, does, or how one gets there. How are the children of the poor able to aspire to higher education if the road to get there is obscured and obstructed? Around the same time, I conducted research on the educational motivations of liberal arts students, the bulk of whom come from solidly middle-to-upper-class families. Without exception, they told me that university was just a baseline expectation for them. They had never considered other options.

Based on my research, I argue that the Dutch educational system is a finely tuned machine for reproducing class differences. Detractors will counter-argue that there has been a continuous influx of first-generation students at Dutch universities since the 1960s, particularly in my own university in the post-industrial city of Rotterdam. This is true, and a credit to working-class families' hard work and perseverance. Upwards mobility, while difficult, is (still) possible. However, downwards mobility is significantly rarer; we don't often find vocational school pupils hailing from wealthy families. I'm sure they exist, but I have yet to meet one. When class mobility works only one way, entrants are expected to conform to the *habitus* of their new environment (Chapter 3). The result is not so much social justice, as reinforcing the system by cladding it in meritocratic clothes. First-generation working-class academic Lisa McKenzie noted at a debate at the Oxford Union in 2017: 'until the middle class allow their stupid children to fail, we will have no social mobility'.[23] While I take issue with the choice of wording, I empathize with the sentiment.

Fortunately, most educational systems are less structurally rigid than the Dutch one. I often serious-joke that it is easier to get a girl from the slums of Harare to university than it is to do the same for a kid from Rotterdam South, because it's true, on paper. A child who passes the ordinary-Level (now called GCSE in the UK) and advanced-level examinations in Zimbabwe is permitted to move on to the next level, even if they pass by the skin of their teeth. Thus, a few of our scholars in Zimbabwe have managed to recover from a string of D's to successfully attend medical and law school thereafter, without significant delays to their studies. On paper, they did not have to jump through any of the hoops that being funnelled into the vocational education track in Holland entails. The same can be said of the American, British and French systems, which allow students to attempt SATs, A-levels or the Baccalaureate without rigid structural pre-requisites. However, I have witnessed the immense challenge that comes with attempting to defy the educational odds for children from poor backgrounds, even within systems that appear to provide equal chances on paper.

In 2017, I began mentoring a brilliant teenager in Zimbabwe as she attempted her first year of university after a lukewarm A-level performance. She was undergoing immense personal stress, as the child of a violent, fractured family. She was homeless at the time I met her, working long hours as a disability assistant to scrape together enough money to pay fees, housing and food. She failed her first semester, which was hardly surprising under the circumstances. Progressively, I took on a parenting role with her, supporting her financially, helping her with everything from homework to health and matters of the heart. From 5000 miles away, at a time when the internet in Zimbabwe was slow and expensive (it still is, but has improved significantly with Chinese investments), we exchanged thousands of text messages, videos, voice notes and calls between my sparse visits to Zimbabwe. Yet even with the extra help, every course throughout her entire bachelor was a struggle. She needed extensive coaching on academic writing, including referencing and plagiarism. Part-way through, she failed a mandatory module and had to repeat a semester, increasing the cost and frustration. Then came Covid – the university closed its dorms, so she was homeless once again, expected to study 'online' with an old phone and no Wi-Fi. Against the odds, she finally graduated from the University of Zimbabwe in 2022, with a 2.1 UK equivalent classification in public administration. She earned her place in a master's programme in law in Europe, where the stress of dealing with endless paperwork for her right to reside in the EU and the necessity of holding down side-jobs to pay part of her living expenses compounded her struggle with the tacit codes and conventions of European academia. This has nothing to do with intelligence; she is a very bright person. Intelligence and academic success are two entirely different things. Her experience reminds me of a memorable quote by one of the founders of the Frankfurt School of critical pedagogy, Oskar Negt:

> A production of knowledge that is directed in such a way can only compile specialized knowledge and cannot organize the experience of society as a whole. The modes of expression of this specialized knowledge as well as its content can thus not be adopted by the majority of the population. This does not have to do with the extreme limits of academic speech or with the 'backwardness' of the experience of the people; the very coexistence of the proletarian production of experience and that of scientific and scholarly knowledge is based on their diverse material foundations.[24]

If one forgives the archaic Marxists speech, what he meant was that the university system is designed by and for the upper classes. Young people from poor backgrounds, like my ward, will always struggle to make sense of it, because it does not speak to the concrete foundations of their life experience.

What I find the most enraging about the cruelty of modern education is the way poor children internalize the injustices of the system as personal failures. I cannot bear to hear another child call themselves 'stupid' or 'lazy' because they could not succeed in a race that they ran from a hundred feet behind the starting line with weights tied to all four limbs. Individualizing systemic failures is the most brutal form of denial of modern education. The blame for this specific ideological shift falls largely on neoliberalism.

So much has been written about the impact of neoliberalism on education, from near-enough the entire catalogue of Henry Giroux's works, to Stefan Collini's *What Are Universities For*,[25] including the vast sum of articles on the subject in academic journals. My aim is not to produce a meta-analysis of the existing literature on neoliberal education. Rather, I'd like to explain the collapse of modern education in light of what I know best: a political economy grounded in material, physical and biosphere realities. I want to show that, in terms of its own goals, neoliberal education has succeeded remarkably. But in so-doing, it has functioned as a catalyst for collapse: an education of despair.

Learning in despair

I've shown that the modern education system, from primary school to universities, was designed in conjunction with and in support of the Industrial Revolution. Curricula were built to justify and maintain the colonial empires, oppressive gender roles and class differences necessary for the workings of capitalism. Throughout the period beginning in 1800 and ending around 1960, the racist, classist and sexist goals of education were stated quite openly from imperial governments down to schoolteachers.

However, this changed in the wake of the revolutionary movements of the 1960s, including a wave of successful anti-colonial revolutions in the crumbling British and French empires, the civil rights movement in the United States, the student revolutions of Berkeley, Paris and Copenhagen, the anti-war movement opposed to the Vietnam War, and second-wave feminism across the Western world. Many of these movements supported alternatives to capitalism: newly decolonized states experimented with various forms of socialist governance, protest movements tried to develop anarchist, communitarian and decentralized group structures. This was the decade that birthed Critical Pedagogy, including the masterworks of Paulo Freire and Oskar Negt, and the reformed Universities of Europe. However, the revolutionary fever was short-lived. A sharp contraction of the energy supply, first in 1973, then in 1979, refocused global attention away from social justice issues, and ushered in the neoliberal era.

Neoliberal education

The late 1970s can best be summarized as a long and painful hangover from the energy glut of the 1960s and early 1970s. In response to the oil shocks, demand-side economists pushed for more government intervention to rekindle dying economic fires. In other words, more of the same Keynesian medicine prescribed since Roosevelt's New Deal in 1930's America. On the other side, supply-side economists pleaded to rein in governments and free the markets, brandishing copies of Friedrich Hayek's *Road to Serfdom* like bibles. Hayek wrote his magnum opus in 1944, so it wasn't hot off the press by the time it landed on the desks of Ronald Reagan and Margaret Thatcher, but there's naught like a crisis to give old ideas a new lease of life.[26] And what a crisis it was! The economic situation was so dire that it generated a new economic term: stagflation – a contraction of stagnation and inflation. It doesn't take political genius to figure that this would be a lethal combination for politicians in power. The unfortunates in power at the time, James Callaghan in Britain, and Jimmy Carter in the United States, both softcore Keynesians with the charisma and leadership qualities of grandfatherly bureaucrats, were completely rudderless against the raging economic storm and the appeal of market fever. Thatcher and Reagan burst through the doors of power riding a unicorn of deregulation, tax cuts and meritocracy. Thus, neoliberalism, birthed in the obscurity of university halls during the Marginalist Revolution (Chapter 1), bred in the shadow of postwar Keynesian glory, finally came to light.

The next thirty years, leading to the financial crash of 2008, are chronicled by Marxist historian David Harvey in *A Brief History of Neoliberalism*.[27] Between the end of the Soviet Union and the Great Recession, the consensus was that neoliberal economics were a wonderful thing, and neoliberal logic should be applied to as many aspects of society as possible, including education. Parties nominally on the political Left, including Tony Blair's New Labour and Bill Clinton's Democrats deregulated and privatized everything they could get their hands on. Left-wing politics at the time was free-market economics with a pride flag on top. For a while, nothing really challenged the consensus. People all over the developing world suffered catastrophic drops in living standards as a result of structural adjustments programmes upon them by the International Monetary Fund in exchange for loans. As noted by a contemporary analyst, this involved devaluing local currencies such that basic necessities were no longer affordable to the average household, curtailing the public sector employment opportunities upon which many locals depended, the suppression of public education and healthcare, the removal of price controls on basic necessities, and the destruction of local industries.[28] Yet these deleterious consequences in no way challenged the no-pain-no-gain economic mantra of the neoliberal trifecta. The generally accepted philosophy held that anything the markets broke, they could fix.

The period from 1991 to 2008 marked the heyday of neoliberalism in education. This period witnessed the rollout of New Public Management across parts of the capitalist world that had hitherto preferred a more social model of education – including The Netherlands, Sweden and Denmark.[29] Policymakers, inspired by Gary Becker's *Human Capital Theory*, shifted from the Dewey-inspired viewing of education as a public good, designed to improve society, and therefore worthy of government support.[30] Instead, they adopted a view of education as personal investment in human capital, with the decision to invest (or not) left to private individuals and educational markets. At first, the changes were not so noticeable, as public funding shifted from supporting public institutions, to supporting riskier semi-private schemes, such as charter schools in the United States, or Academies in England. These institutions come with the profit-making advantages of the private sector and the government funding of the public sector in a win-win financial outcome for the school's owners, though not necessarily for the school's pupils who are left in the cold when these schools go bankrupt. In higher education, tuition ticked upwards, and student grants were replaced with loans. As a result, student debt began building up in the 1990s and early 2000s, especially in the US and the UK, but also in The Netherlands.[31]

The real blow to public education came after the global banking crisis of 2008. It should have been a moment of reckoning for neoliberal deregulation. Instead, governments, suddenly finding themselves strapped for cash after bailing out banks to the tune of several hundred billion dollars of tax-payer money, doubled down on privatization. They sold off public assets, cut spending on public services and constricted the welfare state. In the educational sector, privatization, the precarization of employment and defunding of higher education accelerated.[32] During this period, fixed-term, part-time contracts increased dramatically at all levels of education, public money was syphoned into private sector subsidization schemes, school directorates and university boards were reformed to work like corporate board rooms, student debt ballooned, funding for public schools decreased and the difference in quality between public and private education expanded.

New factories, new schools

In essence, it is not so much that the purpose of education has changed since the nineteenth century, but rather, the nature of the production system that schooling is designed to serve has changed. In other words, if we have new schools, it's because we have new 'factories' that need workers with different exploitable skillsets. As explained in Chapter 1, the immense energy surplus released by fossil fuels in the last century made it possible to create ever-longer production and distribution lines stretched across the world at very little cost. Global capitalism is a physical reality of supply chains that criss-cross political borders under the umbrella of fewer, larger corporations that are multinational and transnational: they have headquarters and subsidiaries in multiple countries, and operations that transcend national borders. Susan Strange, the pioneer of *International Political Economy*, wrote in *The Retreat of the State* that neoliberal governments deliberately gave up political power to these corporate behemoths by deregulating trade within their own borders, and building an international legal architecture that favours big companies at the expense of national governments – in the (unsubstantiated) belief that the benefits of global wealth accumulation would trickle down the lower rungs of society.[33]

A global production system operating on such a large scale can only work well if materials, procedures and distribution are standardized across the world. Global capitalism without standards would fall apart in short order. If you've ever felt frustrated when you realize that there isn't a single charger in your pile of ancient cables that fits the socket of your new phone, then you understand why standardization is essential to the production chain. You can't have cable and socket issues when you're expected to deliver stuff in a seamless, just-in-time manner. What's true for cabling is also valid for people: transnational corporations need workers with a standard set of skills and competences that can be plugged into any part of the supply chain, in any country in the world. It used to be that standardization was something for the working classes only, like Charlie Chaplin's Tramp in *Modern Times*.[34] But under neoliberalism, middle and upper management were also standardized.

The burden of preparing a workforce with standardized competences falls on schools and higher education institutions. Kids come in all shapes and sizes, with variations of talents, creativity, inspiration and abilities, but from the youngest age, they must comply with strictures of standardized testing and reporting. The most egregious example of standardization in recent years is the *No Child Left Behind Act* of 2001 in the USA.[35] The act created an educational framework based on standardized and quantified learning objectives for all students in primary and secondary education, particularly in reading and maths. It established a rating system for schools and teachers based on the students' performance on the standardized tests. Unsurprisingly, the result was that students spent a lot more time doing tests, and a lot less time learning anything that wasn't mandated by the federal government.

The UK witnessed similar developments: around the time of the *Education and Inspections Act* in 2006, the Office for Standards in Education (Ofsted) began crunching numbers on pupils' exam performance and classifying schools on a scale from outstanding to inadequate.[36] Back then, student performance on the GCSEs and A-levels was rated using a scale from A to F (the grade system changed to 1–10 in 2017, but the same logic applies). Since Ofsted ratings depended to a significant degree on the number of students obtaining grades between C and A, teachers contorted to produce the highest number of C grade possible. Several teachers explained to me that they abandoned excellent and failing pupils to concentrate on borderline students who could be made, with significant effort, to scrape a C on their finals. After research was published showing that schools were 'teaching to the test', in 2019, Ofsted reduced focus on exams, but increased focus on school discipline, monitoring student behaviour (both inside and outside of classrooms) and school management practices.[37] In other words, the same fundamentals of discipline and control are alive and well 200 years after the first public schools emerged in industrial England, with an added veneer of bureaucratic rationalization and a sprinkle of New Public Management.

In higher education, standardization and reporting have become increasingly international. Universities compete for a top spot in international ranking systems like the Times Higher Education Ranking and the Academic Ranking of World Universities, both of which are private ranking systems based mainly on narrow research output metrics.[38] Universities pay close attention to these rankings, that influence lucrative international student intakes, grant awards and other financial incentives. To make comparisons easier, universities have been aligning their degrees, facilitating international mobility and providing easier like-for-like CVs for employers to compare in a globalized marketplace. Europe led the way for standardization with the start of the Bologna Process in 1999, making the three-year bachelor and two-year master's degrees the standard for universities in participating countries.[39] The idea was that after finishing their undergraduate studies, students could apply for graduate studies in any other participating country. Universities with integrated four- or five-year programmes faced enormous difficulties implementing the Bologna requirements. They chopped up their programmes and gave up on of some of their educational principles to fit new European standards. But the cogs must be made to fit in the machine.

The purpose of national standardization and international alignment in education isn't to develop well-rounded, self-actualized citizens who can face a future in collapse with sobriety and courage. It is to produce standardized workers who will integrate the global production system at the level dictated by their class. It has been very successful in doing this for the last 200 years, but has produced a system that cannot self-correct, and seems unable to prevent its own demise. When collapse comes, at least some among the working classes still master essential survival skills, such as food production, nursing and construction. But when the production apparatus falls apart, there will be nowhere for the masses of degree-wielding graduates to go, and deep down, I think they know this.

Teachers of the world, despair

The productive system is already crumbling, energy supply is contracting, prices are out of control and supply chains are breaking down; rationality would recommend immediately retooling our educational system to prepare for planned degrowth. But schools cannot offer this kind of physics-based realism since their rationality is grounded in abstract economics, and their main purpose is to produce market-ready workers. In response to the increasing visibility of environmental problems in the public sphere, education has instead been retooled to encourage bargaining and belief in technological salvation, because both psychological processes are required for capitalism to push beyond its physical limits. The main reason adults with full cognitive capacity passively watch the screws come off the machine without taking any steps to protect themselves from the coming implosion is because they were conditioned from the youngest age to believe that science and technology will come to the rescue.

Our schools serve up euphemisms, half-truths and outright fabrications. They teach children about the physical mechanisms by which CO_2 and methane act as greenhouse gases, but they perpetuate the lie that with a little elbow grease, we can put solar panels on every rooftop and solve the problem. Teenagers leaving high schools today haven't got the faintest idea about the energy systems underpinning the world around them, the rapidly approaching production peaks of most of non-renewable resources, and the scale of the losses incurred by the living world. They're told that if they place their plastic waste in the recycling bin, turn the lights off when they leave the room and cycle to school, all will be well. In my view, the blame for this falls on policymakers and educational managers who determine the content of public school curricula at the behest of *the market*. I'd like to think that teachers are not blind to what goes on in the world, but crushed by standardized testing requirements, mandatory monitoring and reporting, inspections, underfunding and understaffing, most have neither the time nor the space to speak the truth. Those that would dare would soon find themselves out of a job. It's no wonder teachers around the world are quitting in droves.[40] Our schools have become sites of despair, breeding grounds for denial and bargaining, churning out market-ready students on a conveyor belt to collapse.

By the time they arrive in my classroom at the ages of eighteen to twenty, students have been living under illusions perpetuated by the school system for fifteen years. It's not surprising that my classes hit them like a ton of bricks. Some of my students are so shocked that they are unable to speak in class for a couple of weeks after my first lecture. I try my best to implement trauma-informed teaching practices (Chapter 5), but I see my students for a mere seven weeks. How can I unravel fifteen years of conditioning in such a short amount of time without driving home truths in sometimes painful ways? I do my best to hold my students' grief, to guide them gently down the rough road of anger and depression, but I'm only one human against a tidal wave of denial and despair. I can only hope that our brief, intense encounter provides them with enough tools to look to the future once they leave my class.

It's neither fair to them, nor to me, that the burden of truth befalls us, when almost every class they have taken in the previous decade has peddled, either implicitly or explicitly, the lie that everything can continue more or less as it has in the last fifty years. Every year, just before Christmas, I update my slides to reflect the bad news coming out of scientific studies published in the last twelve months, and I rage against an education system that prioritizes cramming trigonometry and vocabulary lists into children over preparing them for humanity's greatest test. I'm not saying that we shouldn't teach children maths and languages – those are important; we will still need engineers and linguists in a collapsing world. But I hope to have demonstrated with sufficient force that standardized maths and language tests are mostly used by schools as selective instruments that perpetuate class reproduction. I want students to come to my class aware and appraised of the scientific consensus, endowed with intimate knowledge of the plant and animal world, undaunted by the prospect of fixing a broken pipe or upcycling a torn shirt, so that we may spend the precious time we have together preparing the world that comes next. I want a learning in dialogue with the physical realities of the world and its inhabitants. I want pedagogies of collapse, not the collapse of pedagogy.

Learning in revolution

I want to acknowledge that while *most* schools have served capitalism, for so long as there have been schools, there have been people who dreamt that education could breed emancipation. The pedagogies of collapse owe a lot to the romanticism of *Bildung* and the loving rage of critical pedagogy, both of which I encountered by fate along my educational journey.

Bildung

I begin with Bildung because of its historical precedence, but in fact, I encountered Bildung by accident some years after I started my work with critical pedagogy. In late 2016, I received a request from a colleague to stand in for him at an education conference in the quaint Dutch city of Leiden. This was, it turned out, one of the early meetings of what would become the Global Bildung Network – an alliance of practitioners from all walks of life – teachers, academics, musicians, artists, indigenous activists and NGO volunteers – working together to activate the transformative power of this curious Germanic concept. On that cold morning in Leiden, I met Lene Rachel Andersen, founder of the network and author of the definitive volume on Bildung, *The Nordic Secret: a European Story of Beauty and Freedom*.[41] For curious readers, *The Nordic Secret* contains a comprehensive account of the antecedents, history and practice of Bildung. I cannot do justice to the book or to the lengthy conversations Lene and I have held on the subject since those days, but it's fair to say that the pedagogies of collapse were influenced by discussion within the Global Bildung Network.

Bildung is a German word related to the term 'bild', meaning image, originally referring to the Christian concept of Man, made in the image of God. Until the eighteenth century, the word was exclusively used in a religious context to denote the kind of faith that brings men closer to God. This changed towards the 1770s to mean a general educative engagement for self-betterment, self-growth, personal aesthetic, and, quite often, nationalist pride and commitment. Anthony Ashley Cooper, third Earl of Shaftesbury and one of the earliest proponents of a secular Bildung, was British.

But Bildung's aims were radically opposed to the cold rationality of the English school-factory. The evolution of Bildung at the hands of German poets, playwrights and philosophers followed an arc beginning with revolutionary calls for beauty and freedom and ending with unbridled nationalism at a time where nation states were just forming geographically and conceptually. Throughout, Bildung was associated with the Romantics, from Christoph Martin Wieland, Johann Gottfried Herder and Johann Wolfgang Goethe in pre-revolutionary Europe to Friedrich Schiller, Johann Gottlieb Fichte and Wilhelm von Humboldt in the early nineteenth century. It can be seen as a rebellion against the ugly materialism and rationality of the nascent Industrial Revolution. Proponents of Bildung believed that the human calling is primarily aesthetic and moral, not shackled by material subsistence and productivity.

While the core ideas of Bildung were nurtured in Germany, Bildung's passage from philosophy to educational practice took place in nineteenth-century Denmark. At the time, the border between Denmark and Germany shifted regularly, and as such, German intellectual movements played an important role in Danish public life. The man credited with bringing Bildung to Denmark is Nikolaj Frederik Severin Grundtvig, a pastor, philosopher, poet, and one of the architects of the Danish constitution. Whereas the Germans tended to view Bildung as the purview of aristocrats and bourgeois elites, Grundtvig originated the concept of folk-bildung: a call for the nation-wide educational emancipation of peasants and workers, including the women of the lower classes. This emancipatory project was accompanied by the development of a romantic and aesthetic sense of Danishness, reconnecting people with their past and culture. Despite Grundtvig's broad ambitions, the first folk high schools, which opened in the Schleswig region in the 1840s, catered to the wealthy. The emergence of a Bildung education for the masses came after the Prussian-Danish war of 1848–51, at the hands of Christen Kold, a lower-class man who pioneered a genuine movement to educate the peasantry. The folk high schools were experiments in self-governing, democratic communities: teachers lived and dined with their students, in a relaxed atmosphere combining art, poetry, music, song, civics and moral education, alongside experimental farming practices and farming innovation management. Kold opened his first school for young men in 1851 and for girls nine years later. By 1900, 135 folk high schools had been established with 100 or so surviving into the twentieth century. The ideals of folk-bildung began permeating through Norway and Sweden in the 1860s, where folk high schools also opened in droves. The folk high school movement has been credited for fostering the high levels of societal trust at the heart of Scandinavian economic and social success.

In the spring of 2022, I went with Lene to visit Christen Kold's folk high school, two hours outside of Copenhagen. The (now empty) building looks like a farmhouse; it has none of the austere trappings of the school-factories of England and France; there was not a bench in sight, nor even the space for rows of tables. The ghosts of *hyggelig* times past flittered through the thatching.

After our short tour of the place, we headed to one of the seventy modern folk high school currently operating in Denmark, where well-spoken Danish teenagers talked us through their daily routine and walked us through art studios, theatres and construction workshops. They shared with us their experiences of living in this family-like, non-formal, growth-oriented environment – a kind of steppingstone between formal high school and university. They then marched us to the chapel, where we were handed songbooks and invited to partake in a rendition of Beatles classics (to be fair, 95% of the songs in the book were in Danish, so our choice was limited). As we headed for the exit, I paused to observe boarders fooling around on the school lawn, and then it struck me. I leaned over to Lene and said: 'they're all White!'

It must be said, Denmark is not an especially ethnically diverse country: in 2023, for just over five million inhabitants of Danish origin, there were 405,000 migrants and 174,000 second-generation or more inhabitants with origins in the Global South, so perhaps the composition of folk high schools merely represents the general make-up of the population, but then one would have expected to see at least *some* minority faces there.[42] Economic factors could come into play, while state-subsidized folk high schools still come at a cost of around 5,000–7,000 euros per year, per student. I spoke to the chair of the Danish Association of Folk High Schools, who stated that 75 per cent of students pay their own way, meaning they will likely take two gap years – one to earn the money, and the other to join the folk high school of their choice. About 10 per cent of all young adults in Denmark attend a folk high school before moving on to work or higher education, and most, by the Chair's admission, are from the upper and middle classes. What do folk high schools focused on Danish lore and the pursuit of personal and aesthetic ideals have to offer families struggling with economic deprivation, social exclusion and migration? There is, in my experience, suspicion towards the arts and humanities and a strong preference for financially and socially rewarding education pathways like engineering, medicine and law among working class and migrant-background families. Gap years to 'find oneself' are not really customary in those settings.

So, on the one hand, the aesthetics and practice-oriented activities of Bildung could contribute to future-proofing education. On the other hand, by positioning themselves as extracurricular production centres for the kind of flexible skills prized by employers, folk high schools could allow middle-class children to leapfrog into upper management positions in the production system, while working class and migrant children steer clear. In other words: they could end up reinforcing rather than challenging the social dynamics of capitalism. However, I think it would be possible to revive the early aspirations of Bildung – the kind of emancipatory education for the lower classes envisaged by Grundtvig and Kold – by combining it with new pedagogical methods and inclusivity approaches.

Critical pedagogy

In the winter of 2012–13, I was collecting data in Canada and Denmark for my doctoral research on the educational revolutions of the 1970s. The beauty of modern history is that eye witnesses abound, and many in their twilight years crave the opportunity to record their story for posterity. My academic career thus began with hundreds of hours listening to humans figure out their place in the grand scheme of things, with humour and nostalgia. Having wrapped up my work on problem-based learning in Hamilton, Ontario, I traded the wet Canadian autumn for snow in Roskilde and Aalborg, the homes of the two Danish reformed universities.

On a gloomy day in January 2013, I entered the unassuming office of Henning Salling Olesen at Roskilde University, a man whose name was completely unknown to me at the time. I did not seize his historical importance as one of the founders of the reformed universities movement until later, when I had interviewed dozens of Danes of different academic persuasions. I had scheduled forty-five minutes for our interview, but when Henning began speaking, in a soft voice, often searching for the correct English words, I felt bound to my chair with strong adhesive. The meeting lasted four hours. I'm not sure Henning ever knew the impact this encounter had on me. I returned to my room and immediately e-mailed my Dutch supervisor – I didn't really understand what had just happened, but I knew it was significant. With hindsight, I can put it into words: it was my first introduction to Critical Pedagogy.

On Freire and Negt

Critical Pedagogy is invariably associated with the Brazilian pedagogue and activist Paulo Freire and his followers, from Henry Giroux to bell hooks. Freire's *Pedagogy of the Oppressed*, which I first read towards the end of my PhD, has been one of the most influential readings of my intellectual life and a foundational inspiration for this book.[43] Grounded in Marxist and existential theory, it critiques the oppression inherent in 'banking' education, advocating for the empowerment of 'problem-posing' education instead. Salling Olesen came from a different school of thought: the German Critical Pedagogy movement led by Frankfurt School scholar Oskar Negt.[44] *Kritische Erziehungswissenschaft*, as it was called, developed as an offshoot of German Critical Theory during the same historical period as Brazilian Critical Pedagogy, in the revolutionary 1960s and early 1970s.

Both branches of Critical Pedagogy gave a Marxist reading of the world, with class oppression at the centre of the educational system. Freire's understanding of oppression, expounded in *Pedagogy of the Oppressed*, is explicitly grounded in Marxist class analysis.[45] Negt was a student of Theodor Adorno, the famous Frankfurt School philosopher, and most of the scholars associated with *Kritische Erziehungswissenschaft* claimed Marxist heritage. In both traditions, mass education was understood as a tool for class reproduction; a system in which schooling promotes certain kinds of knowledges to benefit the upper classes while disempowering the working classes. The main difference between the two approaches lies in their answer to the question: Why do the working classes not revolt and overthrow this unfair system? Freire and Negt agreed that the core issue was a lack of class consciousness, but disagreed on the underlying cause.

For Freire, inspired by Erich Fromm and Jean-Paul Sartre, the underlying mechanism was a political-economic system that creates oppressive materialist relationships between people. In this system, both the oppressors and the oppressed treat each other like objects, and therefore, neither can be fully human. This creates a perverse situation where some of the oppressed escape their condition and leave the working class, only to become oppressors in turn. In such a system, success is a zero-sum game, and solidarity becomes impossible.

Negt, in line with Frankfurt School tradition, offered a psychoanalytic explanation for the working classes' inability to challenge their position in society.[46] He argued that workers' children were deprived of the very words to articulate their situation by the schooling system. He called this the 'speech barriers' problem – curricula are designed by the upper classes, for the upper classes, using vocabulary that reflects upper-class reality.[47] The content of schooling is so alien to the experience of workers' children that when they grow up, workers lack words to make coherent demands in the public sphere. They rely on trade union leaders to do this on their behalf, but unions mostly focus on incremental demands and don't challenge the ideology underlying workers' alienation. For want of words, workers occasionally erupt into the public sphere with inchoate emotions, like rage, using symbols such as flags and slogans to express themselves. These spontaneous manifestations release just enough pressure that the cycle can start again, until the next eruption, but the underlying causes of unrest are not addressed.

For Freire, the solution was a humanizing education with dialogue at its core. True dialogue dismantles the hierarchical relationship between teachers and students, turning students into co-creators of knowledge. Knowledge, in turn, is never merely theoretical, but always moves between action and reflection, a cycle known as *praxis*. When enacted with love, the critical practice of dialogue enables students to name the world – that is, to undertake a thematic investigation of the problems at the heart of social, political and economic oppression. Critical Pedagogy, for Freire, was a problem-posing education.

For Negt, the solution was an exemplary education with history at its core. He used the concept of exemplarity to mean learning grounded in the lived experience of workers. Examples from life in the factory, the township or the trade union should be used as access points for workers to understand their place in history. The ultimate goal of education for Negt was the transformation of splintered working-class (un)consciousness into collective class-conscious actions. Exemplarity allows students to look beyond scientific specializations and the chaotic information overload of the bourgeois curriculum. The principle of exemplarity is rooted in the *Sociological Imagination* of C. Wright Mills that connects the individual experience of people to the historical development of society.[48]

Freire is best known for his literacy programmes for the Brazilian peasantry, and Negt for his adult learning projects with factory workers in Germany. Neither of these neatly translates into a usable pedagogy for mass education in the age of collapse. So, as a bridge to the pedagogies of collapse, we cross over back to Denmark, to the place where I first discovered Critical Pedagogy.

Roskilde University

Salling Olesen was not just an avid reader of Critical Pedagogy. He was also a leader of the Danish Student Union (DSU) during the student uprisings of 1968–70.[49] The student revolt ostensibly began as a dispute regarding the governance of psychology programmes at Copenhagen University, Denmark's oldest higher education institution. But really, the target was the entire obsolete model of professorial authority at a time where Danish universities were bursting at the seams with student number increases. The boomer kids wanted more democratic oversight of the curriculum; the professors were having none of it, and soon enough, students barricaded the Rector's office and demanded systemic reforms in Danish higher education. The DSU made an alliance with the Social-democratic (SD) party, supporting their rise to power in the Danish parliament, and quid pro quo, the SD-led parliament then approved the establishment of Roskilde University, 30 kilometres outside of Copenhagen, as the first Danish Reformed University.

The founders of Roskilde University Centre (RUC) had an empty field and carte blanche to come up with a new model of higher education fit for a modern Denmark. Thus, a group of student representatives from the DSU, left-wing professors and SD politicians gathered between 1970 and 1972 to hash out the principles of the world's first Critical Pedagogy university. The model they came up with had a clunky name: 'problem-oriented, participant-directed project learning', later shortened to 'PPL'.[50] It came with three core principles.

First, learning was oriented by social reality. Students began by problematizing aspects of the world around them, then examining these through different theoretical frameworks (to be fair, in the beginning, it was pretty much Marx, Marx and more Marx). This led to the second principle: rejecting academic disciplines. Interdisciplinary, as it was called then (today we would call it transdisciplinarity), was both a fact of the social world, since real-world problems don't fit into neat boxes, and a political project to break down the authority of disciplines. The third principle aimed to dismantle educational hierarchies and empower students and professors to learn and work together. Learning was viewed as a kind of research collaboration rather than knowledge transfer.

The three principles were bundled into a new learning format – the exemplary project. These were semester-long projects, co-created by students and their supervisors, during which students investigated social issues in a cycle of theoretical reading, fieldwork and research. Professors did not lecture, unless explicitly invited to do so by project groups. Disciplinary specializations were only allowed from the third year of study onwards, following two years of interdisciplinary 'basic education'.

The architecture of the university was designed to facilitate this new learning approach: no office towers and no vast lecture halls. Instead, student learning was organized in 'houses'– convivial learning spaces containing group project rooms, a kitchen, a copy room and the 'theory room', for invitational lectures.

In some ways, Roskilde has changed since those early days. For a start, it's a lot less Marxist and more attuned to the complexities of the twenty-first century. After a fraught political battle with the Conservative parliamentary majority that nearly shut the place down for being too Marxist in 1975, a compromise was reached to reinstate traditional, lecture-based courses for half of all study credits in every programme, and the left-wing revolutionary fervour was kept in check by a government-imposed external Rectorate. Roskilde was already struggling with increasing competition in the Danish education market when, in the early 2000s, the Bologna process messed with the two-year interdisciplinary education structure, forcing RUC to introduce specializations earlier in the curriculum. Then, the onslaught of neoliberal reforms under right-wing governments, ranging from the banning of group project exams to shoving industry barons on university boards, left the university scrambling for survival by the time I arrived there in 2013. However, from 2014, RUC found a new lease of life under the leadership of Hanne Leth Andersen, Denmark's only woman Rector (at the time of writing). She revived Roskilde's critical heritage, founding the Critical Edge Alliance of universities.[51] The alliance includes the erstwhile alma mater of bell hooks, the New School in New York, Evergreen College in Washington, Paris 8 University in France, Tata Institute of Social Sciences in Mumbai, among others. These universities (try to) tell the truth about climate and collapse, engage in dialogue with their communities on what solutions students and professors can help bring to the table, and use pedagogy as a tool for catalysing action, even if, in my view, they increasingly suffer from the same misguided perfectionism as many social justice movements.

Danish education has been a great source of inspiration for pedagogies of collapse. Many ideas contained in this book were born around cups of (very, very black) coffee with critical pedagogues and Bildung scholars in Copenhagen and Aalborg, many of whom I still collaborate with. But in the decade since I started working in Scandinavia, I found educational institutions there to be more interested in historically successful learning models than radical innovation to meet the challenge of collapse. I did get a sense that on the whole, some amount of resting on laurels impedes their capacity to fully meet the educational moment. Yet, if we want half a chance of raising a generation capable of navigating collapse, the time has come for radically rethinking what we know about learning.

Learning in dialogue

Indeed, time is ticking on the doomsday clock; collapse is already here in many parts of the world. What kind of radical rethinking am I talking about? I will close this chapter with the four principles of pedagogies of collapse that shape the outline of the rest of the book. I structured this section into four dialogues, because the pedagogies of collapse aren't an instruction manual, but an invitation to take ownership and share in turn. The dialogues open a conversation which continues in subsequent chapters.

Dialogue 1: Speak the truth

We owe learners an honest, scientific account of what is happening to the world around them. I tried to embody the first principle of pedagogies of collapse in Chapter 1. From kindergarten to university and beyond, educational programmes must reckon with climate change, biodiversity collapse and the end of abundance, in an age-appropriate but factual way. Learners must be told that infinite growth is not possible on a finite planet, and economic degrowth means their lives will be less materially prosperous than their parents'. They must be told that oceans, which were once full of wondrous life, are now depleted and filled with plastic. They have a right to know that the snow will disappear, and in its stead storms, droughts, heatwaves and gargantuan fires will rage until the end of humanity's time. We must cease feeding them fever dreams of physics-defying technological revolutions and broken promises of international collective action. The world is most probably going to warm by at least 2°C. And if that happens, we will lose almost all the coral in the ocean, the arctic will be ice-free, sea levels will rise and cities will flood. Millions, if not billions of people will lose their homes. If we do not teach these truths that will shape the future like oceans shape the shoreline, then what world are we preparing students for?

Speaking this truth will be painful. Colleagues have argued that sharing scientific evidence will cause students too much distress – but who are we really protecting? The young will discover the truth sooner or later, if nothing else, with their own eyes and ears. Lies, omissions and half-truths in childhood only aggravate traumatic shock in early adulthood, breeding unhealthy psychological responses. Fellow teachers, school administrators and education professionals, perhaps the real fragility we seek to shield with cheerful 'recycling will save us' mantras is our own, because we don't have the capacity to address our own grief, let alone hold space for that of our students.

What I'm asking is no mean feat. In my courses, lecture breaks are an emotional battlefield where truth grenades land with devastating impact. Students come to me during those fifteen-minute intervals to ask whether they should have children, tell me about their personal stories of grief and share with me tales of dinnertime family crises engendered by the course materials. The pedagogies of collapse call for educational courage. So take heart and feel, dear colleagues, because the classroom entered catastrophic times, and you have the unenviable task of revealing the extent of the damage to your students.

However, my colleagues are right: there's a real possibility that truth alone will trigger catastrophic psychological effects. Discovering the truth plunged Greta Thunberg into a deep depression and triggered an eating disorder that stunted her physical development. Paulo Freire said that words without action are meaningless verbiage.[52] In this case, words of truth alone could trigger a psychological paralysis which only action can reinvest towards change. This calls for a two-step strategy: making space for grief and taking appropriate action now.

Dialogue 2: Make space for grief

Educators and learners are grieving deeply right now. Some of this mourning relates to felt material and spiritual losses in the present, but much of it, I suspect, derives from what climate grief researcher Ashlee Cunsolo called 'grief associated with future losses' – anticipatory mourning for losses not clearly defined, with no temporal or geographic limit.[53] Our students are not quite sure what they should be grieving: it could be anything from losing the ideal of progress, the anticipated deterioration of material life conditions or the curtailment of their and their children's lifespan. Nobody knows yet which pathways collapse will take, so grieving the hurt to come is all the more difficult. Yet we cannot adequately rethink education for times of collapse unless we understand how grief affects learning and learners. I will sketch here briefly the definition and relevance of grief, so that we may pursue this dialogue in Chapter 3.

Current thinking on grief owes a lot to Elisabeth Kübler-Ross, a Swiss psychiatrist who wrote on the experiences of dying patients in the 1960s and 1970s. Her most famous work, *On Death and Dying*, published in 1969, modelled the five stages that most people associate with grieving today: denial, anger, bargaining, despair and acceptance.[54] The five stages are simple enough to grasp: upon learning of their imminent death, patients first experience shock. To cope with the news, their mind blocks it out; they either deny it outright or act as though nothing is amiss. When reality sinks in, patients become angry and find someone or something to blame for their fate. Sometimes, anger turns inwards, into self-loathing. Then follows a period of bargaining, when patients make deals with themselves in the hope of staving off the inevitable. They promise to change their diets, to exercise and to finish unfinished business, but when they see that no amount of deal-making will prevent disease and death, they fall into despair. In the depth of depression, patients no longer have the strength to fight or enjoy the time they have left, which may paradoxically accelerate their demise. Finally, patients come to accept their end, calmly reflecting on their lives and making peace with the present. Kübler-Ross indicated that the five stages were not linear. Patients sometimes skip stages, move forward, then backwards again, or experience the stages in a different order. Even though it has been criticized in academic circles for not being sufficiently evidence-based, the five-stages model is now part of the way we generally understand grief.[55]

So what can the study of death and dying offer educators, on the cusp of civilization's collapse? Though the end of the world as we know it is all but certain, there is a key difference between terminally ill patients and our predicament. Their fate is sealed, but ours is not: humanity can still change course. I worry that if we leave our students held up in grief, they risk passively accepting the worst instead of fighting for the best, even if the best is tragic compared to what they were promised. In Chapter 3, I will offer a deep dive into the psychoanalysis of grief and an existential account of what 'acceptance' could mean for education in the context of collapse.

Dialogue 3: Take appropriate action now

For this dialogue, I need to add a caveat to statements made in Chapter 1. While it is true that the poor and marginalized will be hit hardest by collapse, concluding that they will falter and die while the wealthier populations of the Global North will merely be inconvenienced is a grotesque fallacy with more than a tinge of misplaced White-supremacist logic. It needs to be reminded that the USA was rated most pandemic-ready by the WHO in 2019, with the whole of Africa languishing at the bottom of the preparedness ranking table.[56] I hold out the (probably vain) hope that countries of the Global North will show a modicum of humility, learning the lessons of their misplaced confidence during COVID. This caveat conditions the kinds of actions educators should focus on right now. Here is the second principle of pedagogies of collapse: we should be teaching students how to survive collapse first, and then thrive, in that order.

Discussing this book with my Zimbabwean ward, it seemed obvious to us that Zimbabweans are better prepared for collapse, having lived through it twice in twenty years, than middle-class students in The Netherlands. Truth be told, I worry about my students – it's not just that they don't know how to grow and preserve food, save seeds, regenerate soil, filter water and perform basic maintenance and construction tasks; some actually take offence at the suggestion that these would be useful skills to learn. A whole generation has been brought up to believe that manual labour is beneath them – that it's something Eastern European, African and Latin American immigrants do for low wages. Yet collapse will not be kind to the manually inept. When the services industry begins to crumble, farmers, farriers, builders, seamstresses and nurses will be more useful community members than international relations, economics and gender studies majors. I say this with great affection for my fellow economics and international relations graduates, since I once stood in their shoes. But I was lucky enough that, as the daughter of a working-class mother, I was taught to use a sewing machine and work fabrics and yarn as a child. I also worked on equestrian farms for much of my teenage years, so I was no stranger to working outdoors in pouring mid-winter rain with mud and horse dung up to the knees. Switching to practicing permaculture wasn't too difficult. Few of my students have experiences and skills of the kind; I ask every year and usually see 5–10 per cent of hands raised.

Fellow educators of the city-dwelling world, the reason your students don't need to grow their food, make their clothes and build their houses right now is because of fossil fuels. That is going to change dramatically and unpredictably in the next twenty years. It is, in my view, an act of negligence to let students end their educational journey without basic survival skills. By the time children leave primary school, they should know planting seasons and methods for common fruits and vegetables for their soil and latitude, be able to recognize edible plants and mushrooms in their local ecosystems, participate in soil regeneration, comfortably manipulate weaving and sewing tools, and know how to build basic survival kits like a fire pit and a water distilling pan. Upon leaving secondary school, every child should have basic farming skills, including animal husbandry, as well as first aid, fire safety, metalwork, self-defence and other practical skills for community life.

As someone limited by chronic pain, I understand that students with disabilities may feel excluded from physically demanding work. However, collapse will demand a community of skills. Thus, disabled people must be given a place according to their abilities, and it goes without saying that we have an extra duty of care and compassion for the most severely disabled. There is even more reason for those of us who can work with our bodies to learn to do so.

With the basics for survival addressed (but by no means guaranteed since the future will be unpredictable), possibilities for thriving emerge. Thriving looks different to different people and places, but once food, water, shelter and basic medical care are in place, a wide array of practices become possible. Thriving will require more creators, facilitators and teachers and less bankers, consultants and middle-management white collars. There's still a place for specialized higher education during and after the collapse; we will need doctors, mechanical and civil engineers, linguists, psychologists and legal scholars. I also don't think that the state, or private enterprise will disappear entirely; we will still need qualified administrators and business managers in significantly smaller numbers than our universities currently produce. As for liberal arts, I would suggest that elitist colleges need to disappear, for the same reasons that folk high schools need to change. Liberal education shouldn't be a tool of class reproduction. Students, rich or poor, who learn to sow a field should also learn poetry, political economy, psychology and other academic contributions worth taking with us into the post-collapse world. International relations and gender studies majors, take heart! You're halfway there, you just need to spend as much time with your hands in the mud as you did with your nose in books! In Chapter 4, I will offer a roadmap to reviving Bildung and Critical Pedagogy for taking appropriate action now through the learning framework of *Experimental Pedagogics*.

Dialogue 4: Don't make perfect the enemy of good

It should be clear by now that everything we know about learning needs to change in short order, yet schools are either in denial, or dragging their feet. It's not entirely their fault: educational institutions find themselves squeezed by contradictory injunctions – on the one hand, they should be more sustainable and future-proof; on the other, they must run like a profitable business and churn out market-ready graduates. As a result, school sustainability strategies have become an art in promising much while changing nearly nothing. Leadership with moderate ambition finds itself challenged by rigid bureaucracy, budget deficits and loud minorities of students and staff who either want nothing to change or everything to change at once and object loudly to incremental progress. Where do we even start?

In Chapter 5, I will argue that educators and students whose ambition is to overthrow capitalism and associated oppressions settle for nothing less and refuse to engage in incremental, negotiated progress with actors who don't share their world view end up backing the status quo. I think this tendency feeds from and into an academic habit of perfectionism. From curriculum development to research output, educators generally work under the baseline expectation of perfection, and students take their cues from this.

Pedagogies of collapse require nothing of the sort. On the contrary, they call for imperfection of the highest order – the messy building of solidarity wherever and however we can. I argue instead for *imperfect solidarities*, the art of finding gaps in the system, places where it doesn't have a firm hold; start there and make the best of it, mistakes and all. I have already begun this work in the slums of Lusaka, the township of Marondera, the chaos of Varanasi and the suburbs of Rotterdam South. The kids I work with already have survival skills, so we're sharpening them, innovating, experimenting, working on integrating practical work with spaces of thriving, places for dancing, music, art, karate and, yes, also training doctors and lawyers, as needed. A lot of the legwork is done by local community associations and charities run by committed community leaders. It's also very much a work in progress; we're discovering every year that we can do much more than we thought was possible.

So I would tell teachers: take your caring energy and create learning places of your own in your communities! Seek out places of despair and help birth within them places of joy. Find people like you and join forces. It will take a few pioneers to show what is possible, and when desperate governments, finally awaken to the educational catastrophe of their own making and clamber to find an alternative, those creations will mushroom like the folk high schools of old. Even if they don't, and you're on your own, what have you got to lose? Collapse will strip us of our golden (and not so golden) cages, so it's worth engaging with intent, come what may.

3

Reflecting on Collapse

I ran several studies on the impact of climate education on learners, and came away with the same conclusion each time: without space to reflect and process grief, students devolve to psychological coping mechanisms that impede their capacity to act and change.[1] However, with the right reflexive framework, students can engage willfully with mourning and meaning, finding the courage to let go of what can no longer be and fight for what could be.[2] This is why, today, I focus much of my climate education on guided reflexivity, through practices of journaling and feedback.

The purpose of this chapter is to provide you with an understanding of the psychological processes students go through when they learn about collapse. I cannot stress enough how important it is for educators to understand the psychology of their learners if they want to succeed as guides and facilitators. With a foundation in environmental psychology, I feel I have been able to guide young people to change their lives. After nearly every lecture and workshop, one or two students write to say how much the theories presented in this chapter helped them understand themselves. In my view, no revolutionary pedagogy can succeed without a sound psychological foundation, and that foundation should be made explicit to learners.

In the interest of intellectual honesty and to demonstrate the power of reflexivity, I want to begin with an account of my own reckoning with collapse, the way I ask my students to do in their self-reflection assignments. I didn't write this book as an impartial observer – I have been through despair, and come out the other side. That experience was the birthing pool of the pedagogies of collapse.

A painful reckoning

I can genuinely say that I left university with two master's degrees and not the first inkling of the facts on climate and collapse. It was 2009: the facts were definitely out there for those who wanted to look, but I didn't know that I should be looking. I studied five years at one of France's elite *Grandes Ecoles* in the field of political sciences – the place where future decision-makers are supposedly bred. And not once did anyone so much as mention climate change. There could be some deep-seated denial on my part, but going over my university textbooks and essays, not one of them covers the potential collapse of modern civilization.

My first memory of a discussion on climate was during the last real winter of my life, in 2010. I was living in a charming cottage near Canterbury, at the south eastern point of England. The snow started falling around the first of December and did not stop until mid-January. I didn't know it then, but it was likely one of the last white Christmases I will ever experience. It was the dawn of social media, and I remember a flurry of climate denial proliferating on my Facebook timeline as the snow heaped up in the yard. Atmospheric sciences wasn't my area of expertise or interest, so I didn't give it much thought. It seemed like something that might or might not happen in a future too distant to care about.

I had just taken up a professional opportunity in Singapore and spent the next few years blithely flying around the world, wolfing down steak and consuming large quantities of plastic packaging. In hindsight, I'd like to think that I felt guilty about my actions, that I knew deep down that something wasn't right, but I just didn't. I waltzed up to the business class check-in counter of Changi airport every other week, brandishing a gold membership card and off I flew. What I mean is: don't mistake me for a tree hugger. I come from a conservative Christian family, elevated from the working class by corporate America. My great-great grandparents were servants, my great-grandparents were village tradespeople, my grandparents were factory workers, and my father worked for large American companies and lifted us into the middle class. We rode that social elevator hard, and in my early twenties, I believed that I could not call myself successful until I had blown my father's extensive air miles record to smithereens.

My social awakening happened a few years before my environmental awakening. I graduated from law school with a master's degree in human rights, and within months of working in the non-profit and development sectors, I began suffering cognitive dissonance. I grew up being told incessantly by church and family that the poor are lazy, taxes are evil and socialism is close enough to devil-worship. Yet my experience of the world was that the poor work the hardest; they are poor because the rich don't pay their taxes, and socialism doesn't necessarily mean Soviet Russia. So I left the church and cast my vote for progressive parties – a series of practical decisions that set me at odds with most of my family (more on that in Chapter 5).

I began my teaching career at a new progressive liberal arts college in The Netherlands at the age of twenty-seven. Barrack Obama was president of the United States, the arc of history seemed to bend towards justice, and though by that point I knew about climate change, I sincerely thought the problem was under control. At that time, environmental breakdown was not on the menu at our college. Of the first cohort of students who graduated from the college in 2016, many did so without having encountered planetary boundaries during their studies. The Paris Climate Accords were signed, and Hillary Clinton was going to be the next president of the United States.

I was twenty-nine years old and four months pregnant on 9 November 2016. I went to bed early that night, fatigued from the pregnancy and from last-minute preparations for my doctoral defence, which was only days away. At 3:00 am, I woke up, as pregnant women do, and hobbled over to the kitchen in the dark, looking for something to eat. My phone was on charge on the counter. I couldn't resist; I hit refresh on the home page of *The New York Times*. This is the moment it truly hit me. I leaned on the window sill of our 29th-floor apartment, looked at the flickering city lights below, and realized we were f*cked.

Of course, as I explained in Chapter 1, thermo-industrial civilization was done for anyway, with or without Donald Trump. As a fervent neoliberal, and stalwart defender of industry lobbyists, Hillary Clinton's contribution to the environmental cause would have been, at best, marginally better than Trump's. Paradoxically, we should perhaps thank the Republican Party for hoisting us out of the comfortable illusion that all will be well. That night, I well and truly realized that it won't. The morning of the 10th November, I exited my denial and entered a long, bumpy stage of despair.

Eight months after my daughter was born, I began a two-year postdoc in sustainability education research at an engineering school in Denmark. I started my new position by reading all the science I could get my hands on – climate, resources, biodiversity and planetary boundaries. What I read disturbed me profoundly. I turned to colleagues at home in Holland, and in Denmark, to sus out answers: What are we doing about this?

Let's start with the Danish engineers. The technology-will-save-us mantra was everywhere among my colleagues. They chided my anguish. I was accused of at best, not understanding engineers and, at worst, being deliberately obtuse. What worried me was that the engineers around me spoke of technology in a quasi-mystical manner. Many banked everything on technological innovations like nuclear fusion – a technology which is decades away from maturity, may not ever be commercially viable, and in no way addresses resource shortages or inequality. The fact that we don't have decades to spare was conveniently brushed over by engineering hubris, convinced that what technology broke, technology could fix.

My colleagues in the Humanities department were more realistic about the facts. The debate among humanities educators wasn't whether collapse would occur, but when, how and how bad. However, most humanities colleagues were content to ruminate over doomsday. I had several conversations throughout that period that ended with: 'then we will hit 3 degrees of warming and it's over', followed by a shrug and a sigh. I found little comfort in this culture of cultivated despair. It beats denial, but not by much.

I felt quite alone during this time. For the first time in my life, I experienced crippling anxiety attacks. I stood in the metro on the way home from work, feeling like a sinkhole had opened beneath my feet. All of this beautiful social order, the quiet assumption that trains run on time, that they carry well-fed, healthy individuals seamlessly from home to work and back, the wiring that brings electricity into millions of homes, the water pipes that carry clean water in and sewage out, the trucks that flitter in and out of cities, bringing affordable produce and merchandise into stocked shops . . . all of this will end, and I will live to witness that end. I will perhaps even die in that end. I began to see the hidden nuts and bolts of society everywhere I looked – I could not unsee the monstrous fossil machinery behind absolutely everything around us. It was like a deconstruction software constantly running in the background, and it was exhausting.

In October 2018, shortly after the coup that deposed Robert Mugabe, I travelled to Zimbabwe to shore up my foundation's project in the midst of a dire fuel shortage, with inflation creeping up to double, soon triple digits, eighteen-hour rolling power cuts, cholera outbreaks in the townships, political violence erupting on the streets, and brutal repression in response. I thought to myself: 'what is happening here will happen in Europe too. Except we are far less resilient and less resourceful than the long-suffering people of Zimbabwe. It will be a sh*t-show'.

Tired of confronting nothing but denial and despair, I closed off. I became physically ill, ended my postdoc early, and took medical leave from my academic work. Then came Covid.

In the early days of the first lockdown, I pulled through long days of childcare-while-working-from-home with a cocktail of caffeine and codeine. When the child was finally in bed, toys cleared from the living room and the work laptop put away, I flopped onto the sofa, doom-scrolling through the case countdown. The advent of pandemics was a long-predicted side-effect of our real-time global experiment on nature. We knew it would happen. Just like we know that much of what I discussed in Chapter 1 will, one way or another, come to pass, likely in the next few years. I had just finished teaching the first edition of *The Climate Crisis* at the college, so I knew. And still, the shock hit me intensely.

During those first few weeks, students, colleagues and friends pined for a return to 'normal'. Shared playlists, kitsch zoom high school reunions and online soap-making classes offered opportunities to dream of the day this would all be over. Students joked about telling their future children of *the great pandemic of 2020*, imagining bright eyes opening with wonder at what their parents lived through. Perhaps the reason I found this all so hard was because I knew that no such innocence would be possible. If my students have children, their offspring's lives will be so much harder than that of their parents that the pandemic of 2020 will be fondly remembered as a time when we still had it so good. I realized then, and still believe now, that we have reached the peak of industrial civilization, measured in material wealth, resources, energy per capita and all the things they make possible. The problem with peaks is the descent on the other side. And since we completely failed to prepare for the end of abundance, the downward journey will be a messy fall down a steep slope, bouncing off rocks all the way down, from pandemics to wars, famines and everything in between. That was the lowest point of my environmental reckoning.

Our predicament has worsened since those days. War is here, at our doorstep. Famine has made an unwelcome return. The United States is making steady, determined strides towards a dystopian theocracy, and the rest of the democratic world may follow not far behind. As I wrote this chapter, record-breaking heatwaves relentlessly tore through Europe from late spring to early autumn, and every night, news programmes began with footage of out-of-control fires, while heads of state openly talked about nuclear Armageddon. And yet, while I have bad days, I usually get up in the morning with resolute calm and the willingness to fight on.

When I participate in public interventions, I am regularly asked by anxious audience members how I climbed out of despair. In response, I will end this autobiographical narrative with an account of the three psychological decisions that turned the fight around for me.

Three decisions: Learn, love, live

Learn

My first decision was to confront my breakdown as an existential crisis. I realized that the terror inside me was connected to deeper fears about dying, living and the absurdity of human hubris in the grand scheme of the universe. Contemplating a world without God (as He is understood within Abrahamic religions) was relatively easy when the march of history pointed towards progress. Doing so in a world in collapse triggered overwhelming thoughts in me.

The circumstances that brought me here are barely fathomable: 4.6 billion years of evolution, five mass extinctions, three million years of pre-history, 10,000 years of history, and from the unbroken chain that ties me all the way back to the first single-celled organism, I have been carried into the world by astronomical genetic odds to witness this moment. Of all the possible times in which I could have been born, I landed right here, atop humanity's highest peak, trembling before the fall ahead. What a wicked taunt: my parents were born among the most greedy generation to ever walk the Earth. They pillaged nature, decimated life, ravaged land and water, and are now dying before the price comes due. By the time my daughter, born into a dying world through no fault of her own, will be old enough to affect the fate of humanity, that fate will be sealed. And here I am, alive on the knife's edge with my entire generation. All standing, eyes wide open, mouth agape as the cataclysm sets in motion, when we should be all hands on deck to save what may still be. Denial, guilt, despair . . . young and old, praying to the Gods of technology, consuming away the fear and jetting to the next escape. Anything but to confront the painful truth that life as we have known it for the past fifty years was a historical aberration, a wild frenzy before a spectacular crash.

I occasionally pause in awe at the privilege of living through the zenith of human civilization. When crystal clear photographs of the deep universe filtered through from the James Webb telescope in early 2022, I felt a kind of vertigo.[3] Contemplating the breathtaking images on the screen in the palm of my hands, I realized that I was holding nothing short of the entire history of the universe. Of all the souls to walk the earth, I know the philosophy of Plato, the folly of Erasmus, the art of Da Vinci, the music of Mozart, the dark side of the moon, the ice caps of Mars and the stars that birthed our world. From the Pharaohs in all their splendour to the Sun King on his throne, what would they have given to know what I know now? When I think about my life, the places I have been, the things I have seen, the knowledge I have gained, and the beauty I have witnessed, I feel overcome with existential wonder. The thrill of being alive in this moment – could that not be enough, come what may on the other side of the mountain of progress?

This, I told myself time and again. But every day, around 5:00 pm, a curtain of anxiety would descend. I needed to understand, to dig deeper, so I powered my way through the abstruse existential canon (curse the idiosyncratic syntax of dead Danes, Germans and Frenchmen). I read ecofeminists, indigenous writers, critical theorists, African and African American authors. I discovered psychoanalysis, trauma theory and grief frameworks. I searched far and wide for people who could show me the way and talk me through new ways of apprehending collapse. I held life-changing conversations with strangers, some intensely scientific, others more spiritual, until, one day, I landed on Simone de Beauvoir's *Ethics of Ambiguity*.[4] I read the book cover to cover, and the pieces fell into place. That was when I made my second life-changing decision: to love.

Love

I'm not naturally comfortable with love. It was a word scarcely spoken throughout my childhood, except in a biblical context. As a result, I have always found it difficult to make sense of the burning highs and weighty lows that draw me with passion and compassion for fellow humans of all genders and races, in a rainbow of emotions not covered in Bible study. That changed when I read Paulo Freire's *Pedagogy of the Oppressed* during a short visit to the UK while I was writing my PhD.[5] The pages of this revolutionary book dripped with a love so profound that I sat for hours, transfixed by the text, in the Templeman library of the University of Kent. The *Pedagogy of the Oppressed* gave me the words to make sense of what I had experienced during my time in the development sector, to understand human suffering as a consequence of oppressive forces that converge to keep the poor in their place. This spurred my decision to change academic fields from education psychology to social and environmental justice, to build and lead a women's empowerment organization, and to take up the fight against injustice in the public arena. But Freire's love is all fire and righteous fury, born of struggle and oppression in his native Brazil. It is something rather felt than analysed. My logical mind needed an explanation, lest it replace one irrational faith with another – why love? I could not find the source of Freire's passion in the works he cited. Karl Marx and Jean-Paul Sartre are hardly the epitome of love.

The Ethics of Ambiguity provided the answer I was looking for: we must love because our distinctly human existence depends on it. Generous love, as opposed to narcissistic or obsessive love, is the commitment through which we become fully human. To love nothing is to fall into destructive nihilism. To love only oneself is to wallow in empty narcissism. To love only one person or thing obsessively is to abandon ourselves, surrender our freedom and demand that they do the same. Generous love is a passion for our fellow human in all of their messy, stubbornly different freedom. We love them because we do not own them or lay claim to them, and as free beings, they whisper back to us: 'I see you, you are fully human.' We birth each other's humanity by giving each other generous love. Generous love is both a personal commitment to freedom and a political commitment to fighting oppression.

We cannot love all humans equally. There will always be shades of love: some wholly benevolent but dispassionate, some burning hot with desire, others fierce and loyal, and many difficult and burdensome to carry. Even the most generous love can be spurned. Even the most loving person can make serious errors of judgement, and love in suffocating, narcissistic or oppressive ways. Love without learning is a dangerous path to walk.

As I put down *The Ethics of Ambiguity*, I realized the reason my privileged existence felt so anxiety-inducing in times of collapse: it was a privilege neither shared with the vast majority of the inhabitants of the planet nor with those born after me. Part of my humanity was wilting in the heat of others' suffering.

At first, I sought refuge in dispassionate, humanistic love. I found it comforting to alienate myself in social justice work, to care for others at arms' length, content to watch them grow from afar. But then something discomfiting happened: some people demanded love in praxis – not in the stoic manner in which I had approached it, but in real human ways. I was hostile to this intrusion. It demanded that I wade into the fray of living, with all of the cumbersome ups and downs of attachment and, inevitably, loss, with the tangled tests of racial, class and gendered dynamics. I pushed people away, earning a reputation for being prickly, even haughty. I'm grateful to those who persisted.

Now, I believe that generous love cannot be only stoic. Attachment and the inevitable grief that ensues is the condition of living. I still find this difficult. Sometimes, I cannot give back as much as I am given, driven by the fear of erring and loss. Other times, I burn too hot and leave a trail of destruction in my wake. As I watch the world crumble, the love that binds me to children birthed and fostered, to siblings by blood and bond, to lovers straight and queer, to friendships forged in common purpose, that love also binds me to hope. And when hope for the future falters, it binds me to the belief that the moment matters. I would prefer a meaningful life in collapse over a life of comfortable alienation. It was love that finally gave me the courage to make my third decision: to live without pretence.

Live

Most people go about their business like tomorrow will be exactly the same as yesterday. I was on the train recently, overhearing an agitated conversation about an insurance marketing campaign. A lady and two gentlemen in suits debated the most profitable manner to utilize their canine mascot. All I could think was that within ten years, most risks will be uninsurable because damage will be too frequent and costly to offset with premiums. Even within progressive circles, too many colleagues focus conversations about diversity and inclusion around getting marginalized people into board rooms, rather than saving lives from climate chaos.

I went along with this collective delusion for as long as I could. I graduated from my doctoral studies cum laude, chased grants, impact factors and H-indexes for the illusive promise of a research career. I sliced and diced data into as many papers as I could squeeze to increase my numbers. I put up with the ritual flagellation of peer-review. But I hit a breaking point in late 2021. It was mid-December, at the end of a very difficult Covid year, just as the Dutch government ordered another round of Christmas lockdowns. I was staring at my computer screen, contorting my work to fit the conflicting expectations of peer-reviewers for the third round of minor edits on a paper that nobody would read, that would contribute exactly nothing to the survival of humanity, and I thought to myself: 'the world is on fire, what the hell am I doing?'

Academic research is a broken system that often promotes quantity at the expense of quality, bureaucracy at the expense of creativity, and crushes young scientists at the best of times. But the times are not the best; they're catastrophic. No one currently in their thirties is going to retire at a ripe old age with hundreds of papers and books to their name, a comfortable pension and cozy consulting contracts to finance a couple decades of silver-haired globe-trotting. We are in the fight for our lives, for our children's lives and for the lives of all creatures with whom we share this planet. So I quit my research career, and I have not looked back. Now, I do not write one line that does not, in some way, contribute to the battle. I turn down review requests for papers that do not address our existential predicament. I won't fly to the other end of the world for a conference, not even one on climate.

Liberating myself from pretence allowed me to make space for grief and anger. It also allowed me to focus on my own resilience. The fight for tomorrow requires nothing less than the best of us, the mentally and physically strongest version of ourselves. The time to build that resilience is now, while we still can. In Chapter 6, I describe the concrete steps that I took to include resilience practices into my personal and professional life.

I'm not saying that I have it all figured out. Collapse weighs heavily on me, and there's only so much joy home-grown cucumbers can bring when it's 40°C outside. All the love in the world could not wish away the terror I feel when, aching from the latest report of atrocities on the battlefield, I hear the military build-up around Taiwan announced on the evening news. I struggle to sleep at night and need all sorts of practices to keep my mind and body from buckling under the strain (Chapter 6). I lose patience a little more often than I'd like. I get especially exasperated by the chest-thumping of wealthy White men whose grandiloquent monologues on transitions drip with greenwashing, and I'm less and less inclined to hide it. As a result, probably aggravated by the fact that I'm a woman, I'm often branded as emotional, aggressive and irrational, and I'm not sure that these labels do me many favours. I'm still learning to love more generously, which includes the courage to be hated and feared when necessary. I long to listen and learn better, especially from those with fewer privileges than me. I reckon with the painful truth that I cannot offer perfect solidarities, and in the absence of perfection, learning through imperfection must be embraced and loved in turn, as hard as that is.

So, I'm still a work in progress. But I'm no longer paralysed by grief. The present has taken on almost sensual, poetic qualities. It feels deeper, stronger and more alive for its inescapable end-date. I pause to feel wonder, to marvel. Quoting the final words of Leonardo Di Caprio in *Don't Look Up*, the best film ever made about climate denial, 'the thing of it is, we really did have everything, didn't we'? – just before he is vaporized with his entire family by the comet-climate-metaphor.[6]

I am so grateful, in my bones and through my veins, that I realized the staggering glory of being alive in this moment while there was still time. Though I may no longer be strictly speaking religious, I hope that I may live through what little time of abundance is left with a modicum of grace. I shared my story to hold my hand out to you and let you know that if you are in the depth of despair right now, you are definitely not alone. Your personal journey through this is important, and I invite you to take your time with it. I hope that this book contributes to bringing about understanding and hope for you.

Guiding students through collapse

When I guide learners through collapse, I present them with three psychological perspectives: cognitivism, psychoanalysis and existentialism. I invite students to reflect on the applicability of these theories to their personal psychological journey, through the practice of regular journaling. For each course that I teach, I give a lecture and readings from each of the theoretical lenses, then assign three formative diary assignments and one summative overarching reflection. In the diaries, I prompt students to theorize their emotional and cognitive experiences with the course material using the lenses. In a classroom where an atmosphere of psychological safety and understanding pervades, students' diaries are most often intensely personal, honest and emotionally raw. In many cases, students experience the theories as a lifeline to understand the whirlwind of thoughts and feelings swirling inside of them, hanging onto the words of Melanie Klein and Simone de Beauvoir as a drowning person to a rope. That's because these theories also offer ways to deal with the psychological turmoil; therein lies their power in the classroom. So we now dive into the paradigms of the psychology of collapse.

Cognitive biases

Cognitivism looks at how thought patterns are created and used by the mind to structure our understanding of the world. In environmental psychology, cognitive research has focused on the role of mental biases in stymying action on environmental issues, in particular, the impact of cognitive dissonance and other biases. I must say that this is my least preferred of the three paradigms because I do not believe it sufficiently deals with subconscious and emotional states. However, it appeals to many of my students, particularly those from science, business and economics majors, and is usually quite popular with young men. My experience is that these kinds of students are generally unaccustomed to reflection; therefore, an easy entry point that puts them at ease and 'speaks their language' serves them well.

Cognitive dissonance

Cognitive dissonance is a psychological theory from the 1950s that focuses on the psychological discomfort experienced by people who hold two or more contrary cognitions at the same time.[7] A cognition is a structured pattern of thought – it could be a belief, an attitude, a set of facts or a behaviour. Think of it as a box for your thoughts with a label on it. Your mind is pretty much Marie Kondo on steroids: it loves harmony and tidiness, and hates disorder and contradictions.[8] So much so, that it literally hurts to have two boxes with contrary contents in the same mental space. Psychologists call this pain 'dissonance'. To reduce the pain, people must either add 'consonant' cognitions (new boxes that match the dominant box set in the mind) or reduce the discrepancies between the boxes. They can do this by changing one or more of the boxes (e.g. a behaviour, a belief), or by making one box bigger and the other one smaller.

One of the most cited studies on cognitive dissonance and climate was done by Stoll-Kleemann and colleagues in Switzerland.[9] They interviewed people in focus groups to compare their attitudes towards changing their lifestyles for the sake of the environment, and their actual behaviours. They found a great deal of unresolved cognitive dissonance, eased with denial and displacement (i.e. shifting the blame). While most participants recognized that there was a serious climate issue, they were unwilling to take action in line with the scale of the problem. In other words, they had environmentally conscious attitudes, but environmentally destructive behaviours and suffered cognitive dissonance as a result. To deal with the mental pain, participants relied on two main strategies: first, they displaced personal responsibility for action ('why should I do anything if nobody else will?'), and second, they rejected behavioural change on the grounds of their personal comfort ('I need this level of comfort to live meaningfully'). To boost their 'comfort is good' mental box, they expressed trust in technology as a climate saviour, diminished the urgency and severity of the crisis, and blamed inaction on governments. The authors concluded on a pessimistic note regarding the ability of democracies to shepherd citizens towards climate action. They did recommend a rush of positive stories about behaviour change to encourage the association of good feelings with giving up personal comfort for the planet.

In my class on dissonance, I use something I call 'the box exercise' with my students. I begin by confessing that earlier in life, I very much enjoyed steak. I draw a box on the white board and write 'steak is good' in it. I write down pleasant memories of steakhouse outings with friends, the smell of barbecue, the texture of grilled meat and other associations that come with it. I explain to students that so long as I remained unaware of the catastrophic environmental impact of rearing beef, I could indulge happily, there was no box with contradictory contents lying around in my mental space. But then I learned about the impact of beef rearing on the environment. So I draw a new box next to the old one, and label it 'steak is bad'. There are now two boxes with contradictory labels on my board. At first, I try to make my 'steak is good' box bigger by writing down cultural grounds ('eating beef is an important part of my culture'), social grounds ('I will be a social outcast in my family if I become vegetarian'), health grounds ('I need a low-carb, high-protein diet to combat my illness') and practical grounds for eating steak ('I don't know how to prepare a dinner without meat'). I try to squeeze my 'steak is bad' box into the smallest space possible on the board using phrases that sound like soft denial ('my beef is organic, bought from a family butcher'). But I also keep adding evidence on the harms of beef to the bad box, blowing up its size. Meanwhile, I keep making my 'steak is good' box smaller as I wipe justifications off the board: many people among my friends and family have stopped eating meat, so the social justification falls away (wipe). Documentaries like *The Game Changers* convinced me that it is possible to build muscle and stay healthy on a plant-based diet (wipe, wipe).[10] Then, as I started preparing vegetarian dishes more regularly, I got much better at vegetarian cooking (thanks, Ottolenghi).[11] So now I draw a new box that dwarfs the 'steak is good' box: it comes with the label 'vegetarian food is awesome'. I merge the 'steak is bad' and 'vegetarian food is awesome' box and together they boot out the 'steak is good' box from the board. After this demonstration, my students have a go in small groups, using large sheets of paper and permanent markers. Popular topics for this exercise include 'flying', 'fast fashion' and 'technological gadgets'. I think there's more to this story than cognition, but the exercise serves as a useful illustration of the theory's application to environmental issues, and you can do this in 30 minutes in your class with paper and a couple of markers.

For me, the exercise also served to illustrate the findings of Stoll-Kleeman, showing that I was only able to make the switch to vegetarianism when I gained positive associations with vegetarian cooking rather than just bad associations with eating meat, so there is definitely value in changing the story.

Heuristics and biases

Cognitive dissonance is an example of what psychologists call heuristics and biases. These are evolutionary mental short-cuts designed to save us from imminent danger.[12] Heuristics and biases help the brain to make quick decisions, often at the expense of rationality. They affect all humans and cannot be educated away: they're built into our psychology. They can only be corrected after the fact, which requires us to be aware of the bias, notice how it has warped our decision-making, and consciously redress the decision, even if it conflicts with what our primal senses are telling us. For instance, humans tend to stick to decisions they have invested time, money and effort into, even if it would be more rational to give up, a bias known as sunken-cost fallacy.[13] Humans also have a hard time thinking out of the box when dealing with familiar situations because their perception is steered by prior experience, a bias known as functional fixedness.[14] Researchers in cognitive psychology have identified two dozen biases and heuristics over the last fifty years, but are just beginning to make the link with environmental psychology.

Two researchers from Scotland and the United States, Johnson and Levin, suggested that there might be four biases in addition to cognitive dissonance that prevent people from taking action on environmental issues.[15]

The first challenge for our minds is the *positive illusion* bias. We have a kind of invincibility complex, an 'everything is going to be okay (for me)' blindspot. How many times did I hear students declare that Elon Musk will save us, and even if he doesn't, climate breakdown is sad for people in Bangladesh and sub-Saharan Africa, but being rich, White and European would be a safeguard against collapse. This is part of a wider category of biases called 'availability biases': our mind tends to overestimate the probability of what we know best, and all we know is prosperity, peace and stability. The good news is that there is a cure for the positive illusion bias. The bad news is that it involves living through disaster. Running for your life as your house burns down in raging wildfires tends to convince you that everything isn't going to be okay. An overwhelming majority of my students recognize this bias in themselves and struggle with it even when they are made explicitly aware of it. The fact that this bias persists among students even after the very real experience of COVID shows how difficult it will be to overcome.

The second challenge, called *fundamental attribution error*, is a little more complicated. It means that people tend to blame their own environmentally damaging behaviours on external factors, while blaming other people's bad intentions for identical behaviours. When you line up, boarding pass in hand, at security checks in overcrowded airports, you might think to yourself that you would definitely have gone by rail or road if you didn't have a work meeting tomorrow or if the car wasn't broken down. But then, you might look around and think, 'all these people jetting off on holiday without a care in the world, they're climate vandals!', even though they are likely thinking the same about you. On a broader scale, it might translate as a tendency to think, 'We're trying so hard here in The Netherlands, but we're such a small country, we can't control global forces', while simultaneously thinking, 'China is intentionally triggering global climate chaos and collapse'. Since Dutch politicians have a vested interest in convincing voters that China and India are the problem, not the billions in pandemic relief donated to its national carrier KLM, or the earth-shattering profits amassed by the oil giant Shell since the start of the Ukraine war, it only makes the bias stronger.[16]

The third challenge is even more difficult. Researchers call this *prospect theory*. In short, people take more risks when they are faced with only bad options. As we noted in Chapter 1, we now face a choice between controlled demolition or uncontrolled collapse. The former is widely preferable to the latter, but neither is going to be pleasant. Faced with these two awful options, the mind tends to gamble on the possibility that scientists calculating the odds of apocalypse are incorrect, and therefore, it's worth taking the risk of doing nothing. Prospect theory is a potent combination with the positive illusion bias, in a self-reinforcing doom-loop. The more we do nothing, the worse the options look and the worse they look, the more we are willing to risk doing nothing. The cure is, again, for disaster to force action.

Finally, a fourth challenge comes from social psychology, namely our tendency to favour members of our inner circle – a phenomenon known as in-group/out-group bias. Social scientists have established that even when groups are formed on the most arbitrary criteria (like 'people wearing a blue shirt'), with the flimsiest of identity markers, people will still tend to behave favourably towards the in-group and disparage the out-group.[17] We can probably thank our prehistoric ancestors for this trait that, while useful in the competitive tribal setting of early human history, hinders trust and cooperation in a globalized world. One concrete effect of this bias is the tendency for people to perceive themselves and their national or political grouping as more environmentally virtuous, and others as more environmentally culpable than the facts warrant. Without a doubt, leaders deliberately titivate this sentiment to suit their own political agendas and distract from their dismal failures on the politics of collapse. But their work is cut out for them by the cognitive biases that make us want to believe them.

The cognitive paradigm offers useful ways for students to understand and arrest some unhelpful thought patterns. It's accessible, comprehendible and evidence-based, which is probably why students like it so much – their first learning diary often takes an explicitly cognitive perspective. But I find cognitivism to be quite superficial. It offers simple, quantifiable explanations to complex emotional phenomena. Although it's a good entry point to reflection, cognitive psychology doesn't delve into deeper issues at the core of our conundrum, limiting its power to engage students in profound emotional transformations. That's why my next move is to introduce environmental grief through a psychoanalytical lens.

Grief and psychoanalysis

I first encountered an adaptation of Kübler-Ross's model of grief to societal collapse in Slavoj Žižek's bizarre book, *Living in End Times*.[18] That the book is strange should come as no surprise to anyone familiar with Žižek. In the words of Alex Miller from Vice:

> Slavoj Žižek is a big, friendly Marxist intellectual. He spends as much time blathering on about Batman films as he does about Hegel. He's written about 75 books, most of which remain impenetrable to me. But it's his public appearances . . . which have really cemented his position as the most broadly popular anti-capitalist philosopher working today. This is because, unlike pretty much every other anti-capitalist philosopher, he actually has a sense of humour.[19]

A friendly warning: there's a lot to unpack in Žižek's (at times barely coherent) philosophy and its underlying psychoanalysis. Žižek is a lot for students to handle. I don't recommend assigning his books to undergraduates, except within the humanities. I like to play online videos of him, as it's always funny to watch students' reaction to his entirely neurotic demeanour the first time they see him on screen. To smoothen the transition between the reassuring science of cognitivism and the mad world of Žižek, I begin by giving students a short, user-friendly introduction to psychoanalysis that goes something like what follows:

Psychoanalysis is a branch of psychology famously founded by Sigmund Freud in the early twentieth century.[20] Its main purpose is the study of the relationship between the conscious and unconscious minds. Psychoanalysis supposes (without too much hard evidence) the existence of a primal subconscious part of the mind, called the *id*, from which our most basic drives emanate. In non-human animals, the *id* is all there is. There are no mental constraints to the drives: if an animal wants to eat, it will try to eat. If it wants to defecate or copulate, it will try to do so without restraint. If it fails, it will lash out, growl, cry and howl. At birth, babies are also exclusively driven by their *id*. But as humans grow, they become aware of powerful social norms that constrain animal behaviour. Those norms exists to make social life possible. A society in which we would all give in to our instincts without restraint wouldn't hold up for very long. These norms create a mental architecture that Freud called the *superego*. It constrains the *id* at a preconscious level (i.e. we are not fully aware of it). The conscious part of the self, which Freud called the *ego*, arbitrates between the *id* and the *superego*. But it's not a rational, orderly process. The *ego* is constantly battling to stabilize these two warring forces that it cannot consciously perceive or control. Our sense of self, the inner voice that we typically think of as 'me', emerges from this fraught cohabitation. To keep the peace, the *ego* resorts to defence mechanisms, some of which are quite well known, like repression (in which uncomfortable memories are suppressed into the unconscious) or projection (in which our own unacceptable feelings and thoughts are pasted onto someone else). Others are a little more obscure, like sublimation (redirecting socially unacceptable behaviour into acceptable alternatives that satisfy the same instinct) or reaction formation (acting in the opposite way to your impulses). I like to imagine my *ego* as Kermit the Frog running like a lunatic between my *id* and *superego*; it helps me to take my *ego*'s defence responses less seriously. Cue a GIF of Kermit the Frog on the screen, and that, dear students, is Freudian psychoanalysis in very broad strokes.

Žižek combined Kübler-Ross's five stages of grief with a social psychoanalytic analysis of collapse.[21] Where Kübler-Ross described the experience of individual patients, Žižek tried to draw larger insights about the behaviour of societies faced with collapse. He compared each of the five stages to some of the defence mechanisms of the ego, implying the existence of a kind of unresolved collective grief about the end times.

> One can discern the same five figures in the way our social consciousness attempts to deal with the forthcoming apocalypse. The first reaction is one of ideological denial: there is no fundamental disorder; the second is exemplified by explosions of anger at the injustices of the new world order; the third involves attempts at bargaining ('if we change things here and there, life could perhaps go on as before'); when bargaining fails, depression and withdrawal set in; finally, after passing through this zero-point, the subject no longer perceives the situation as a threat, but as a chance of a new beginning.[22]

We have spent the past fifty years in a state of collective denial. It should have been evident that infinite growth was not possible on a finite planet. The Meadows report of 1972 spelled it out for us.[23] Yet, Žižek suggests, our collective ego has been locked in a particularly insidious defence mechanism: fetishistic disavowal. Deep down, denizens of the Global North know very well that the material constraints of the world meant their socio-economic choices will eventually lead to collapse, and that the damage inflicted by those choices on the poor and marginalized makes them at least partially complicit in racist and classist oppression on a planetary scale. However, in the practice of their everyday lives, by getting up in the morning and going to work for companies whose existence relies on the illusion of forevers (growth forever, resources forever, productivity increase forever . . .), by spending their salaries on consumer goods, these same denizens participate in maintaining the illusion. From a psychoanalytic perspective, iPhones, Nikes, BMWs

... and increasingly, 'green' products like Teslas and Dopper bottles are fetishes. They are voodoo objects that maintain the fantasy that the consumption frenzy will never end. A psychoanalyst might argue that consumer objects allow us to cynically disavow reality – because we know full well that the end of the glut is coming, but with every purchase, we buy the fancy that for now, all is well. The effect is self-contradictory: the objects we buy to maintain denial are the very object that contribute to making denial increasingly difficult (because they visibly harm the environment).

But indeed, at some point, the impact of consumerism on the planet becomes so visible that it leeches into our mundane reality. We now live our lives alongside fires that rage every night on the evening news, fierce droughts that suck rivers dry, torrential downpours causing flash flooding all over the world, all the while the prices of gas, electricity and food rise threefold to tenfold, and the global supply chain grinds to a slow chug. Under the circumstances, while outright denial still persists, Žižek notes that many have turned instead to violent protests – in Chile, Paris, the Middle East, the United States and so forth – to express their rage. The *gilets jaunes* were emblematic of the explosive potential of ecological countermeasures. The movement has mistakenly been taken as proof that *the people* are not prepared to sacrifice one inch of personal comfort for the planet. French political economist Thomas Piketty makes the counterpoint that what the *gilets jaunes* were really protesting wasn't the imposition of an eco-tax on fuel per se, but the fact that the receipts from this tax were to be mostly allocated to financing tax cuts for the rich enacted by Emmanuel Macron's neoliberal government.[24] The anger wasn't merely another kind of denial, as was claimed, but a protest against a society in which collapse makes the rich richer while the poor foot the bill. For now, anger has been remarkably subdued on a global scale. If the 2023 Hamas terror attack on Israel and ensuing all-out assault on Gaza is any indication, there are warning signs that rage could blow up into full reign-of-terror proportions in more parts of the world in short order. Žižek goads his readers by suggesting that 'slapping thy neighbour' may be the best wake-up call from denial, and one suspects that he may not be entirely averse to violent revolution, but the nightly news is a reminder that any bloodlust will come with a cost.[25]

Our response is quite predictable: we bargain to stave off the inevitable. Žižek concentrates on society's attempt to save neoliberal capitalism by turning it into social capitalism. Green New Deal in the United States, Green Deal in the European Union, plans abound for changing everything without really changing anything. Žižek's particular call-out is Universal Basic Income (UBI), a proposal to endow all citizens with a state-funded monthly pay-out to cover basic needs like housing, food, energy and education, regardless of whether citizens work or not. Dutch historian Rutger Bregman called it 'an idea whose time has come' – producing pages worth of statistics to show that pilot projects in UBI were successful on an economic and human level and that UBI makes people less stressed, healthier and generally more able to live full human lives.[26] Despite predictable opposition from right-wing politicians, interest in the UBI as a stopgap measure that would save capitalism from collapse by improving wealth redistribution is growing. Žižek points to the unlikely beneficiaries from this bargain: millionaires and billionaires. After the financial crisis of 2008, in which ordinary tax payers bailed out casino capitalists, there was legitimate concern among the billionaire class that the pitchforks were coming for them. Prominent progressives in the United States, like Bernie Sanders and Elizabeth Warren, have openly questioned the morality of the existence of billionaires.[27] However, the introduction of a UBI would provide a social justification for maintaining a millionaire and billionaire class. Here's how it works: the wealthiest agree to a capital tax (a tax on the machines they own) to provide the funds necessary to support UBI in exchange for keeping the whole production side of capitalism just the way it is, while redistribution provides some social legitimacy to the whole thing. It's a win-win. There's only one problem with this bargain: you can't redistribute wealth on a dead planet.

We are witnessing the failure of this bargaining strategy in real time. Collapse is knocking randomly at our door: parents and friends suddenly died from a COVID-19 infection, jobs were lost in lockdown, or because companies went under the pressure of increased energy bills, and now houses are swept up in uncontrolled wildfires and floods (sometimes both one after the other). The overwhelming majority of the world's population, including the middle classes of the Global North, are only one disaster away from destitution. Disasters are now coming in fast and furiously, leaving more of us in a permanent state of depression and anxiety. Žižek argues that the violence inflicted by the present collapse differs from previous historical violence. In the past, rebellions, revolutions and even wars formed part of a bigger story – a story of freedom, nationalism, progress and so on. Even for those of the losing side, the fight had meaning; it drove history forward. But the collapse of thermo-industrial civilization risks leaving us with nothing – a big blank, meaningless void – a feeling currently expressed on the faces of the boys sent to die in Putin's pointless war in Ukraine. Since we more or less did away with religion as the main vector for dealing with catastrophes, the permanent catastrophe we're living through may leave survivors to haunt the Earth like zombies, deprived of past and future, in a state of permanent trauma. Collapse risks sapping away our lust for life, without which, in psychoanalytic terms, we are only left with a death-drive.

If the current situation leads us to a state of collective depression, is the next logical step some form of collective acceptance? And what would acceptance look like? Some might argue that religious fundamentalists are already way ahead in this regard, welcoming collapse with open arms with the promise of salvation thereafter. I find Žižek's answer to this question at best unsatisfactory, at worst outright dangerous. He harks for a return to some kind of collective emancipation, a neo-communism of sorts. The picture he paints is chaotic, confusing, and I struggle to draw any concrete path forward from it. Having spent time discussing the 1980s with locals in my husband's home country, Romania, the fief of the notoriously despotic Ceaușescu family, I would caution against any revival of communism, in whatever form.

So, what next? My students get a lot out of engaging with the five stages of grief. I give them time to think through some of the more complicated concepts, like fetishistic disavowal and death-drive, inviting them to relate these to their personal experience with grief and discuss it in small groups. I see these concepts come up regularly in learning diaries, so with the right guidance and explanations, Žižek's interpretation of grief hits home with learners. It's not uncommon for students to claim that learning about psychoanalysis changed their relationship with collapse.

I enjoy teaching Žižek's psychoanalysis of collapse; it offers deep insights about what is going on with the world. But Žižek focuses on collective processes. I was interested in exploring unconscious motives at a more personal level. So I would like to close this section by presenting my proposal for a psychoanalysis of collapse based on Melanie Klein's object relations theory, based on my most popular lecture to date: 'Why do we love d*ckheads? On cowboy billionaires, phallic-techno magic and environment grief.'

Why do we love d*ckheads? An object relations perspective

After Freud's death, psychoanalysis was reinvented by Austrian-British children's psychologist Melanie Klein.[28] Her biggest contribution to the field was *object relations theory*. Observing her own children, Klein realized that the superego forms much earlier than Freud supposed.[29] Newborns already develop a proto-superego by splitting the world into good and bad objects, starting with their mother's breasts. Klein explained that babies experience intolerable anxiety when they realize that their mother is a separate person. Unlike in the womb, where foetuses and mothers shared food, warmth and comfort symbiotically, now mother comes and she goes; breasts (food and comfort) come and they go. To cope with this painful randomness, Klein claimed that babies separate the mother into two distinct objects: a good breast and a bad breast. The good and the bad are just projections of the baby's own feelings of satisfaction and despair, as babies can't tell the difference between their inner states and the outside world. In infancy, toddlers separate most of their world along good and bad lines, according to their inner feelings, which gives children the impression, at times, that they are literally swallowing external objects and feeling them from inside their bellies. As children get older, they develop ambivalence towards the world. They realize that there is a separation between their inner states and the outside world and that you can't literally swallow objects. They come to see that most external objects share a mix of good and bad characteristics; nothing is as black and white as it seemed in childhood. Healthy growing up comes with a kind of grieving for a simpler world. This is quite a distressing experience, which is why Klein called it the *depressive position*. However, not all children evolve this more sophisticated perspective, while other children revert to binary thinking when confronted with something seriously anxiety-inducing. Klein described adults who continue to obsessively separate the world into good and evil, confusing the boundaries between their inner feelings and external objects, as being stuck in a *paranoid-schizoid position*.

My analysis is that we have collectively regressed to a child-like state of paranoid-schizoid phantasy. Like children, we phantasize that we have swallowed the world whole: the production of life-like satellite imagery of our planet, from the first clumsy photographs of the DODGE space missions in the 1960s to the 'pale blue dot' image taken by Voyager 1 in 1990, six billion kilometres from the Earth; the concentration of the sum total of human achievements within a digital network available to anyone with a wireless connection; the intimate knowledge of everything since the dawn of time itself, from the hot miasma of the first inflationary seconds of the Big Bang to the accelerating expansion of a cooling universe fourteen billion years later. In the twenty-first century, the Earth has no vast, inscrutable horizon. It is no Gaia, no mystical gateway to the divine. It's a ball, and it feels like we have swallowed it whole. From an object relations perspective, we have developed the delusion that the Earth lives inside of us. As a result, we can no longer disentangle our troubled internal representation of the planet from external reality.

Bruno Latour suggested that the Anthropocene erases the boundaries between nature and culture in a way never observed before in human history – even geological forces are now entangled with human activity![30] From a psychoanalytic perspective, it also erases the boundaries between the geological reality of the planet and our internal representation of it. Just like the infant splits the maternal breast into a good and bad breast, we have split the planet into a good, benevolent, sexually pure and fragile Mother Earth, and a bad, wild, destructive and sexually out-of-control Mother Earth. The image of the Good Mother merges with our most noble moral impulses, while the Bad Mother merges with our destructive consumerist impulses. In this paranoid-schizoid position, we fear for and want to protect the Good Mother, and therefore also the good parts of ourselves. Meanwhile, every storm, flood, heatwave and wildfire is experienced as a terrifying manifestation of the Bad Mother, and therefore also the destructive parts of ourselves. Some people experience this paranoid-schizoid confusion so violently that they express suicide ideation (while they phantasize about death, I don't think most really want to die). I interpret their expressed desire to end their life as a desperate attempt to liberate the persecuted Good Mother from the rampaging destruction of the Bad Mother, one part of the self killing the other (perhaps this is associated with the phantasy that the good part somehow survives?). The trouble is that a quick reality check will easily convince people that almost every action they undertake participates in planetary destruction to some extent. As such, external reality merges uncomfortably with internal terror, and paranoia takes over, hampering the ability to imagine a future in which capitalism dies but humanity survives. I would like to suggest that this vicious feedback loop is the basis of a traumatic psychoanalytical experience of collapse, often manifesting before collapse hits in a material way.

There are two unhealthy responses to this trauma: grandiose narcissistic delusions and melancholia.

The first and most visible response is harboring grandiose narcissistic delusions. The best example of this kind of pathological response is the space race between billionaires Jeff Bezos, Elon Musk and Richard Branson. Here are three men whose delusions of grandeur led them to build rocket ships literally shaped like penises to send themselves to space so they could phantasize about swallowing the Earth from the vantage point of their spaceship window. Critics will argue that vagina-shaped objects are significantly less aerodynamic, but *come on!* Bezos' *Blue Origin* rocket is literally a flying metal penis. The cowboy billionaires, manifesting their phantasies of rugged masculinity with symbolic hats, claim that their phallic vessels are an expression of their love for humanity. But it's clear that they identify as omnipotent Gods with the power to penetrate the planet.

It's easy to see how men with such money and power might develop pathological narcissism. But why do we indulge them? Why do we love d*ckheads (I am referring here, *of course*, to the phallus-shaped machines)? From a psychoanalytic standpoint, cowboy billionaires embody omnipotent father-figures who subdue Bad Mother Earth by penetrating her with machines (some might ask, 'Isn't that a bit rapey?', to which I would respond, 'Yes, it absolutely is'). The reason we love techno-billionaires, I would argue, is because we have psychologically regressed to a state of child-like terror and powerlessness, seeking a masculine parent figure to rescue us from Mother Earth's aggrieved rage. Our collective relationship to billionaires resembles what psychoanalyst Wilfred Bion called a 'basic-assumption dependency group'. That is a group in which the dominant energy is geared towards maintaining the group's delusion that a magnificent leader will save them all, rather than doing productive work. In other words, instead of putting in the hard work to save ourselves from apocalypse, society at large is willing to entertain the phantasy that a handful of insanely rich yahoos will save humanity from destruction by taming the unruly, rebellious Bad Mother with phallic techno-magic.

The irony of this situation is that billionaires are building bunkers in faraway places and hiring private armies to protect them from an apocalypse of their own making, unwittingly revealing a paranoid fear of their own perceived omnipotence and a desire to crawl back inside Mother's belly when all hell breaks loose.

There's a second possible psychic response to the trauma of environmental loss: unresolved mourning, also known as melancholia. Sometimes, people can leave the paranoid-schizoid position and enter a tussle of ambivalent feelings in the depressive position. But ambivalent towards what? This is part of the problem. Psychoanalyst Renée Lertzman studied the emotional responses of locals living around the highly polluted Great Lakes in the US.[31] The lakes have been ravaged by industry for decades, creating all sorts of environmental and health hazards, many of them invisible. Lertzman concluded that the lack of a specific object to grieve made it hard for local people to process their loss and complete their mourning. She described her interview participants as wandering through life in a kind of disengaged daze, an environmental melancholia that resulted in detachment and apathy. Healthy mourning in psychoanalysis supposes the capacity to let love for our objects eventually overcome the hate and anger we feel connected to their loss.[32] Our capacity to verbalize what we have lost enables us to libidinally disinvest, creating the space for new attachments that make a world without the lost object bearable. But in the case of environmental loss, we don't really know what we're losing; much of our grieving is by anticipation. We know the worst is yet to come, but we don't know when, where, or how we will be affected. That makes it hard to verbalize and process feelings of love and hate, repressing grief into unconscious melancholia.

This ambivalence is further complicated by complicity and guilt. Over the last thirty years, capitalism has destroyed a large part of life on Earth, but it has also lifted billions of people out of poverty and squalor. Having been swept up in humanity's wild ascent, many people are reluctant to voice concern for capitalism's rampant destruction, for fear of sounding like an ungrateful child. Industry is internalized as a benevolent, authoritarian father who gives so long as he is not displeased. To many, not just in the Global North but also in countries that adopted capitalism after the Cold War (in Asia and Eastern Europe), expressing overt feelings of hate and anger towards capitalism amounts to betraying the father. I see this vividly in my own family: my husband escaped a miserable existence in communist Romania for a life unimaginably better in The Netherlands. He, like billions of others, loves the system that gave him a ladder out of poverty and despair. But he is also acutely aware that the very system that liberated him will likely leave our daughter at best insecure, at worst destitute, and living the very kind of life he sought to escape. This ambivalence, compounded by guilt, can trigger two reactions – either people attempt to flee from the discomfort and revert to the paranoid-schizoid position, or freeze in the depressive position, stuck in apathy. Apathy, as Lertzman points out, is not a lack of caring, but rather too much care that has no appropriate home. So long as either of these reactions dominate, we will continue to let cowboy billionaires tear open the earth and the heavens, some cheering them on, while the rest of us observe in melancholic apathy.

But as I said in Chapter 2, our fate is not written. We are not pre-destined for uncontrolled collapse, untold misery and possible extinction. If we collectively rise up against the system and its enablers and demand its controlled demolition, we may yet preserve some form of organized civilization and a habitable planet for generations to come. But that requires breaking the spell of the casino capitalists and the hurt of melancholic apathy, before it's too late.

Freud thought that mourning relates to the capacity to speak openly about the love and hate for what we have lost, so that we can disinvest and close the grieving process.[33] That means we need to find it within ourselves to both love capitalism for the opportunities it has undeniably brought billions, from Paris to Mumbai, and hate it for the violence it has wrought on the biosphere, communities of colour, women and the working classes of the world. Speaking that ambivalence out loud, rather than letting it sit as amorphous, semi-conscious feelings, could trigger a first move towards action: reparations. Lertzman concludes her book on the potential of reparations for jolting people out of apathy. She means this literally: people need to feel like they are repairing the Earth, with their hands. I witnessed the power of reparations in my own climb out of environmental despair – caring for the critters beneath the soil in my backyard opened up psychic spaces for transformation (Chapter 6). These kinds of small-scale reparations are by no means sufficient to overthrow the system, but they re-ignite our life force, our libido and subdue our death-drive. This enables us to look at ourselves in the mirror and see something other than death and destruction. Repairing takes away some of the weight of the guilt and complicity, and with that weight lifted, it might free us to imagine ways of living beyond collapse.

Psychoanalysis is a difficult but worthwhile paradigm for students to engage with. To teach it, I break up my explanations with opportunities for students to reflect on manifestations of what I have just described in their own lives, giving them space to verbalize their losses and share with their peers. Judging by their diaries, these exercises sometimes help them to interrupt their melancholic ruminating and move towards more directed forms of mourning. Constrained by the rigidities of the academic schedule, I am not yet able to integrate material reparations as much as I would like in my classroom, but this is something I intend to challenge in my next educational projects (Chapter 4).

If cognitivism and psychoanalysis help students understand their mental barriers to action and change, this does not adequately answer the question: what next? For that, I introduce a third psychological paradigm: existentialism.

Identity and existentialism

When I announce that we're going to study existentialism, the very mention of the word sometimes triggers existential dread; it's a step in the dark for most students. Few courses have ever asked them: Why are you here? What is the meaning of your life? Many students find this initially uncomfortable – not merely thinking about purpose, but thinking about it *in a classroom*. To them, classrooms are comfortably numb places of meaninglessness. How they describe this reminds me of sitting at Dubai airport in the middle of the night, waiting for a connecting flight: nobody really wants to be there; it's just a waiting space to collect tickets before the real destination shows up on screens. So, when we crack open the hard questions, they tell me: Who knew education could be so personal? To ease students into the subject, I begin by discussing identity, which was for me the entry point into existentialism.

Identity crises in times of collapse

Identity is one of these Rorschach concepts, whose meaning depends on who you ask. Broadly speaking, there are two camps in the identity debate: those who think identity is socialized through family, schooling, peer group and work, and those who think it's something you have the power to shape yourself.

For the first camp, initiated by French sociologist Pierre Bourdieu, identity is 'habitus' – a series of habits that people pick up from their environment.[34] People are not necessarily aware of it, but these habits define which social group they belong to and reproduce the conditions for being part of that group down the line. Nineteenth-century political economists defined social groups by economic class – landlords, capitalists and workers. But in the early twentieth century, Bourdieu suggested there might be more to class than economics, adding social and cultural dimensions.[35] He claimed that society values some social and cultural activities more highly (e.g. opera, art galleries) than others (e.g. football, beer festivals). That's not because there's anything intrinsically better about opera and art galleries, but because it's the kind of activities that upper classes reproduce among themselves. Sometimes, a lot of economic capital is necessary to access activities with high cultural value, like collecting art or golfing. But in modern societies, there's also a group of people with little economic capital, yet high cultural capital: teachers, attorneys, accountants and other professionals that form the intellectual middle classes. Defining class through culture as well as economics has advantages and disadvantages. On the one hand, it means that people with little economic means can improve their social mobility by increasing their cultural capital. My grandmother understood this very well, and though she was the kind of person who prayed before cutting a piece of fabric because she knew that she could not afford a mistake, she also spared no expense to elevate her five surviving children's cultural standing. My mother had no fridge or washing machine growing up, but she did have piano lessons and an endless supply of books. On the other hand, cultural capital pulls an invisible curtain between classes, such that even those who make it economically remain socially shunned because they do not adhere to the social codes of the upper classes.

The second camp in the identity debate was initiated by British sociologist Anthony Giddens, who refers to identity as 'self-identity'.[36] Giddens was inspired by existentialism – the work of German philosopher Martin Heidegger in particular.[37] At the core of existentialism is the belief that human consciousness is radically free, offering incalculable possibilities for action in every moment. Yet this freedom comes with a radical contradiction: it will one day be cut short by death, and there's nothing we can do about it. From the moment we're born, the only certainty is that we will disappear into nothingness. Existentialists did away with God since Friedrich Nietzsche, so when they say nothingness, they mean it: you're born, you die – there's no higher reason or purpose, save those you create for yourself.[38] This is so anxiety-inducing that people have for centuries sought comfort in traditions, religions and superstitions to hold their world together and provide meaning. Giddens explains that in the old world, you didn't have to think much about your freedom because tradition dictated your station in life. If you were a man, your father's station determined your own. If you were a woman, your lot was the kitchen and a lifetime of pregnancies, miscarriages and stillbirths. All of this was unchangeable, ordained by God, or Gods, depending on the culture. Though Giddens doesn't make the link, I believe, as explained in Chapter 1, that the release of fossil energy into the world loosened the social ties that bound societies in tradition, allowing individuals to survive without as many rigid social collaborative arrangements. The Industrial Revolution gave wealthy young White men the power to advocate for more freedoms and the right to a personal identity beyond social dictates, often at the expense of women, people of colour and the poor. I would argue that the odes to individuality in the nineteenth-century poetry of Goethe and Lord Byron probably owe more to coal than any intrinsic change in human genius.[39]

Incrementally, over the next couple hundred years, as the quantity of fossil energy increased, women, people of colour and the poor were formally granted the same freedoms as White men. Though Giddens missed the underlying energetic considerations, he argued that late modernity, the society of radical freedom, forced a reckoning with unprecedented powers to shape one's life. The late-modern human is mandated to create 'lifestyle projects', which are both radically liberating and radically anxiety-inducing.

The obvious catch is that while global human rights and freedoms may be *de jure* recognized since the Universal Declaration of Human Rights,[40] *de facto* freedoms and rights available to humans vary. Many countries still operate under authoritarian regimes, with advances in technology allowing states to control the lives of their citizens to extreme extents. For instance, China's surveillance system of social credits assigns ratings to citizens based on their allegiance to the Communist Party, thereby turning regime opponents into pariahs.[41] Even among more democratic countries, many places retain strict social and gender roles, with deviations sometimes punished with public violence, sexual violence and murder.[42] Giddens' society of radical freedom is, therefore, largely a Global North phenomenon. And while the latter may offer de jure equality (to varying degrees and subject to arbitrary regression, as women in the United States are finding out), most wealthy countries maintain institutions that systematically disadvantage women, people of colour and the poor, such that freedom remains a contentious and contended issue.

Therefore, the kind of lifestyle projects described by Giddens might actually form part of the habitus of cosmopolitan middle classes. This begs the question: are post-millennial generations, whose lifestyle aspirations translate into curated social media feeds, exotic travel preferences, cosmopolitan friendship groups and worldly cultural tastes, experiencing real choice? Or is this a form of highly individualistic, alienating and environmentally destructive socialization existing symbiotically with neoliberal capitalism?

I wanted to understand what happens when middle-class socialization meets planetary boundaries, so during my postdoc, I interviewed sustainability students from the liberal arts and engineering departments where I was working.[43] Looking at the data, I realized that the students defined environmental issues as a moral question. Caring about climate change and the loss of the natural world was defined as a moral good, i.e. it was perceived that good people should care about the planet, and since most people (except psychopaths) want to be seen as good, students claimed to care about the planet. Yet most of them had only very limited experience of the natural world. Therefore, students experienced the degradation of nature less as personal loss and more as moral conundrum pitting personal comfort and pleasure-seeking against the fate of the living world, the poor and future generations.

Understanding how students got to this line of thinking requires a short step back in history. In the nineteenth century, one of the dominant moral philosophies in Western Europe was the broad utilitarianism of John Stuart Mill. Its lodestar for evaluating the greater good was *utility*, which comprised five social goods to guide moral decision-making: security, individuality, abundance, subsistence and equality.[44] Security, the right not to be arbitrarily detained, killed or have your property taken, was the most important and the basis for all the others. But among the remaining four, abundance was valued as dearly as the right to individuality (being allowed to be and do what you like with consenting adults so long as it harms no others) or subsistence (not starving and having roof over your head). However, during the Marginalist Revolution of the 1870s, described in Chapter 1, this was replaced by a single measure of utility, defined only as personal preferences, with more almost always assumed to be better.[45] Marginalists boiled utilitarianism down to abundance, then wove that moral prescription into their economic modelling as the basis for a scientific understanding of human economic behaviour. Abundance-seeking was first transmitted by universities, then by governance through formal and informal institutions, and has since seeped through to ordinary people through schooling and socialization. This isn't mere speculation – the students I interviewed literally talked about calculating the adverse effect of their environmentally destructive behaviours against the positive impact of their activities on their personal growth and lifestyle projects. Given this view of morality, students could and did easily trade the moral 'bads' of their flights and steaks with other actions perceived as moral 'goods', like being a supportive friend, or committing to better oneself. In this bargaining process, the environmental cost of their actions were no match for the draw of lifestyle project experiences and the curation of middle-class identities.

At that time, most students did not feel directly affected by collapse; this was before the COVID-19 pandemic and the war in Ukraine. I am beginning to see different reactions now that the reality of living in a collapsing world begins to sink in. It happens more often that students experience distress during my classes, manifesting as tears or anger. Once the possibility of bargaining is taken from them, the contradictions of their lifestyle projects appears to many like an insurmountable identity crisis.

The existential fear of finitude

In 1973, the American existentialist anthropologist Ernest Becker suggested in *The Denial of Death* that humans try to escape the absurdity of death and nothingness by crafting 'immortality projects'.[46] Having children, building successful companies, writing books, making movies – these are all attempts to transcend death by leaving our imprint on the living long after we have departed. If Becker were alive today, he might conclude that social media posts are just so many immortality projects – in a quasi-literal sense, since the number of accounts belonging to the deceased grows by the year.[47] Immortality projects allow us to beat back the existential dread of death, comforting our fear of nothingness with a warm balm of remembrance.

Now collapse threatens to sweep away our carefully crafted mausoleums, like matchstick castles. Switch off the internet tomorrow, and the digital memory of billions of people disappears. But the internet is merely the largest and most fragile of our immortality projects; the irony is that while our power over the Earth grew exponentially, nothing we built in the last 100 years was made to endure. In the ultimate stages of consumer capitalism, even our immortality projects are mass-produced. Now enter climate change, burn the forests, flood the cities, scorch the land and take with it our delusions of immortality! Pyramids will still stand a thousand years hence, long after the last sky scraper has fallen to rubble. We can try to hide the truth from ourselves, but cracks appear beneath the selfie-ready smile – the knowledge that collapse could sweep it all away. A century from now, if there are humans left at all, they will be too preoccupied with survival to remember us, all eight billion of us. You and I must face the fact that our existence, with the richness of our inner lives, our traumas and fears, our joys and accomplishments, will all be wiped from the Earth and forgotten. Just as we have silently wiped over 70 per cent of animal life from the planet, much human life may face a similar fate, buried in mass graves in war zones or left for dead in deserts of our own making. Collapse confronts us with our darkest fear: finitude.

Escaping the abyss

The fact is that for the largest part of history, the human condition has been rather miserable. As someone living with chronic illness, I can imagine that one might just about learn to live with awful ailments, but I struggle to wrap my head around the omnipresence and randomness of death in pre-modern times, particularly the grief of losing children. The death of children was, until very recently, an expected part of life. My generation is the first in my family not to lose a baby – I don't mean miscarriage, but the death of an otherwise healthy child through domestic accident or illness. Everyone, from peasants to royals, lost children to what are now preventable illnesses and injuries. And yet, though I can imagine no greater pain, a grief-laden humanity has carried on, enduring loss for millennia, for that was its fate, and its burden: a species condemned to understand its own suffering.

We are alive in strange times indeed: humanity has pierced through the clouds of death and misery and showed us a world in which children no longer need to die, illnesses can be treated and lives can be lived without war and hunger. But that same humanity is now hurtling back down towards the abyss, and I worry that the fall will hurt all the more for knowing what was, and might have been. With all that energy and all those resources, we could have built a civilization so much fairer, more resilient and more meaning-laden. Instead, we let the rich pillage and plunder, grateful for the crumbs of their misdeeds. Now that the abyss is visible once more, rage, despair and revolutionary fever spin around it like the halo of a black hole.

What do we do with the existential abyss? The existentialists' answer to that question is yet another exhortation to individualism. Nietzsche, Heidegger and Sartre would tell you to live authentically, free from the social constraints of those whom Heidegger called Das Man – the 'they',[48] and live for what purpose you can find for yourself as a free man (all three were unabashed misogynists, who didn't think women fit to live free). That freedom comes at the cost of lifelong existential angst, and the constant awareness of death, but is, accordingly, the only way to live authentically in a world without absolutes.

For many people, including me, this is not a very satisfying answer, especially in a world in collapse. Recognizing climate grief as an existential issue, one nonetheless finds little comfort from collapse in existential philosophy. Perhaps this explains the surging popularity of post-human eco-feminism and indigenous philosophy in environmental circles – the works of Isabelle Stengers,[49] Donna Haraway,[50] Ursula Le Guin,[51] Robin Wall Kimmerer[52] and Leanne Simpson[53] to name just a few. Post-human eco-feminism takes inspiration from the biological sciences to offer a different way of thinking about the spaces we share with other living creatures, from blue whales to bacteria. Donna Haraway, the intellectual leader of this movement, dreams of a world in which human thinking becomes entangled with other species.[54] She invites us to pull on the threads of the worldwide production web of global capitalism. At her most literary, she puts forward stories about children genetically modified into animal chimeras to become speakers for extinct species. I came to Haraway with an open mind, since many colleagues were inspired by her ideas, but quickly found limitations to her work. I have written at length about my Haraway hesitations in an essay titled 'The Love at the End of the World', so

I will only offer here a summary.[55] It seems to me that Haraway's philosophy is existentially inauthentic. She hides in the mud with creepy crawlies to avoid the human condition. She offers what Guha and Alier called 'environmentalism for the rich',[56] linguistically placing the lives of bacteria on par with the lives of Black slaves in plantations. She also leaves the depopulation door too wide open to ecofascists for comfort. Although I understand why she focuses on reducing the number of people on the planet, I don't think she does so in a very nuanced or sensible way. The problem, when one starts talking about reducing the human population to 3.5 billion within one century, is that it is usually not long before someone comes up with racist ideas to achieve this.

The works of indigenous women, like Kimmerer and Simpson, offer a more sober and nuanced take on living in community with one's environment. Indigenous people have already lived through the apocalypse, and the longing for what was lost haunts their texts. A recent study suggests that native Americans were exterminated in a genocide so brutal and widespread that it briefly affected the composition of the atmosphere.[57] Survivors were hounded from their lands, packed into reservations and had their children forcibly removed and taken to missionary schools with the aim of erasing native culture. Authorities in Canada and the USA are still uncovering the unmarked graves of indigenous children in the yards of these mission schools.[58] Given the history, it feels dark for former colonizers to come to indigenous people for help with surviving an apocalypse of their own making. Taken seriously, this could be an opportunity for reparations and reconciliation, but I fear this may end up just another extractive operation to save ourselves at the expense of indigenous people. I fear it all the more when I see that the result of raising awareness on questions of moral identity and existential dread plunges many students into a quest for environmental identities instead.

Environmental identities

There's nothing wrong per se with environmental identities, a term coined by Susan Clayton to refer to self-concepts built on feelings of belonging with the non-human world.[59] In fact, her research showed that children who developed their identity around belonging in and with nature in their youth grow up to care intrinsically about nature when they reach adulthood.[60] Their drive to protect the living world is impervious to moral bargaining, since it rests on different foundations. And while environmental identities are mostly formed in childhood, Clayton and colleagues suggested that such identities could also be developed later in life through place-based education that reconnects young people with nature. This is why I advocate for students to go outside, touch the living world with their hands, grow things of their own, and marvel at the resilience of plants and insects, even somewhere so ecologically damaged as the Randstad.

But too many students end up reaching the same conclusion as James Lovelock, one of the authors of the famous *Gaïa hypothesis*: humans are a plague upon the Earth-system, and their numbers must be kept in check.[61] Every year, at least one student says 'good riddance' when we discuss the possibility of human extinction. I find this problematic, on several counts.

First, it shows a lack of appreciation for the fact that not all humans consume resources at planet-destroying levels. Eleven billion people could comfortably live on Earth like present-day Angolans, but to sustain the lifestyle of the average person living in The Netherlands, the human population would need to be cut by close to 85 per cent.[62] That some European students find it easier to wish for humanity's extinction than for the end the planet-destroying political-economic system that feeds western lifestyle projects is, from the vantage point on those on the receiving end of climate chaos, like rubbing salt in the wounds. From our vantage point, it marks the abject failure of the education systems of the Global North to instill solidarity and compassion for humanity.

Second, environmental identities lies are built around intrinsic attachment to the natural world, without the intermediary of moral commitment. While this forms a good basis of taking action to protect nature, it can easily be read as endowing nature with intrinsic value. This is a core tenet of so-called 'deep' ecology – the kind of biocentric ecology that focuses on preserving pristine nature from human intervention.[63] This assertion is fundamentally and practically untenable. Indeed, the word 'valuable' implies an entity capable of assigning values bestowing value upon nature. From a religious perspective, God or Gods could be cast in the role of valuing entities, but in a chemical universe, there is no order of molecular preference. Therefore, I have no reason to believe that assemblages of carbon are intrinsically more valuable than, say, hydrogen or uranium. If valuation comes from neither God(s) nor the universe, it must be coming from somewhere closer to home. Deep ecologists will argue that anything that lives has valuing capabilities, and we should have no reason to place human values above the values of, say, fungi or amoebas. While I am sympathetic to this argument, I have never thought twice about taking antibiotics when infected with potentially lethal bacteria. Even the Jain monks who sweep the floor before they step forward to avoid squashing insects must eat and therefore must destroy some life in order to keep living.[64] Feeding off life to sustain life is in the very definition of living: there can be no life without metabolism. We must therefore accept that living comes with a mandate to dismantle other life forms. Living therefore comes less with a responsibility to do *no* harm than with a responsibility to exercise restraint and care. Students generally find this argument compelling – its gentle ambivalence helps them move away from paranoid-schizoid thinking – but the existentialism of Simone de Beauvoir gives it some ontological punch.

Existential environmental ethics

Since the argument for an intrinsic value of life does not hold up to scientific scrutiny, we are back in the territory of ethics, which is, as we have seen, fraught with the dangers of neoliberal utilitarian thinking and existential solipsism. I suggested in the beginning of this chapter that the power of De Beauvoir's philosophy is her recognition that to be human is to love generously. De Beauvoir is not the first to preach love; the Bible beat her to it, and her philosophy was certainly influenced by her Catholic upbringing.[65] But existential love is a love of freedom, rather than a love of people – thy lovest thy neighbour's freedom. This boils down to fundamental existentialist beliefs about what people are. From an existential standpoint, one can only define a person (i.e. give a person an 'essence') after the fact, based on what they have already done. But what they do next is always up in the air, because having a conscience means being free to choose what happens next – you may have heard this expressed as 'existence precedes essence'.[66] The Austrian-Jewish existential psychologist Viktor Frankl demonstrated that choice is still possible even in the worst possible circumstances in his account of surviving Nazi terror at Auschwitz.[67] You can't really love *a person* in any kind of essential way, as that would be exactly the kind of pathological obsession De Beauvoir rejected. To love generously is to desire that our fellow humans be free to keep making choices and projects. To love them is to fight against the obstacles to that freedom, even, in some cases, by violent means if existentially necessary. Indeed, De Beauvoir's love was not pacifist: she argued for hanging Nazi war criminals, and defended Algerian freedom fighters during the war of independence against France.[68]

This capacity to grasp freedom as an existential necessity sets humans apart from other animals. Indeed, while there may be no intrinsically greater value to human flesh than any other organic matter, humans have the capacity to situate freedom within the arc of history, between past and future. To preserve freedom, they have the capacity to organize politically, defy self-preservation instincts, rally, fight and sacrifice.

I agree with De Beauvoir, not just philosophically, but in lived praxis. There is a humanizing quality to the shared passion of fighting for a world in which our fellows are not crushed by collapse. That quality cannot be quantified or rationalized with preference curves, nor does it boil down to existential self-fulfillment; I see it as humanity itself, pouring forth from love translated into action. Love is both in the doing, and the doing-it-together.

While collapse is upon us, it need not be merely an end, but the chance of a new beginning. We are teetering on the edge – what we decide to do in the next ten years will determine whether civilization falls into an apocalyptic nightmare, or emerges renewed and ready for a fairer, freer future. Being fully human at this moment in time requires nothing less than committing all we have to the side of life – living and loving. On this note, I close my class on existentialism, followed by a heavy sigh in the audience. They need to sit with this, to let it sink in.

What a reflective journey! In some courses, I give the light version, presenting a brief overview of the three paradigms and easily accessible reading materials, in other courses, we spend an entire semester exploring the lenses together with more complicated texts. If you read this chapter wondering how you could possibly teach this without a degree in psychology, fear not; the point was not to require teachers to become experts on Freud and De Beauvoir. I wanted to show that reflection on collapse is, in my experience, at its most powerful when experienced as a praxis between theoretical perspectives and students' personal lived experience. Praxis cannot exist without theory, but you don't need expertise to introduce theory to your students. It's perfectly reasonable for teachers to discover theory alongside their students. I have done so many times in my days as a problem-based learning tutor. I know this is hard for the academically minded, but your students don't need you to publish a dozen articles on climate psychology for you to guide them through their reflections on collapse. They need you to facilitate their praxis, to hold space for their existential reckoning. What this means to me is giving every learning diary personal, heartfelt feedback, and sitting down for coffee with students who feel lost at sea, making personalized reading recommendations based on conversations. It's my personal interpretation of care, but you can develop your own. The knowledge I shared in this chapter is more than sufficient for you to do that; the rest is in the intention you give to the process.

4

Experimental Pedagogics

In the previous chapter, we established a foundational understanding of the psychological impact of learning about collapse on students, as well as some basic reflective practices I use in my classrooms. I'd like now to share *Experimental Pedagogics*, the education framework I developed starting in 2020 to structure the development of pedagogies of collapse. It was my answer to the 'take appropriate action now' conundrum. Experimental Pedagogics isn't a specific teaching technique, but rather a structuring way of thinking about education in times of collapse that allows teachers to organize learning in praxis for students. In this chapter, I will discuss some specific pedagogical practices I use in my courses. You're welcome to take inspiration from these for your own teaching, but the main goal is to provide you with a usable educational framework to construct your own pedagogies of collapse.

Trying something new

As mentioned previously, I spent the first years of my academic career following in the footsteps of great educators – people like Henning Salling Olesen, pioneer of Critical Pedagogy in Denmark, and my doctoral supervisor, Henk Schmidt, who turned problem-based learning from a method of medical education suited to graduate students into a learning approach that could work for all higher education. I mean that literally: I was often trotting behind these *eminences grises* to various archives and libraries to excavate typewritten records of their educational breakthroughs.

Being a history buff (I took extra history exams in high school just for fun), I had a ball writing my PhD. I loved every word I put down on the pages of my monograph, and I think it showed: I was awarded the doctorate cum laude in 2016.[1] As a result, I became known as the 'historian of problem-based education': people still email me from all over to discuss my dissertation. However, my intention was neither to be an historian nor an expert in problem-based education. I studied the history of the educational movements of the 1970s – problem-based learning in Canada and The Netherlands, and problem-oriented project work in Denmark – to discover what makes educational revolutions succeed, because I knew that under conditions of collapse, the time would come to start educational revolutions anew. At whatever scale, in whichever place, I wanted to know the secrets of devising educational innovations that stand the test of time under conditions of social stress. In the mournful words of my dear supervisor: 'you could have been a great scientist, it's such a shame you wanted to change the world instead.' In 2020, I was offered the chance to put the wheels of change in motion, in the most unlikely of places: Russia.

Setting the scene

It was the summer of 2020. We were still reeling from the first wave of Covid when I received a call from an educational acquaintance, Daniel Kontowski, with whom I had crossed paths while he was writing his doctoral thesis on the rise (and fall) of Liberal Arts colleges in Europe. We had lost touch in the intervening years, so I was surprised to learn that he was now managing an experimental Liberal Arts college in Siberia and was hiring teachers to fill the course roster for their English-language master's degree in Education Innovation. Having failed to persuade me to pack my bags and leave for Siberia in the middle of a pandemic, Daniel agreed to let me run a course online, so long as travel restrictions remained. The course was called 'Classroom Experiments', and beyond the title, I had a free rein to design it as I wished.

In line with pedagogies of collapse, I wanted to assemble a course that would place truth-seeking, real-world knowledge and imperfect solidarities at the heart of learning. I didn't want students to merely *learn* about the multitude of problems with education described in Chapter 2 but actually *experiment* with transformative education design, building classroom interventions to address real problems they identified for themselves, so they could experience the messy, imperfect process of wading into the fray. The obvious move was to turn to the approaches mentioned in Chapter 2: Critical Pedagogy and Bildung. However, I felt that neither approach fully encompassed what I was trying to achieve.

I find great inspiration in Critical Pedagogy, but feel frustrated with the way it has veered towards American identity politics in recent years (more on this in the next chapter). This tendency is salient in two regards: suspicion towards education science, and a specific (American) vision of diversity and inclusion. It wasn't always this way: at the dawn of Critical Pedagogy, there were attempts to integrate scientific insights from cognitive psychology into the educational design of revolutionary programmes. For instance, in 1974, Knud Illeris, widely regarded as the founding theorist of problem-oriented project work in Denmark, brought together cognitive psychology and Frankfurt School Critical Pedagogy in the design of the method.[2] However, of the two Danish universities that implemented Illeris' approach, one promoted a stubbornly Marxist reading of Critical Pedagogy, while the other never took as much interest in Critical Pedagogy and focused on cognitivism instead.[3] So the glue binding the two perspectives dissolved. Today, postmodern Critical Pedagogy critiques scientific research as prone to racist and patriarchal biases that serve imperialist and capitalist interests.[4] While there is merit in the contents of this critique, the guilty-till-proven-innocent suspicion that many critical pedagogues harbour towards educational studies conducted predominantly by White men makes integrating their scientific insights into social-critical education challenging.

To my second point, Critical Pedagogy has increasingly shifted towards addressing diversity and inclusion through an American race and gender discourse. This marks a departure from its original emphasis on economic justice and freedom. Dutch critical pedagogue Gert Biesta observed (in 1998!) that economic issues and class justice had gradually taken a backseat to diversity and inclusion, ultimately narrowing the definition of justice.[5] He stated: 'if postmodernism has nothing more to offer than an unqualified celebration of differences, it then creates a situation where other forces – like the forces of the new capitalism – can easily come in and take over',[6] a theme echoed in Chapter 5. Works of postmodern Critical Pedagogy like bell hooks' *Teaching Community*[7] and *Teaching to Transgress*,[8] and Carpenter and Mojab's *Revolutionary Learning*,[9] give the impression that education's primary goal should be tackling racism and patriarchy. They prescribe quite specific approaches to achieve this, with the implication that anyone who does not adhere to these prescriptions participates in oppression by default. While I disagree with Tim Urban's criticism of Critical Pedagogy as a tool for political indoctrination, I can understand how he reached that conclusion if his exposure was limited to its postmodern iterations.[10] And that's on us, critical pedagogues, for not speaking up loudly enough when our tools started being used to admonish more than to liberate.

When it comes to Bildung, my biggest concern is the fuzziness of the approach. After participating for some years in Bildung communities of practice, I find that outside the context of folk high schools in Scandinavia, Bildung means a wide range of things to different people. I recently had a debate with a Danish practitioner who assured me that Bildung was impervious to scientific scrutiny because it is actually closer to a religion than an educational method. While this view is not necessarily representative, it goes to show the extent to which the definition and purpose of Bildung come under debate. The expansion of Bildung beyond its Nordic origins is still in its infancy. The loose collection of educators and civil society activists gathered in the global Bildung community is still looking for its place between modernity and postmodernity, philosophy and method.

Attempting to put together a course design for my Russian students, I realized I needed a *praxis framework*, backed by theory, steeped in action, anchored in planetary boundaries and the science of collapse, mindful of cognitive, psychoanalytic and existential dimensions of psychology, taking inspiration from Critical Pedagogy and Bildung while cognizant of the imperfect nature of transformative education.

In the end, I felt the name 'Classroom Experiments' wasn't broad enough to reflect my aims, so I came up with a different course name: *Experimental Pedagogics*. In October 2020, as the second Covid lockdown loomed, only eighteen months before the start of Putin's brutal assault on Ukraine, I taught the first iteration of *Experimental Pedagogics* online to a group of young Russians in their Siberian bedrooms.

Dimensions of learning

What's in a framework? I'm aware of the tendency towards framework-hyperinflation in the education sciences, encouraged by a scientific publication system that seems to reward framework development for its own sake. So let me clarify how I think about Experimental Pedagogics (I'll use XP for short from hereon): I see it more as an educational meta-philosophy with flexible associated practices than a method. In the rest of this chapter, I aim to help teachers understand what it's about and how I made it work in practice. Teachers will ideally take it home, make it their own, use what works in their context, discard what doesn't and share the results so we can learn from it.

Why *meta*-philosophy? That's because I didn't so much write new theory for XP as structure existing theories and philosophies in a Russian-doll-like system that assembles everything into a coherent, concentric whole. I broke reality down into five dimensions, from narrowest and closest to us, to broadest and furthest away, starting with the brain and ending with the world, passing through individuals, social groups and larger communities. You can apply the framework sequentially, however, in the second part of the chapter, I will show how to apply the logic of the framework to existing courses in ways that do not necessarily follow the order below.

Cognitive dimension

The first task of XP is to provide learners with educational activities that align with the human cognitive architecture and what we know about knowledge processing. In other words, even (especially?) in times of collapse, we want to design education that is efficient, effective and enjoyable. This is what educators generally think of as education design principles, under the headline of pedagogical sciences. This builds on classical cognitive psychology, starting with Vygotsky's work on language in the 1930s,[11] Jerome Bruner's work on thinking in the 1960s,[12] the constructivists' research on knowledge acquisition in the 1970s and 1980s,[13] and the golden rules of learning compiled in the 1990s.[14] These are cognitive triggers of knowledge acquisition, which can be summarized as follows: first, the activation of prior knowledge is needed for integrating new information in the brain – something intuited since Vygotsky's Zone of Proximal Development hypothesis in the 1930s,[15] but evidenced after the cognitive revolution.[16] Then, problem-solving and learning are context-dependent, because knowledge is organized in structures of words (semantic networks) that the brain builds by encoding personal experiences into associations of images, words and storylines (schemas and scripts), which organize long-term memory. In other words, human problem-solving skills are not algorithmic like a computer's but depend almost entirely on what the brain can draw from long-term memory storage (i.e. the more relevant information you know, the better you can solve problems).[17] Third, elaborating on new information, for example, by adding detail or explaining it in one's own words, is key to improving its encoding in long-term memory. Finally, motivation is a core driver for learning.

While there are several major strands of motivation research, XP focuses on Self-Determination Theory (SDT), pioneered by Edward Deci and Richard Ryan in the 1970s.[18] SDT identified three determinants of motivation: autonomy (how much choice students have in their own learning), competence (how well equipped they feel to tackle a task) and relatedness (how much they feel like they belong in the classroom). Based on these criteria, Ryan and Deci distinguished between autonomous motivation, where people feel in charge of their learning, and controlled motivation, where learning is imposed from the outside. Unsurprisingly, the former spurred learning more effectively. SDT was chosen for XP over alternative motivation theories because of its relative accessibility.

The elements presented here form the theoretical basis of the cognitive level. This information won't be news to experienced educators, most of whom will have received a training course or two on educational design. But I've included it as the foundational level of XP because I have seen multiple occasions where enthusiastic educators get so wrapped up in innovative thinking that they forget basic psychological facts about learning and end up overwhelming their students and missing the mark on their goals, which is a shame. I must admit that even though I wrote my PhD on this topic, I still need to check myself every now and again and go back to education design basics.

So what does a pedagogical approach that respects good educational design principles look like? One of the approaches often cited to this effect is problem-based learning (PBL) – here I'm talking about the learning method that originated in medical schools in Canada and The Netherlands.[19] In summary, PBL consists in presenting small groups of learners with ill-defined problems to analyse. Problems are usually made up of text and images gathered in vignettes, but some teachers get creative and use role-play, experiments, games and so forth as problems. The tutorial, which lasts around two hours, takes place under the guidance of a tutor, who acts as a process guide. The crucial distinction between PBL and other methods that use real-life problems (like the Case Method) is that PBL students approach the problem without any kind preparation.[20] Reading materials and lectures should only be made available after the initial discussion phase. This is because tackling problems without prior preparation activates existing knowledge based on previous schooling and personal experiences, opening up pathways for new knowledge to assimilate into or modify cognitive schemas.

PBL has been investigated from all angles, like motivation theory,[21] cognitive load theory,[22] knowledge acquisition[23] and long-term retention.[24] Despite the thousands of articles written on the subject, there is scant evidence that PBL as a whole performs 'better' than other learning approaches, but that depends on what outcomes one seeks to measure.[25] When I was researching the history of PBL, I interviewed Geoffrey Norman, one of Canada's PBL pioneers, and he made the point that looking at processes may be more interesting than outcomes. He recalled a conference held at Michigan State University in 1975, during which he despondently admitted to Lee Schuman, a pioneer of medical education, that there was no evidence of the superior performance of PBL students. To this, Schuman allegedly responded, 'What do you prefer, sex or artificial insemination?'[26] In short: perhaps PBL does increase long-term retention of knowledge somewhat, or perhaps it's just a more fun way to learn. Research has shown that specific elements of PBL, like the skills and knowledge of the tutor who facilitates the class or the quality of the problems offered to students can be tweaked to improve learning outcomes,[27] but it's not the panacea that PBL proponents have often made it out to be.

I taught with and was a strong advocate for PBL for almost a decade, and I will grant that it beats the boring lecture-seminar format I was subjected to at university. I discuss PBL in my XP courses and teacher trainings because I think it's important for participants to see for themselves how a learning approach can build on and feed back into education research. However, I noticed that many universities that were using PBL are now dropping it, and I have almost stopped using it. I sense a general PBL fatigue among educators – a feeling that PBL doesn't provide the answers they were looking for. Proponents of PBL will argue that this is caused by poor implementation practices.[28] That is partly true, and I have written at length about misconceptions that lead to poor implementation.[29] But I don't think this is the full story. It seems to me that while PBL is great at answering the 'hows' of learning, it does a rather poor job of answering the 'whys'. And in catastrophic times, we need to do better than just offer a faster conveyor belt to collapse. Together with leading scholars in the field, I have pleaded with the PBL community to take the 'why' more seriously,[30] but truth be told, the imminence of collapse calls on us to look beyond the comfort of tried-and-tired methods. Good educational design alone is not enough, which brings us to the second dimension of XP.

Individual dimension

The individual dimension of XP aims to get students out of their heads and into their bodies, as living, feeling human beings, capable of projecting themselves into a world of meanings. This dimension was inspired by existential phenomenology, the school of thought pioneered by De Beauvoir and Merleau-Ponty. This isn't as radical an opposition to the cognitive perspective as first appears: Merleau-Ponty was fond of quoting scientific studies on interesting neurological, sensory and cognitive disorders to support his ideas on human perception.[31] What demarcated De Beauvoir and Merleau-Ponty from other existentialists was their commitment to the human body as the starting point of experience. Earlier existentialists and phenomenologists had a more or less dualistic view of the mind-body relationship. De Beauvoir's lifelong companion, Jean-Paul Sartre, placed consciousness and the body into two distinct categories: the mind was there for-itself, capable of determining its own purpose and meaning, while the body was just a thing in-itself, like tables and coffee cups.[32] In starting with the scientifically unassailable premise that consciousness is born in the body, and the body is made up of exactly the same stuff as the rest of the universe, Merleau-Ponty and De Beauvoir operated something of a Copernican turn in existentialism. Claiming that there's nothing chemically special about being in a body, and yet, it is within this fragile envelope of 'flesh', as Merleau-Ponty called it,[33] that the depth of our inner world is possible, they dispelled dualist mind-body fantasies and turned existential phenomenology into a philosophy relevant to a world on the cusp of collapse.

Fossil fuel capitalism did a reasonably good job of taking care of our body's physiological needs,[34] such that in large parts of the world (to varying degrees), it was easy to forget that having water, food, medicine and a safe place to sleep are essential preconditions to making meaningful life projects – until Covid and climate catastrophe came knocking. Centring the body as the source of lived experience calls to mind our dependency upon the material world, but existentialism acknowledges that material preconditions are just that: a situation to which we can freely react. This was epitomized in Viktor Frankl's autobiographic book *Man's Search for Meaning*, in which he recounted his life during the Nazi occupation of Austria, culminating in his arrest, deportation and internment at Auschwitz.[35] He concluded that in the worst situations imaginable, humans retain the capacity to choose their attitudes and reactions, even when the options for actions are limited.

Collapse is taking away bodily certainties taken for granted since the end of the Second World War. Even in Western Europe, students find themselves in the increasingly uncomfortable position of existing in bodies threatened by temperature extremes (too hot in summer, energy restriction on heating in winter), pandemics, food and medical supplies shortages of one kind or another, and imminent dangers like floods, storms and wildfires. Existential phenomenology offers students a hopeful way of reckoning with this, acknowledging that their material situation is changing for the worse, while centring their enduring capacity to find meaning and purpose under the circumstances.

How does this translate into pedagogical practice? I hand my students a copy of *Man's Search for Meaning*, and we go over *The Ethics of Ambiguity* together in the reflection track of my courses.[36] However, I want them to grasp their bodily existence as the heart of their subjective experience. This is where I draw from another pedagogical tradition: embodied learning. A couple of years ago, I was invited to contribute to an exciting project combining university studies with creative, artistic and musical education in Rotterdam, the *Rotterdam Arts and Sciences Lab*, where I met professional dancer and artistic research scholar Suzan Tunca.

Suzan teaches a dance exercise called double-skin-double-mind (DS-DM), a method developed to open the creative space for dancers and choreographers by Emio Greco and Pieter Scholten.[37] The purpose of DS-DM is to bring practitioners into awareness of their existence as beings in bodies, lift them out of preconceived notions and increase their body's sensitivity to the world before going into the creative process. In DS-DM, participants engage in breathing, stretching, shrinking, jumping and moving for over an hour, until the body leads the conversation, silencing sometimes tyrannical cognitive impulses that enjoin them to think and behave in fixed ways. Participants are then invited to reflect, first in silence, then as a group, on the ways their bodies manifested as an agent of learning during the process. As a martial artist, I'm not surprised by the power of embodied learning to release unconscious emotions that conscious cognition would rationalize away. When I said that we need to take appropriate action now, the ability to reconnect the body was among those, as a necessary precondition to meaning-making. I recommend that every course that covers collapse should include a movement-based element of embodied learning, and if you do not know how to teach this yourself, I encourage you to do what I did and make friends with your local dance teachers.

Group dimension

Working with imperfect solidarities in education requires students to work together and overcome conflict, strife, frustration and deal with messy human emotions. Working productively in groups isn't something that comes easily to students. Within higher education, group work is often billed as a trainable skill that improves students' future market position rather than a basic fact of human life. Teachers who work with group-based approaches, particularly within the realm of project-based pedagogies, will be familiar with the usual suspects in group dysfunction training: the free-rider, the dramatic student, the deconstructionist and the over-zealous leader . . . volumes have been written about 'student types' in the classroom.[38] I am not fond of these characterizations and approach the group level in XP from a psychoanalytic standpoint instead, to design group activities that address subconscious patterns underlying destructive behaviour in groups.

Building onto Freud's work, psychoanalyst Wilfred Bion developed a theory of group dynamics in the 1960s, focused on the difference between productive work groups, which are driven by principles of scientific reasoning, rationality and goal-orientation and basic assumptions groups, in which subconscious drives take over the collective process.[39] These groups are called 'basic assumption' because Bion believed this to be the default position unless effective work is put into building and maintaining productive group functioning. He identified three types of basic assumption groups: dependency, pairing and fight or flight groups. Dependency groups happen when the group subconsciously appoints one person as an all-mighty leader tasked with saving the collective from implosion. This is not the same as consciously appointing a group chair or leader, who would be subject to rational scrutiny and follow scientific procedures. In this case, the leader is more like a guru or messiah – they are given unquestioned obedience in exchange for the promise of salvation. If the chosen leader refuses to take up that role, the group will ditch them and pick someone else willing to play God. Dependency groups are unfortunately common in educational settings. Teachers are often appointed as saviours by students, expected to rescue them from the difficulties of learning by providing the answers in exchange for passive cooperation. If teachers refuse to play along and attempt to reveal the unhealthy nature of the group dynamic, they might find themselves aggressively shunned and replaced in the role of saviour by someone else, like the classroom's most popular or studious person. Pairing groups work in a similar way, but the leader in this situation is a dyad, expected to produce a messiah by coupling together. We can allow a metaphorical interpretation of this coupling as producing figurative babies, like an answer or intervention deriving from two people's combined efforts that will save the group. Fight or flight groups, as the name indicates, happen when the group devolves into rage or panic. This happened to me early in my teaching career during a particularly difficult tutorial, where I was teaching an external fellow's materials that I did not fully grasp myself. The group's first line of defence was to adopt a dependency group formation, but as I was neither able nor willing to fulfil the saviour role, a first student broke down in tears, and then within five minutes, half the class was howling, while the others watched with concern. I had to call it quits and end the meeting early. Given the emotional intensity of topics related to collapse, the temptation to fall into basic assumption group patterns is quite high, for the same reasons as the prevalence of paranoid-schizoid thinking at the individual level (Chapter 2). It is therefore important to identify when such patterns emerge and how to build back up to a productive work-group dynamic.

Most of the pedagogical approaches I use in teaching collapse are group-based. However, in my experience, group work concentrates the sum of student frustrations, particularly in topics related to transitions and sustainability, where equally committed passions oppose and clash. Students also need a learning method to *learn* to work in groups. To this effect, XP borrows Elliot Aaronson's model of cooperative learning: the jigsaw classroom.[40] Aaronson developed jigsawing as a learning approach to overcome prejudice in the de-segregated South of the United States. The premise is simple: make students dependent upon each other, and they will cooperate. Jigsawing consists in dividing up class objectives and materials into three or four component parts and then sharing those among the corresponding quantity of 'expert' groups. These student groups research and prepare the same objective and materials.

Students work in their expert group to prepare their share of the class, then when everyone is ready, the groups shuffle into their 'jigsaw' group, such that one expert for each objective is present in each jigsaw group. As an illustration, if there are twelve students in a classroom, and the learning objectives are divided into A, B, C and D, the expert groups will comprise students A1, A2, A3 and A4, B1, B2, B3 and B4 and so forth. The jigsaw groups will comprise students A1, B1, C1 and D1, A2, B2, C2 and D2 and so forth. Each expert is responsible for teaching their share of the class to the rest of their jigsaw group, so they really had better prepare, because the group is assessed on their performance for the *whole* class, and only does well if all experts have prepared accordingly. I have used jigsawing for several years now and find that students come to class significantly better prepared than for regular tutorials or PBL groups. They also feel responsibility towards fellow students – creating space for quieter students, students of colour, queer students and so on to share their perspective on an equal footing with others. As a bonus, it forces teachers to stay quiet: I hover around, intervening only when someone raises their hand, but listening to all the jigsaw groups. I schedule a thirty-minute plenary discussion at the end of the group presentations so we can discuss the class contents together, structuring Socratic questions based on what I heard in the presentations. I shake around the jigsaw groups every week, such that all the students work with all the other students in their class, which also helps them to realize that group dynamics shift radically depending on who is in the group. This process is accompanied by scaffolded reflection guidance to make the group processes explicit (more on that later).

Societal dimension

The goal of XP is to help educators develop education for rapid social change commensurate with the challenges of collapse. When it comes to social change in education, I've already discussed Critical Pedagogy and Bildung. While drawing inspiration from Negt and Freire, I believe it's important to keep an open mind to different views on education for social change. The most popular voice for progressive change in education in the twentieth century wasn't a critical pedagogue but the American pragmatist philosopher John Dewey, best known for his pleas for experiential learning. Perhaps less known to educators are Dewey's political views, which revamped a kind of socially embedded liberalism à la John Stuart Mill (Chapter 1). With *Democracy and Education*,[41] Dewey began where Mill left off on the role of education in fostering collective participation for the protection of individual rights and liberties. These views set him up against dominant (neo)liberal thought since the Marginalist Revolution (Chapter 1). However, in the absence of any hint of Marxism, it would be a mistake to count Dewey among the Critical Pedagogues – he was intent on fixing liberal capitalist democracy, not breaking it. *Democracy and Education* remains, at its core, a book focused on individuals within society.

Understanding Dewey's philosophy offers key insights into the philosophical differences between practically related but philosophically quite different pedagogical practices for social change – service-learning and problem-oriented projects (PPL). Service-learning is a popular community-learning approach inspired by Dewey's plea for experiential citizen-education, sending students into communities to provide a service.[42] The idea is that locals benefit from the services provided, while students gain valuable socially conscious learning experiences. PPL also prescribes sending students into local communities; however, contrary to service-learning, its core objective is to problematize normality.[43] Service-learning doesn't generally question why problems exist in the first place or engage community participants in researching and planning novel ways of addressing these problems. For instance, sending medical students to provide Covid vaccines in pop-up clinics in the poorer suburbs of Rotterdam might be a great learning opportunity for students and provide a valuable service to the community, but it doesn't address the distrust of the medical establishment within these communities, resulting in much lower and slower vaccination rates than within wealthier areas of the city. When it comes to addressing health issues in underserved communities, questioning accepted normality and asking tough questions is essential to addressing injustice and changing outcomes. This is why, despite my admiration for Dewey's work, I use and develop problem-oriented project work in my educational practice on collapse.

Global dimension

Progressive education theory and Critical Pedagogy were written before the epoch of collapse, at a time when impediments to progress were primarily thought to be social and economic. Today, these approaches still do not, in my view, reckon fervently enough with the consequences of material progress coming to a brutal and perhaps definitive stop. As educational approaches, they exist largely in the social realm: a sudden contraction of the energy supply, the collapse of weather patterns necessary for large-scale agriculture, or the depletion of natural stocks do not feature in their roadmap to revolution. That's why, to teach at this level, it's important to introduce students to perspectives that grasp collapse as our defining planetary issue. Although I've expressed reservations about post-humanism (Chapter 3), I still think the work of Bruno Latour,[44] Donna Haraway,[45] Isabelle Stengers[46] and other post-humanists in the field of Science and Technology Studies offer important insights to help us grasp the magnitude of what's happening around us. It's not the most accessible literature, so students need some preparation and accompaniment with it. For students with no background in philosophy, Tsing's *The Mushroom at the End of the World*, an anthropological narrative that follows the Matsutake mushroom and its pickers in the derelict pine plantations of the United States, offers a good introduction into the kind of entangled thinking that defines post-humanism.[47]

To teach at the global level, I use different pedagogical tools, but I'd like to focus on one in particular: a serious game I designed to teach systemic thinking around climate. I used to run a design exercise where students were asked to imagine the world in 2100. I invited them to think about different categories of infrastructure like energy, transport, food production, security, education and so forth, and write everything down using mind clouds on a white board. It was a fun exercise, and some students came up with unconventional ideas. For instance, one group suggested that future adults should partake in Ayahuasca ceremonies as a rite of passage – a suggestion I would, being better informed, now support (Chapter 6). However, many of these ideas were also wildly unrealistic: fusion technology to the rescue, unconstrained global trade volumes, unmitigated 'green' growth – it was closer to sci-fi than science. Students really struggled to imagine a materially constrained world, with finite resources and catastrophic warming that tears things down faster than they can be rebuilt. So I started assigning points to various infrastructure sectors to see if constraining choices this way led to a better systemic understanding of the challenges. I tested the points-based version with a local environmental group, got a designer to make a full deck of cards with five infrastructure categories (energy, transport, agriculture, security, art and culture), bonus cards, disaster cards, tokens to count resources, population, energy production, kilometric distances, yield and well-being, had game boards made, and thus was born 'COLLAPSE!', a climate game which is freely available for download to all interested educators.[48]

Experimental practices

So far, I have organized interrelated theories and pedagogical practices into a framework that can help students grasp their place in the world in times of collapse. However, the core of XP is the integration of the five levels with reflective practice in student projects, and personal and group reflections. By connecting individual levels with group and societal levels, this two-pronged practice gives students a tangible approach to engage in what would otherwise be an overwhelming array of problems.

Projects, rebooted

I introduced the Danish problem-oriented project method in Chapter 2. PPL, as it's sometimes shortened to, is grounded in Oskar Negt's Critical Pedagogy and was first developed for undergraduate students at Roskilde University in 1972.[49] This was followed two years later by Aalborg University, in the eponymous industrial harbour town of Northern Jutland. Whereas projects had been around for over a hundred years in all kinds of learning environments, from K–12 to university classrooms, from vocational training to liberal arts education, these historically tended to apply theoretical knowledge in practice. By contrast, PPL emphasized letting learners figure out what their projects should be about, using them to explore and expand theory, rather than merely applying it.[50] This approach was inspired by the critical concept of 'exemplarity' in Negt's philosophy.[51] Education should give learners an opportunity to use their everyday experience as a springboard to explore the historical, economic and political forces that shape it. In other words, in line with Critical Pedagogy tradition, PPL was designed to help learners question the underlying causes and repercussions of things we consider 'normal'. When he spoke of exemplary learning, Negt had a narrow target group in mind, namely German blue collars, and a quite specific view on which aspects of normality he wanted problematized, namely class relations between the workers on the factory floor and the owners in their mansions.[52] As the Danish Negt scholar Eva Hultengren noted, this wasn't exactly a perfect fit for Danish university students, most of whom had never worked a day in a factory.[53] Nevertheless, the Danish Student Union (DSU), led by Salling Olesen and his friends, was keen to make the round peg of German worker's emancipation fit in the square hole of Danish university education, and devised a project-based pedagogical approach for Roskilde University that built onto Negt's exemplarity. In addition to being exemplary, the DSU decided that projects at Roskilde should be problem-oriented, interdisciplinary and participant-directed.[54] Problem-orientation was another way to describe questioning the fabric of normality – students were invited to investigate and deconstruct everyday paradoxes and anomalies, questioning social structures lying beneath mundane problems.[55] The term 'participant-directed learning' was born to reflect the belief that teachers were co-equal participants with students in the project.[56] Abolishing knowledge transfer, disciplines, and even teachers was evidently a project of its time, straight off the heels of the student revolutions of 1968. However, the pedagogical model has proven resilient throughout the years. Give or take the addition of lectures, individual exams and the shortening of the interdisciplinary study period, the core principles of PPL survive at Roskilde and Aalborg today, despite the fact that Aalborg confusingly refers to the approach as 'PBL'. Even so, PPL was never uniformly applied across the board: Roskilde stayed close to its critical origins, whereas Aalborg, being dominated by engineering and business disciplines, saw projects as a convenient way to educate work-ready professionals. Within the universities, different faculties always had alternative interpretations, with humanities and social sciences sticking closer to critical philosophy, and scientific and business disciplines focusing on disciplinary knowledge and marketable skills and competences.

I observed PPL projects during my postdoc in Denmark, where I witnessed the practicalities of designing and implementing PPL within programmes. Concretely, projects break down into five broad steps: defining a topic (usually based on a theme assigned by course coordinators), formulating an initial problem and analysing it, reformulating the problem based on the analysis, performing further analysis with the new problem, and writing up a problem intervention plan.[57] Themes can be more or less broad, problems can range from theoretical to practical, and interventions can be anything from a conceptual write-up to a phone app or a medical protocol, depending on where and by whom the projects are carried out. Upon my return to The Netherlands, I recommended PPL to some faculties and programmes that were seeking to increase their societal impact, including our medical school and sustainability programmes, and began implementing PPL in my own courses. Reflecting on my experience with PPL, I believe it to be potentially one of the most transformative educational approaches out there, but it needs a strong framework to avoid tunnel-visioning either on cognitive competences or on social-critical analysis. I think the transformative impact of problem-oriented projects can be enhanced by tacking the dimensions of XP into the problem process. That's why in the XP course, where participants have to develop an educational experiment, I fitted the five levels to the projects, guiding them to think through their projects from a cognitive standpoint, an existential perspective, with an appreciation of group dynamics, societal relevance and an understanding of their project's place among planetary boundaries. I developed a matrix (Table 1) that project groups can use to map the relevance of the five levels as they progress.

It's simple to use: they write down the central themes or research questions of their project, then break down the theoretical, empirical and practical considerations they uncover for each level.

I have broad ambitions for XP project work; my next move will be to integrate the 'survival' vocational skills mentioned in the third dialogue on pedagogies of collapse (Chapter 2) into the approach. I will be inviting students from all levels of higher education, from vocational colleges, to applied sciences and universities, to

TABLE 1 The XP Project Matrix

		Project Theme 1	Project Theme 2	Project Theme 3 ...
Cognitive	Theoretical			
	Empirical			
	Practical			
Individual	Theoretical			
	Empirical			
	Practical			
Group	Theoretical			
	Empirical			
	Practical			
Societal	Theoretical			
	Empirical			
	Practical			
Global	Theoretical			
	Empirical			
	Practical			

collaborate on regenerative farming, the circular economy and land and water management projects in which everyone gets their hands in the muck. My hope is that students will share skills across the educational levels: being endowed with practical skills and a sense of working life, vocational learners will shine as leaders in applied thinking, while university students will provide the exemplary link between practice and theory. The whole process will be encased in a non-formal Bildung half-year educational bridge-programme structured with the XP levels. Like Christen Kold's students of 1851, our students will return from a day's hard work with their farming projects to cook, sing, dance, make music, read philosophy, discuss literature and reflect on the meaning of their lives. Unlike Christen Kold's students, they will be imbued with a sense of urgency, preparing for a world in collapse, with reflexive existential and psychoanalytic grief processing at the heart of our approach. This is but a brief sketch of what is to come: at the time of writing, I have set the wheels in motion for this new approach to Bildung, Critical Pedagogy and environmental education, hoping to launch the pilot around the time this book is published. Expect stories, results and reflections in the next book!

Reflection, a reconsideration

Meaning literally to 'bend back' in Latin, reflection has been a topic of interest for educators since Dewey, with the idea that allowing learners to check in the mirror could improve their agency and deepen their learning. However, a closer look at the literature reveals that most of what has been written on reflection focuses on cognitive processes like problem-solving, improving learning efficiency and increasing performance.[58] The famous Kolb cycle represents the archetypal cognitive approach to reflection: start with a concrete experience or event, think about what happened and why it happened, theorize or conceptualize in order to optimize a response, then take commensurate actions to improve the outcomes.[59] There's nothing wrong with teaching students to reflect in this manner. Even if the scientific evidence for its effectiveness in performance enhancement is limited, it's a starting point for students to familiarize themselves with reflective practices.[60] But cognitive reflection alone is not enough: it largely leaves out personal development, group dynamics and social relevance. Even assuming that cognitive reflection positively impacts student learning, in catastrophic times, sticking to cognitive reflection merely greases the wheels of the conveyor belt to collapse.

Inspired by my research with existential phenomenology, I turned non-directive phenomenological interview methods into a self-reflection process that draws out ways in which conscious perception and experience connect with materiality. Starting with Merleau-Ponty and Simone de Beauvoir's perspective on the body-consciousness relationship, I ask students to describe the sensations, emotions and sense of self they experience as the course progresses. This can be both liberating and distressing for students, who are used to being treated as intellectual products and are rarely asked to position their physical bodies and feelings in the learning space. I share phenomenological research articles to help them understand the kind of analysis I'd like them to perform on themselves. Of course, the major difference between research articles and personal reflection is that the double-hermeneutic (the researcher interprets the interviewee's interpretation of their own experience) turns into a single-hermeneutic (the student is both the researcher and the interviewee) in this situation. That has implications for the students' ability to distance themselves from their sensations and emotions. That's why, once the students have written down their reflection, they work in pairs and treat their reflections like interview data for analysis, drawing out themes from their notes. Working on this analysis in pairs allows a healthy sharing of emotions, increasing the capacity to distance from them. It does require creating a learning space where students feel safe enough to disclose themselves.

How do we make students reflect on group dynamics? With the right facilitation, focus groups can get everyone to the table, sharing thoughts and feelings. But we want students to do more than just talk about their inner worlds; we would like them to put themselves in the shoes of their fellow group members, inversing their perspective, especially if they are locked in an unproductive drama triangle, viewing themselves as victims and others as persecutors.[61] Going straight into a group meeting might further perpetuate pre-existing toxic dynamics. As Wilfred Bion indicated, the default mode of a group tends towards dependency, pairing or flight-or-flight.[62] That's why, before a group discussion can productively begin, students should make an effort to piece together their thoughts on their relationships with other group members, and then attempt to role-play the perspective of other people involved in their 'drama'. From the perspective of a perceived persecutor, what might be going on? What does the student look like from the vantage point of the other? Once students have made this conscious effort to de-centre themselves from their reflection, group reflections can move towards what Bion called a working-group scenario.[63] The aim is to create enough critical distance between students and their reflection to allow some scientific scrutiny of what has been going on with them.

Getting students to reflect on their place in the grand scheme of things is hard, especially for undergraduates. Reflection in Critical Pedagogy implies the ability to understand present and personal experiences in reference to past, future, social and global events. The sociologist C. Wright Mills called this the 'sociological imagination', using the example of a soldier on the front line of war to highlight the role of individuals in making history.[64] Soldier don't start wars; they are merely pawns in powerful people's games. But without the service of the individuals who, willingly or by force, wear the uniforms and hold the guns, powerful people find their grasp on history slipping away. Sociological imagination inspired Negt's views on exemplarity; he gave it a psychoanalytic twist and called it 'sociological phantasy' to stress his view that most working-class people only have a tenuous grasp of their place in history.[65]

As the most materially advantaged generation to ever enter higher education, my students struggle to see themselves as part of a bigger whole. Their learned helplessness and individualism, a product of thirty years of neoliberal socialization, is hard to challenge. This is why it's crucial to start with the first three levels of reflection, building a bridge between the comfort of cognitive reflection, and critical reflection. My colleagues and I ran an action research study after we piloted our first multi-dimensional reflection track: we found that, having honed their reflective capabilities in the first part of their reflection journey, students were then capable of reflecting at a social and global level, with the right scaffolding.[66] Our research showed that all of the students felt in some way transformed by their reflection journey. The results weren't evenly distributed: while all of the students engaged actively with the reflective process, only about a third were able to fully engage with the social and global level. We also found that a couple of students went too far the other way, falling into a regress of reflection where the object of reflection was lost in a fractal descent into an existential crisis. Following Simone de Beauvoir, the best cure for existential crises is action – I do hope that in a post-Covid world, we can get students who descend into fractal thought patterns out in communities to work with their hands and break the funk!

Post-script on a Russian adventure

I handed my resignation in to my Russian employers on 24 February 2022, after two successful iterations of *Experimental Pedagogics*. I received heartbreaking letters from some of my students, expressing despair about a future taken away in the blink of an eye. Beneath the despair, there was also hope that somehow these young people could take what we built together into a future free from war and tyranny. The foreign staff might be gone, the emancipatory courses closed down, but the students took something with them, tucked under their coats, into the winter of self-inflicted Russian isolation. Hopefully we meet again, when this is over, to start something new.

Since the pandemic was still raging at home and my field research was cancelled or postponed, I used the time to develop a Minor in Experimental Pedagogics for students interested in becoming educators at my Dutch University, with the help of my mentor Liesbeth Noordegraaf-Eelens and colleague Lorenzo Duchi. We refined the five levels and developed the reflection approach into a self-standing track with a series of scaffolds like reflection diary prompts and workshop tools that can also be used in other courses and programmes. One pilot and a national education grant later, our Minor was the highest rated of the entire university for the academic year 2023–4 (out of eighty-three courses). Elements of XP like the reflection track and the COLLAPSE! game have been adopted into new and existing undergraduate and postgraduate programmes at home and abroad.

Having courses and training programmes to help students and teachers understand and use the XP framework is great, but the point is to change existing practices to address collapse. I wanted to show teachers how to retrofit their programmes with XP, so I began by retrofitting my own climate course.

How to retrofit a course

I took over 'The Climate Crisis', an eight-week second-year undergraduate climate course, when I returned from my postdoc in 2020. The previous coordinator had taught the course with a Science and Technology Studies perspective. With his permission, I researched the outcomes prior to taking over the course, and discovered that students came out of it well informed about the climate crisis, but quite despondent and depressed about their options for living with collapse.[67] So when it was handed over to me, together with a colleague, we went back to the drawing board and re-wrote the course to include insights from history, political economy and psychology, with a marked presence of Black and Indigenous literature in the reading list.[68] Our revamped course contained quite some post-humanist content still, with various assigned chapters by Latour, Haraway and Tsing, among others. But after teaching the new version for a couple of years, it became clear that post-humanist readings mainly appealed to humanities students. Business and life sciences students struggled to understand what they should do with them. I wanted to reach all undergraduate students, regardless of major, to encourage them to consider their career choices and future perspectives in light of the climate crisis. So when I retrofitted the course with XP in 2022, I kept Latour and Haraway on the recommended reading list and translated the post-humanist approach into pedagogical practices that all students could engage with instead.

Before the XP re-write, the course used a combination of lectures and problem-based learning, like most courses at the college. Here's what the XP matrix looked like for the course by the time I was done with the retrofit (Table 2). The XP matrix for course coordinators is nearly the same as the one I used for projects, except 'project themes' are now 'learning objectives', and 'empirical/practical' elements have been modified to 'pedagogical/assessment' elements. Essentially, this is a constructive alignment matrix adapted to XP, and I invite educators interested in using XP to simply replace the learning objectives with their own and try to fill it in.

You'll recognize many of the pedagogies I mentioned above. In designing the jigsaw classes, I combined problem-based learning with jigsawing, by cutting PBL problems into three parts and assigning one-third of the problem to each expert group. So students were still learning with problems and activating their prior knowledge, doing their self-study and reporting on their findings, but their engagement with the materials was enhanced by the cooperative group process and responsibility they felt in teaching each other. With this approach, students met up in their expert groups between classes to prepare their findings together each week, something that I did not see with PBL alone. The only class for which I still used standalone PBL was

TABLE 2 XP Matrix for Course Coordinators Adapted for *The Climate Crisis*

		Learning Objective 1: Understanding the basic science of the climate crisis & Planetary Boundaries	Learning Objective 2: Understanding the history and politics of the climate crisis	Learning Objective 3: Understanding and applying the psychology of collapse	Learning Objective 4: being able to formulate pathways towards transitions
Cognitive	Theoretical			Cognitivism	
	Pedagogical	Jigsaw PBL	Jigsaw PBL	PBL	
	Assessment			Reflective essays	
Individual	Theoretical			Existentialism	
	Pedagogical			Journaling	
	Assessment			Reflective essay	
Group	Theoretical			Psychoanalysis	
	Pedagogical	Jigsaw PBL	Jigsaw PBL	PBL	Project
	Assessment			Group evaluations	
Societal	Theoretical	Political economy	Black & Indigenous studies		Political economy
	Pedagogical				
	Assessment				
Global	Theoretical	Planetary boundaries	Post-humanism Implosion		Future studies
	Pedagogical	COLLAPSE!			COLLAPSE!
	Assessment				Project portfolio

on climate psychology, as this was an individual reflection process leading up to students' personal reflection essays.

I packed the back-end of the course with activities and lectures focused on giving students options for action, inviting guest speakers from the business transition world and civil disobedience groups to share their roadmaps for change. Post-humanism appeared in the form of an exercise devised by Joseph Dumit, an American Science and Technology Studies scholar, which he dubbed *Writing the Imposition: Teaching the World one Object at a Time*.[69] The premise is that students pick an object from their bag and deconstruct it according to the materials involved in producing it, the labour required to assemble those materials, the technologies involved in its production, the legal and political processes that govern it, the economics involved in its circulation, and the sociological aspects of its use. When I ran this exercise, it wasn't long before students realized just how deeply everything in their lives is entangled with global capitalism, fossil fuels and cheap labour. Those interested to read further were encouraged to open their Haraway books, but really, I found that just asking students to stop a moment to think about the nature of their fluorescent pink pens or take-away coffee cups had more far-reaching impacts than complex philosophy. This course ended in raucous playfulness as student teams battled each other with cards and tokens on their COLLAPSE! boards. As for the final assignment, I adapted the XP group project format, with a peculiar deliverable requested from students: role-playing a group of government advisers from the year 2100, students were tasked with compiling a portfolio with a history of the future of a country of their choice, complete with maps, charts, graphs, timelines, oral history accounts and even an artefact from the future. Some students took this very seriously and produced music, artworks, poetry and restaurant menus. Bridging the present with a future in crisis, the assignment nonetheless offered an ambivalent message of hope: someone will still be here to write the history we're making, so the choices we make matter, in the eyes of those that come after, even if they feel futile right now.

What I learnt from retrofitting XP to my climate course is, first, you don't have to follow the levels in a linear fashion; in this case, we started with global issues, moving through individual and cognitive levels in the middle of the course, only to go back outwards at the end. Second, XP offers guidelines, not a fixed to-do list, so educators can pick, choose and modify their pedagogies until they work right with their learning objectives. Third, XP is fun – we managed to have fun while discussing what is otherwise a highly anxiety-inducing topic. Of course, this does apply to everyone – there will always be students who are too caught up in denial, fear, trauma or anger to engage. I have found their numbers to increase worryingly in the aftermath of the Covid lockdowns, occasionally leading to unhelpful classroom dynamics. Which leads me to my final point in this chapter: a framework alone cannot suffice to teach the pedagogies of collapse with hope. This also requires that we, the teachers, be willing to act as guiding lights.

Guiding lights

Collapse follows us into our classrooms, an unanswered question humming in the air that blares loudly with every war and heatwave. How can educators be relevant under the circumstances? From where I stand in Rotterdam, it's on the faces of the refugee and migrant children now sitting on our school benches, whose obliterated homes foreshadow our collective future. In places like Zimbabwe and India, it's in the empty seats left by children who dropped from hunger, or were forced into early marriages to ward off economic distress, especially in the wake of the Covid-19 pandemic.[70] Educators hold a looking glass to society; we see what is really happening in families across nations, beyond political platitudes and sensationalist media coverage. When there is hunger, disease and violence, teachers, along with the doctors, nurses, farmers, social workers, security personnel and all those on the front line of collapse, are the first to know.

Dealing with this is an immense task. I hope the XP framework helps educators align their course designs and pedagogies with what's at stake, enhancing the impact and reach of their work. But I want to close this chapter by addressing teachers at the core of their function.

Who are we, actually?

Who are we, as teachers, and what is our role? Historically, teachers' function was to accustom students to certain kinds of hierarchical relationships necessary for the good functioning of the productive apparatus (Chapter 2). This is the kind of teacher role that Freire decried in his critique of the 'banking' system of education.[71] Though I do not know a single teacher who entered the profession with aspirations to enable the smooth functioning of the economy, this is still de facto the role many of us are forced into when national programmes, inspectors and accreditation bodies dictate what may or may not take place in classrooms. But I would like to address the teachers we have it in us to be to build the education system anew, rather than the teachers we are too often made to be under the present system. In defining what teachers could be, I take inspiration from Dewey and Freire, who wrote at length about teaching in the emancipatory classroom.

As the chief architect of the progressive education movement in the early twentieth century, John Dewey inspired young radicals to rethink education. As is often the case, some of his followers tried to outdo the master and flipped the teacher script on its head, suggesting that the presence of teachers was at best superfluous, at worst actively harmful. None were more vocal about this than William Kirkpatrick, famous for writing an educational pamphlet in 1918 in which he stated: 'the teacher's success – if we believe in democracy – will consist in gradually eliminating himself or herself from the success of the procedure.'[72] Dewey responded in a 1933 re-edition of *How We Think* with a new section criticizing this trendy call to abolish teachers.[73] In this addendum lies, in my view, one of the best descriptions of the role of teachers ever published. Dewey declared:

> In reality, the teacher is the intellectual leader of a social group. He is a leader, not in virtue of official position, but because of wider and deeper knowledge and matured experience. The supposition that the principle of freedom confers liberty upon the pupils, but that the teacher is outside its range and must abdicate all leadership is merely silly.[74]

Dewey called on teachers to take responsibility for two aspects of their profession: firstly, they should know their stuff inside out, read broad and deep, do their research and keep their knowledge fresh. This is not to drown students in information or recite findings with authority, but so that they may have their hands free to focus on classroom processes, pedagogy and students' understanding. In other words, Dewey foresaw what cognitive psychology later confirmed: that the markers of a successful teacher are a combination of subject-matter expertise and social congruence that together brew a key ingredient of teaching success: cognitive congruence.[75] Most of us don't need scientific jargon to understand intuitively that having abundant knowledge makes it easier to scaffold learning, just like we know that the capacity to intuit students' struggles makes it possible to guide them forward, yet these truisms are under attack from the exacting demands of neoliberal governance and technocrats who salivate at the prospect of replacing qualified teachers with an army of AI-enhanced teaching assistants.

Freire called upon teachers to provide *hinge-thematics* to learners, that is, to help students articulate the relationship between their personal lives and the broader societal context.[76] This is quite similar to the sociological imagination we saw earlier. As teachers, we can ask questions, provide pivots and impetus for students to question scripts, events, relationships and structures otherwise taken for granted. Freire described his approach for doing this in Chapter 3 of *Pedagogy of the Oppressed*, and it looks remarkably similar to PPL.

Having outlined what teachers are, it's important to dwell for a moment on what we are *not*, lest the threat of collapse push us to plug holes in a sinking ship.

Firstly, teachers are not therapists. We are not qualified to hold and process the trauma and emotional dysfunctions of students. Mental distress has never been higher among the young.[77] Ever larger numbers of students come to school with mental diagnoses like ADHD, depression and anxiety.[78] This is only getting worse as anxiety about the future spirals, especially in the wake of Covid lockdowns. Unfortunately, in the absence of affordable and accessible mental healthcare, we are often treated as frontline therapists by students who have no other outlet for their grief. Students have come to me to discuss all kinds of mental health crises. It was particularly salient during the COVID lockdowns, when the trickle of breakdowns turned into a stream. Most teachers are not equipped to deal with these situations, and no educator should be asked to do so.

How to respond when students call upon us with highly distressing personal information? Some teachers do not feel capable of responding at all, in which case the message should be forwarded to the relevant support person, such as a student counsellor. Personally, I will usually hear students out. I am happy to talk to them one-on-one (or by email) about existential dread, fears concerning the future and the search for meaning. Depending on the student, their age and their situation, I would recommend drawing the line at receiving confidential medical information, requests for help with personal trauma, and details of personal mental breakdowns, drawing the necessary boundaries to protect your own safety. For me, this means that I will hear students out if they want to talk, but I will invariably refer them to people and places where they can access the right expertise to deal with their emotional distress, rather than take that emotional burden on myself.

Teachers being by nature endowed with an overabundance of care, it's quite difficult to maintain boundaries. Yet this is essential to the longevity of our stay in the profession. The result of not abiding by these rules is often burnout.

Secondly, teachers are not service providers. Under New Public Management, we might be fooled into thinking we are. With the cost of education skyrocketing and students taking on large quantities of debt for what was only a couple decades ago a public good, students and parents expect value for their money. I have seen a difference in student attitudes in institutions with higher as opposed to lower tuition fees, with demands and expectations rising with the cost of the education. I have received arrogant, borderline insulting emails from high-fee-paying students demanding re-grades because their perfectly adequate pass did not fit their plans for a cum laude award or master's degree application. I have received pleas from parents begging me to allow their child a special exemption to retake an exam, expecting me to produce and grade a test just for one student. End of course evaluations feel increasingly like Yelp reviews, with teaching careers made or broken based on aggregate scores and anonymous reviews. I don't blame students for their confusion about the role of teachers. Their own governments have been beseeching them to treat education like any other product for decades, while jacking up the price. As difficult as this sounds, we must resist. We must refuse to be treated as products. When our institutions dare us to submit or walk away, we must find the courage to pack up and leave. The last shreds of education as a public good are in our hands, when we walk, the education system falls apart and we can build anew.

Finally, within the confines of the classroom, teachers are not political activists. This is a confusion that comes about with rising frequency, as social justice fights make their way through educational institutions. Tim Urban reported that in the United States, teachers are increasingly expected to demonstrate appropriate political beliefs and credentials before being allowed in the classroom.[79] The nature of the required beliefs depends on which political 'tribe' the school adheres to. One might dismiss the conservative agenda as predictably reactionary, but things are also changing for the worse within progressive educational circles. Within these circles, students may be exposed to only one discourse on progress and justice, and told that anything else is not only wrong, but also racist, sexist and queer-phobic. Urban expressed concern that, given the social punishment for saying the 'wrong' thing in the classroom, many US students either toe the line or remain silent. If a recent survey at my own university is anything to go by, the problem seems to have found its way outside America.[80] It goes without saying that no Critical Pedagogy classroom can exist where students are afraid to speak their minds.

This is not to say that teachers can't be passionate activists outside of their teaching roles; I would certainly consider myself as such. I have strong opinions on certain topics that I share in the public space. But it is crucial that the classroom be a space where dissent is possible, and teachers do not abuse their moral authority to impose a viewpoint. I appreciate that this is difficult to achieve – teachers with big personalities share their knowledge with an inflamed passion that can make students feel like they can't offer a counterargument. It's vital to make pedagogy work for us in this case. I'm not condemning lectures: in the hands of passionate and articulate speakers, they can inspire, enrich and fascinate. But there's a time and space for that fire, in small quantities, with the caveat that lectures are not mandatory and should be considered more like opinion pieces than knowledge transfer, with a well-furnished reading list that provides alternative viewpoints. For the majority of our contact time with students, we must allow them to make up their own minds and exchange freely (within the realm of scientific reality and respectful discourse). This is why I use pedagogies that decentre the teacher, like jigsaw and project work. This allows me to fully engage in the process of guidance and support, saving the TED-talk style delivery for the occasional lecture.

So, if I were to summarize what teachers are for, in times of collapse, I would say we're here to give students just enough courage to face the difficult questions raised by collapse, the persistence to seek out answers and the stamina to see them through.

We have one dialogue still to address, perhaps the most important: pedagogies of collapse require a continuous forward movement, flooding the cracks in the crumbling old world with beautiful, imperfect hope. To achieve this, we must cast aside the shackles of loneliness and the impossible quest for perfection. Only then we can build and commit to imperfect solidarities.

5

Imperfect Solidarities

I recently hosted a sustainability meeting with educators from the different faculties at my university. We discussed how we could engage students within our schools with a grassroots revamping of the university's sustainability strategy. A colleague pointed out that targeting students was not so simple in an institution where perhaps as many identified with conservative right-wing politics as they do with American-style social justice movements. They were right: our community has increasingly been subjected to the 'culture wars' of American campuses, with opposing conservative and Green Left parties regularly topping the vote tally at the campus polling station. If discussions on the university's sustainability strategy were already fuel for campus polarization, the war in the Middle East accelerated the rise in confrontational rhetoric in our community.

In this chapter, I argue that polarization and identitary hostility are not external interferences that hinder progress on managing transitions, but a traumatic manifestation of collapse in educational spaces. This is a chapter about trauma, trauma reflexes and the ways in which these reactions jeopardize the very things involved parties claim to cherish. I will argue that the only way beyond traumatic rage and hostility is through imperfect solidarities and all the hard, messy work this implies.

Positioning the dialogue

I have alluded to my skin in the game in previous chapters, but I must position myself more precisely before I kick the hornet's nest of trauma. I have lived a peculiar life, to say the least. Having at times experienced wealth, privilege and opportunities, and at other times poverty and powerlessness. Privilege is often spoken about in a static, binary way: you have it or you don't. Privilege narratives aren't overly fond of ambiguity. Many would find it hard to reconcile the experience of dining with billionaires and living on a squalid council estate within one lifetime, and yet, this has been my experience.

I sit at a crossroad of classes. Within my (large) family, many aunts, uncles and cousins are still firmly working class, while others have become solidly middle class. This has been a source of simmering tension, misunderstandings and resentment. As internationally educated, well-travelled English speakers, my brother and I were treated with some suspicion by our French relatives. In childhood, I experienced this as painful rejection. In adulthood, I came to understand the ways in which unintentionally flaunting a cosmopolitan *habitus* could paint me as a class-traitor. I have certainly benefited from privileges and material advantages not afforded to my cousins. Most people assume that the hard work of climbing out of the working class was entirely performed by my parents while I confidently navigated a middle-class world, having never known any different – as if the intergenerational trauma of poverty could be erased with the magic wand of a white-collar job and a pay rise.

Given this, it might come as a surprise that due to difficult circumstances in early adulthood, I lived through several years of poverty in a crumbling terraced house on a council estate in South-East England. Looking back, the sticking point wasn't so much counting pennies at the grocery store, mould running up the walls, collapsed ceilings with no money to fix them, letters from the bailiff hidden in a drawer and the screams of the teenage mother next door day and night. Rather, as Rutger Bregman has cogently argued, a lack of cash can lead people to make bad decisions,[1] and even though poverty was a temporary state of affairs for me, the impact of the poor decisions I made during those years stays with me to this day. As difficult as those years were, I am grateful for experience scrubbing floors for a painfully low wage, coming home at two in the morning smelling of frying oil, or rummaging through the 'reduced to clear' aisle to find something affordable to eat. I treasure the friends I made throughout those years, even if we seldom speak these days. Though I no longer worry about grocery bills or the physical toll of standing for an eleven-hour shift, I am not comfortable in privileged echo-chambers. I find it difficult to relate to people who never experienced material hardship. I feel empathy with those who have such experiences, even if they are, as a result, more difficult people.

Even so, I will never know the impact of *growing up* in poverty or racial discrimination. I have an idea of the first, from the stories shared by my husband about his difficult childhood in communist Romania, and of the second from the stories shared by my Zimbabwean foster daughter. I have seen the destructive impact of class and racial trauma in both of them. I tried to fill the gaps in my experience as best I could through reading, but some things I will never *know*.

So what I'm about to say comes, I hope, from a place of nuance, a depressive position of ambivalence, psychoanalytically speaking. I am painfully aware of what I know, and also cognizant of how much I do not.

Alone in the darkness

I vividly remember a student in despair, sobbing the words 'I feel so alone' at the end of a classroom conversation about future climate scenarios. This was the moment I realized the extent of the relational damage caused by thirty years of neoliberalism and two years of Covid lockdowns. Of course, the end of the world you know is terrifying, if you believe you have to face it alone! Doing anything alone is counter-natural to our species, which is biologically wired for social interaction and collaboration.[2] And yet, students of the Global North and increasingly large parts of the Global South have been raised within cultures that glorify individualism. The epicentre of this disease can be found in the Anglo-Saxon world, but it is rapidly growing elsewhere. The advent of fossil fuel capitalism released us from physical interdependency, providing an ever larger share of humans with enough machinery to feed their material needs and wants on their own. This is not equally shared, and we see something of a relationship between increasing access to energy and technology, and decreasing social cohesion around the world.[3]

A few years ago, a group of my students conducted a research project on Ubuntu, the African philosophy of reciprocity and sharing. They found that Ubuntu (Hunhu in the Shona language) was alive and well in rural Zimbabwean communities, whereas it was being replaced by market competition and individualism in urban centres. The project centred on the experiences of women in these different settings, and it was clear that the social cohesion of rural areas was preferable for the well-being of women compared with the dog-eat-dog informal capitalism practiced in cities, even if income was slightly higher in cities. Whereas fossil fuels reduced the physical need for interdependency, our brains have not changed much in response to this shift; we still crave community, belonging and the sense of being part of a larger, meaningful whole. Access to fossil energy was a necessary, but not sufficient condition for the advent of individualistic mindsets and behaviours. The development of individualism also required a lot of ideological work.

Individualism as ideology

Before discussing the ideological framing of individualism in the capitalist world, I need to say a word about state communism, given the popularity of communist and socialist ideas among my students who identify with progressive politics. I would like to bat away the notion that, for all of its flaws, state communism had at least succeeded in achieving a measure of collective solidarity. I have never witnessed such individualistic mentalities within former communist countries – from Eastern Europe to South-East Asia. This is not merely a mentality that prioritizes individual achievement but a common understanding that cheating, stealing and serving one's own interest at the expense of others are socially expected practices. Those who did not practice this still expected it from others, and therefore behaved under the assumption that their fellow citizens could not be trusted.[4]

From speaking with citizens of these countries – those who stayed and those who left – it seems to me that beneath the veneer of collectivism, communism broke down the basic fabric of trust within societies. Rural folks were forcibly removed from their ancestral homes and taken to urban centres, where they were parked in squalid concrete towers to fill factories as a matter of ideology – regardless of whether these factories actually produced anything. Towards the end of the communist regime in Romania, giant glory-project factories stood empty while workers went hungry. The only way to survive in countries persistently plagued by state-induced shortages of all kinds was to cheat, steal and make deals on the side. Those who did not ended up like the workhorse in George Orwell's *Animal Farm*: dead.[5]

When my husband was a child, the only way to get eggs and meat in communist Transylvania was to know someone who worked at the food processing plant and could trade on the black market. Corruption was a norm, and stealing from the amorphous, overbearing state (the same state that was starving its own people) didn't come with the moral stain or social retribution of theft in pre-communist societies. At the same time, communism encouraged neighbours to denounce each other as social traitors, creating a culture of fear and suspicion well described in Milan Kundera's *Unbearable Lightness of Being*.[6] Far from enhancing social cohesion, state communism blew it apart.

Meritocratic mythology

If fear and mistrust were the main drivers of individualism under communism, capitalism relies on a more subtle range of emotional triggers to alienate people from one another. It's not just that access to fossil fuels reduced interdependency: capitalism *needs* to alienate people from each other as a matter of principle because, as Polanyi explained in *The Great Transformation*, markets need interchangeable, standardized commodities to function properly, including labour.[7] When people stick together to form large families, groups or tribes, the emergent properties of these collectives tend to make the people within hard to interchange – they don't usefully lend themselves to the fiction of standardized units of labour. Capitalism still needs families because someone must produce babies that will grow into labourers, but the most efficient productive unit to achieve this while maintaining a perfectly competitive market structure is the nuclear family (foisting the reproductive labour upon women). By fostering social ties that conflict with the invisible hand, larger groupings work against market efficiency.

But people are naturally inclined to group together and form powerful social bonds, so how did capitalism manage to breathe into being the self-serving, asocial *homo economicus* of the Marginalist Revolution (Chapter 1)? How did capitalism convince a fundamentally social species to become atomized individuals? In his book *Capital and Ideology*, Thomas Piketty offers a suggestion: individualism is fostered and supported by the ideology of meritocracy.[8] The basic premise of meritocracy is that under competitive capitalism, personal social and economic success is primarily a product of individual hard work, skills and intelligent decision-making, while failure is a sign of sloth, lack of aptitude and poor decision-making. Meritocratic ideology dismisses structural barriers to success such as class, race, gender, disability and so forth by hailing education as a great leveller that provides equal opportunities for success to all, regardless of initial structural disadvantages. And since, under capitalism, education is essentially a competitive endeavour for the best grades, best college places and best degrees that give students an edge in the labour market, an individualistic, competitive mindset is the surest path to success within that system. Meritorious individuals get rewarded for their efforts with high-paid jobs and wealth, while the undeserving poor reap the consequences of their poor decision-making with low-pay, low-skill work.

The most influential proponent of this view was Gary Becker, a leading Chicago School economist, awarded a Nobel Prize for extending neoliberal thinking to social sciences. Becker's *Theory of Human Capital* is one of the most influential ideas shaping modern educational politics.[9] Becker agreed that education is a hefty expense. Even in countries where tuition fees are subsidized by the state, taking three to five years out of the workforce to pursue vocational training or a degree comes with living expenses and opportunity costs. However, he argued that these financial constraints are efficient because individuals are free to decide whether investing in their personal human capital is worth the return. Those who don't have enough capital to invest in education could simply borrow, and include interest payments in their returns calculations. So far, so logical – we might disagree that the ultimate purpose of human life is individualistic competition, but on the surface, this seems like a fair system.

Except it isn't. In *The Economics of Inequality*, Piketty thoroughly debunked the fairness and efficiency of this approach.[10] First, he argued that the poor are much more likely to be credit-constrained, meaning they struggle to borrow money (or borrow on less favourable terms). They might miss out on study opportunities for lack of funds, even if that investment would yield good returns. This surely holds for the Global South, where rural populations are still largely excluded from the global banking system. Second, the expected return on investment of education for marginalized people is depreciated by prejudice. Employers expect these groups to underperform and, therefore, pay them less in anticipation. Knowing that they are likely to be underpaid, many people from underprivileged groups do the math and find that the return does not justify the investment, thereby creating a self-fulfilling prophecy of exclusion. Third, as I showed in Chapter 2, many of the decisions leading up to higher education need to be made while the person is still a child, that is, by the parents, who, within economically excluded groups, often lack the information necessary to make the most profitable decisions. We end up in the situation illustrated by Piketty, where, in France, 1 per cent of the children of factory workers make it to university, *against* 80 per cent of the children of people in the professions (doctors, lawyers, accountants, architects etc).[11] While legal class privileges were legally abolished after the first French Revolution, de facto (in practice) has replaced de jure (by law) class reproduction in the intervening 230 years. And yet, despite evidence of its limitations, the mythology of meritocracy has a stranglehold on quite a hefty proportion of our students' imaginations.

It's lonely at the top

Does individualistic competition actually work for the winners of the game, even if it's rigged? If it does, there might be an argument for making the game more inclusive, increasing the number of winners, without changing the fundamental premise that individualism is the way to go.

Let's dive into the psychology of winners. It starts in childhood: economically advantaged parents understand that the game plays out in schools, so they provide their children with the best quality education money can buy. Upon graduating from the best schools, these children are in a good position to access excellent universities, where they can build the right networks to start their professional lives under advantageous conditions. An honest analysis would reveal the extent to which inherited financial and social advantage contributed to the success of wealthy children; however, confronting this fact is psychologically uncomfortable. Psychology has long established that humans like to think well of themselves. Seeing ourselves as upstanding, moral people strongly contributes to our 'positive self-identities'.[12] We want to believe that we possess superior moral qualities like assiduity, graft, intelligence and so forth because it makes us feel good about ourselves, like agents of our destiny. Nobody likes to feel they had it easy or think that success was facilitated by rules that lift some up while pushing others down. Our brains tend to reject that information and embellish our story of merit to maintain positive self-identities. This was tested empirically when social psychologists ran an experiment involving a rigged game of Monopoly in which one player was randomly selected for favourable treatment.[13] That player received more money and preferential rules, inevitably leading to their victory. Despite the obvious advantages in their favour, winners began displaying superior attitudes, flaunting their wealth and claiming credit for their success in front of the other players. In this case, there was obviously no merit involved, and *still* the winners claimed moral superiority. In the real world, success comes from a whole host of factors, in which merit does play a part, even when it is heavily bolstered by structural advantage. Therefore, it's even easier for winners to single merit out as the cause of their success.

Why does this happen? I think that knowing the game is rigged causes an uncomfortable feeling we've already come across: cognitive dissonance (Chapter 3). Believing that the poor morally deserve to be poor and the rich to be rich helps to alleviate the psychic pain of dissonance. This helps winners to feel good about having more income and wealth, even if they know that these benefits were in part acquired through structural advantages, including educational advantages.[14]

This creates a situation where the wealthier and more successful one is, the stronger the dissonance, the more powerful the compensatory meritocratic narrative. Among winners, this encourages a social landscape where anybody less successful is seen with suspicion and scorn, and anybody more successful, with envy. The handful of high net-worth individuals I have met, for all their bravado about pulling themselves up by their own bootstraps, were mostly insecure (bordering on paranoid, in some cases), unhappy and unloving individuals. I recall a prime example in Singapore, one of the world's hotspots for the excesses of the wealthy. An investment banker showed up to a party already drunk and passed out on the club couches while the women (including me) posed for cheeky photographs around his slouched figure. At the end of the night, someone forged his signature to pay the bill, which ran into the thousands while he lay comatose. He had something of an awakening (literally) after this event, and went to work in an orphanage. Good for him. Everyone deserves the chance to regain their humanity.

This episode, I must admit, also reflected poorly on me. Even though I had just come out of several years of biting poverty, I fell straight into the meritocratic trap of believing my own bullshit just because I had a couple of shiny diplomas to show for it. While I lived the high life at Marina Bay Sands, and drank enough at airport business class lounges that I nearly missed my flight on several occasions, I have never been lonelier, more depressed and isolated than during the years I was living large in Singapore. I felt untethered from the world: I could go anywhere, do anything, but none of it mattered anymore. One morning, during a work trip to Malaysia, I woke up alone in a hotel room crawling with ants, sticky with monsoon air, listened to the whirring of the fan above me, and realized I was lost. It was my 'passed out on the club couch' moment. I left Singapore and began a decade-long journey to find my way back to humanity. I am convinced that the ideology of individualism, like a malignant cancer, serves nothing but the reproduction of the system itself. Atop this system, wealth breeds materially excessive, relationally mean, spiritually void and emotionally empty lives. A quick browse through the recent spate of reality-TV shows about the super-rich illustrates that the lovelessness of wealth knows no racial boundaries.[15]

Meanwhile, losers in the meritocratic game have invested so much energy in the belief that they too could become the next tech-billionaire if they just put in a little more elbow grease, that they find it hard to let go of the sunken-cost fallacy, even when they hit rock bottom. I saw this during my postdoc in Denmark, when I ran a qualitative study of the lived experience of working-class White male students.[16] I heard their depression, loneliness, dispossession, frustration and self-hatred. I listened to their uphill battles with education, unresolved grief and despair about the world. I realized that they lacked words to make sense of their pain. But while they struggled with undiagnosed, or recently diagnosed neurodivergence, unsupportive or outright hostile home environments, and classist discrimination in early education, they persisted on blaming their failures on personal laziness and lack of ability. They were trying hard to work their way up the class ladder, but it felt like running the wrong way up a moving escalator. One of the men, after failing his calculus exam for the second time, said to me, 'I just need more time' with a tremolo of defeat in his voice. I believe that with time, space and institutional support, he could do very well indeed. But instead of addressing these men's struggles with empathy and dismantling the structural barriers standing between them and educational success, society tells them to man it out on their own. The United States shows us the consequences of pushing this ideology to the extreme: homeless people on the streets of San Francisco, pushed into desperation by the tech industry's rapacious grasp on the housing market, peer outside of their shabby tents, look up to the shiny buildings above, and blame themselves for landing on the pavement.[17] America is a country where over 500,000 homeless people,[18] millions of people on the verge of destitution and over 200 million people living paycheck to paycheck could feed the ranks of an almighty revolt,[19] but shackled by individualism, blinded by the meritocracy, they are merely struggling individuals with little in the way of class consciousness.

Individualism and trauma

We've situated the roots of individualism in neoliberal economics, but ideologies can only thrive if they find fertile ground. I believe the reason individualism has been such a successful brainworm for the modern era is because it feeds on trauma.

I owe my understanding of trauma to Pamela Armitage, a Canadian violence prevention specialist who, after escaping domestic violence, dedicated her life to educating others on trauma. I spent a year going over the canon of trauma theory with her, including the works of Gabor Maté, Bessel van der Kolk and Pete Walker. I'm fascinated by Maté, a Hungarian Jew whose mother gave him away to a stranger as a baby to save him from the Nazis, and whose life was shaped by the resulting trauma. In *When the Body Says No*, Maté delved into the physical consequences of unprocessed childhood trauma, resulting in cancer, auto-immune disorders, dementia, fibromyalgia and other diseases of self-destruction.[20] I like to put Maté's podcasts on just to listen to his soothing, empathetic voice. Psychiatrist Van der Kolk is more scientific in his approach; in *The Body Keeps the Score*, he focused on the neuropsychiatry of trauma, citing fMRI studies to locate trauma as a physiological response in the brain, with its dire consequences on behaviour, relationships and overall health.[21] Van der Kolk tried, in vain, to have trauma listed in the Diagnostic and Statistical Manual used in clinical psychology practices around the world, but psychiatry and clinical psychology remain in denial about trauma. Walker is a survivor of childhood trauma with a pragmatic, experience-based approach to trauma-management. In his self-published book *Complex PTSD*, he analysed the four main trauma responses – fight, flight, freeze and fawn – their triggers, manifestations in behaviour and methods for overcoming them.[22]

So, what is trauma? First, it's not a discrete biographical event or even a series of events, it's the psychological reaction to those events. In that sense, trauma, like pain, is always subjective. But just because the causes and experiences of trauma vary between individuals, it doesn't mean that trauma is a figment of their imaginations – as Van der Kolk showed, we can actually locate trauma pretty specifically in the brain with fMRI studies. Those studies show that trauma is a neurological response that prevents the assimilation of painful memories into the autobiographic sections of the brain, leaving them instead in a kind of permanent present that keeps re-enacting itself. That permanent present can be experienced vividly, as in PTSD, or latently, through bodily and psychiatric disorders like the ones examined by Maté. Living a painful past as a permanent present makes it hard to relate to other people – human contact will often be perceived as a hostile, painful intrusion, triggering the reflexes raised by Walker.

With this understanding of the impact of trauma on the human body, mind and ability to connect with others, I realized that the pull of individualism is so strong among our students because it invites a flight response from trauma. But what trauma are we talking about? With all the material progress of the past fifty years, is trauma really that prevalent in society? It's true, a lot of potential triggers for what Maté called 'big-T' trauma (the kind of violence-induced psychological hurt we typically think of as trauma) have been curtailed over the past two generations.[23] As Hans Rosling pointed out, there's been remarkable reductions across the globe in terms of violent deaths, war, poverty and destitution (though this trend is already starting to reverse as collapse accelerates).[24] But trauma isn't an event, it's a psychological reaction to lived experiences. Taking Maslow's perspective on human needs, recent material progress only provides the most basic layers of the hierarchy.[25] Giving credit where it's due, fossil fuel capitalism dramatically improved people's capacity to cater to their physiological and safety needs. But it also created an environment in which it's difficult for children to get the belonging, love and esteem they need to move up the pyramid. In *The Myth of Normal*, Maté described how this created an epidemic of 'small-t' trauma; a pervasive, society-wide phenomenon which is both a product of and contributing to the toxic culture of late-modern capitalism.[26]

I was recently visiting a community of untouchables in Uttar Pradesh, Northern India, when I noticed that none of the babies were crying. They were being passed around from person to person, held, kissed, cuddled and played with all day long. Among the material misery of the shanty village, which would be wiped from the map during the next monsoon season and rebuilt from the leftover mud the following year, there was a potent, unmistakable scent of love. These children will grow up poor, and most of them won't go to school. They face a life of hunger, begging on the streets and an early death to boot (life expectancy was forty-five years, I was told). There is not much to envy here, and I wholeheartedly support the fight to elevate these people through land rights, infrastructure and education. But one thing these children will grow up with is belonging.

Following Maté, I argue that most children raised under capitalism will struggle to know plentiful love, acceptance and belonging because capitalism broke villages down into productive nuclear family units, where the care of children generally rides on one or two individuals, at least one of whom has to work all day to keep food on the table. It's an untenable proposition, even with the money and time to make it work on paper. No single human, no matter how functional, is capable of giving the kind of consistent nurturing attention that an entire village can provide. And the fact is that most of us don't have it together all that much. Most parents raise their children to the best of their ability, but the reality is that it's nearly impossible for them to replace the nurturing of a village, providing everything their children need to grow up feeling whole. As a result, their children may struggle with a sense of emptiness that can last a lifetime, hampering their capacity for self-actualization in adulthood. If these feelings are not addressed, the next generation may also inherit this same small-t trauma, creating a destructive cycle of lovelessness. Material disadvantages compound the challenge to provide warm and nurturing homes – people from marginalized groups are more likely to bring the scars of intergenerational trauma with them into the next generation, and less likely to have the financial and social means to seek help, through therapy, childcare assistance, social support, etc. It's really hard to heal from your own hurt and provide a nurturing environment of love, belonging and esteem for your children when you also have to work two jobs to keep food on the table. But these issues affect everyone – looking at the former president of the United States Donald Trump, it's not hard to see the shadow of a loveless family environment behind his raging narcissism, a point made by his niece in her scathing biography of the Trump family.[27] Things get even more complicated when societies face environmental breakdown: the global response Covid-19, our biggest reckoning with collapse to date, was to create even more social dislocation and trauma by forcing people into isolation with fear and state-sponsored repression. I ran a research project on the impact of lockdowns on students, which showed that without critical educational interventions like XP, isolation reinforced their pre-existing individualistic tendencies.[28] This does not bode well for our ability to manage coming threats.

Where does this leave us? Describing the *flight* reflex, Walker explained: 'many *flight types* stay perpetually busy and industrious to avoid being triggered by deeper relating.'[29] Therefore, flight doesn't just mean physically running away but often manifests as workaholic behaviour and an overburdened diary that deliberately leaves no time for meaningful relationships. I think a lot of students reading these lines will feel transparent, all of a sudden. Many students embrace competitive individualism because conveniently grants them an out from building relationships with others, an otherwise painful experience for egos damaged by trauma. The price to pay for escaping the pain of connection is getting sucked into the meritocratic vortex, alone in the darkness with our successes and failures.

Revolutionary myths

While neoliberal individualism feeds a flight response to trauma that breeds loneliness and despair among some of our students, a fight response has also been steadily developing on our campuses, within social justice movements, and among left-wing political groups. This trauma reaction is significantly more difficult to discuss within academic circles, particularly in America, but since American identity politics are rapidly spreading as a framework for national and international political discourse around the world, thanks to the internet, we must discuss this issue. I believe the reason American identity politics are such a prized ideology is because they trigger a fight trauma response that feels empowering – making people who subscribe to it (on either side of the culture wars) feel seen, heard and validated. But its capacity to push real progress can be questioned.

On moral purity and performative perfection

I have been in and around social justice movements for over fifteen years. I abandoned social justice as a career in the early 2010s because I was disgusted by the neo-colonialist tinge in much global development discourse and practice at the time. So the reckoning on what bell hooks termed 'White-supremacist imperialist capitalist patriarchy' within the non-profit world, incomplete as it was, still felt like a welcome relief.[30] When I founded my own social justice organization in 2015, working in partnership with local leaders was core to the mission. Either local leaders had ownership of the projects, or they weren't worth doing. This was bound to be an exercise in imperfect solidarity, with lots of learning-as-we-go, mistakes and misunderstandings to correct, and unintended outcomes, positive and negative. The imperfect nature of the work drew in talented and committed people, many of whom also had a foot (or two) in education, understanding that social justice could only ever be work in progress. I was quite hopeful at the time that real change was afoot in the non-profit and academic worlds.

Then something changed in the second half of the 2010s.[31] It started in America and steadily crept its way into Europe, first through educational campuses and activist circles, then through national politics and the corporate world. Social justice movements became more interested in performing perfection, and less interested in messy processes and outcomes. Progressive issues were packaged together in an indivisible bundle, resulting in a more binary world view. One either toed the line on the entire creed, from climate change to trans rights, or risked being branded anti-progressive. The internet began functioning as a modern public pillory, with increasingly severe punishments for straying from the progressive package: careers were set alight, characters assassinated and people's personal safety threatened.[32] Honest mistakes and well-meaning but uninformed opinions were trashed, and their authors thrashed, sometimes with more zeal than that directed at outright intolerance and hate. It seems to me that the public focus of diversity and inclusion shifted away from materially improving the lives of marginalized groups, instead expending energy on reforming language perhaps with the (rather post-modern) expectation that changing linguistic structures would disrupt underlying power structures.

In response, people began using social media to confess their social justice sins and promise to educate themselves. Surprisingly, the loudest and most shrill voices were often White, middle class and highly educated. They were egged on by people who made a career out of chastising – like Robin DiAngelo and William Watson, who calls on Whites to repent, atone and seek redemption for their racial sins.[33]

I'm all for bold action to mitigate historical wrongs. I recognize that challenging systemic injustice starts with acknowledging the ways we personally contribute to the problem as part of a privileged demographic. But the present direction of progressive discourse has the contours of religion: confession, performative self-flagellation, repentance, redemption, down to priest-like influencers on social media, ready to hear our confessions of social justice sins.[34] Having spent a decade escaping the mental hold of the Catholic Church, I am bothered by this cult-like language. I might reluctantly adhere if this proved to be the best way towards rapid social progress to stave off planetary collapse. But I do not believe it is.

First, nobody goes to confession because they actually intend to stop sinning, but because each confession wipes the slate clean for more sinning, which will be expunged with the next quick trip to church. Likewise, I would argue that the performance of moral rectitude doesn't create meaningful behavioural change, but serves as a substitute for action that yields positive regard and social validation, particularly online. Confessing your sins online, then promising to educate yourself sounds like the beginning of change, but since the work of educating oneself is never truly done, it's easy to put off action indefinitely and deflect further accusations by reiterating one's confession and claiming to be doing the work. I'm not against books – quite the opposite – but at some point, you have to put the books down and take action.

Second, social justice literature is mostly written by and for a highly educated audience, many of them academics. I recently came across a paper on queer environmental theory, the title of which sounded promising.[35] But I could not make heads or tails of it, and wondered: Who is the intended audience? It can only be a vanishingly small circle of self-referencing peers in English-speaking gender studies departments. In *Capital and Ideology*, Piketty mapped the lurch of left-wing politics towards highly educated, urban-dwelling middle classes. This phenomenon has occurred all over the Global North since the heydays of the neoliberal Left in the 1990s.[36] Left-wing politics has shifted away from being a social programme aimed at improving the lives of the poor, towards becoming a social club for urban youth with college degrees, where they engage in linguistic one-upmanship with each other. It's basically middle-class *habitus* formation disguised as moral benevolence, with the ultimate sign of class-adherence displayed as disdainful tutting at less educated people who commit linguistic blunders. But if the working classes feel like they require a PhD to support the progressive package, and nothing short of full, perfect adherence is acceptable, then they make easy pickings for anti-intellectual populists who sing songs about 'the people' having enough of experts.[37] Populists tell the poor that left-wing parties are more interested in playing word gymnastics than attending to their material concerns and, unfortunately, they are to some extent correct. Of course, solutions proposed by populists (like tax cuts for the rich) offer little material benefits to the working classes either. But in my experience, among the less educated, awful things said with simple words land better than commendable things said in academic riddles, a fact well known to populist propagandists. After thirty years of disdain from liberal elites that were supposed to be on their side, feeling heard and seen matters as much to working-class people as material progress does. Conservative media outlets know this. That's how the Murdoch empire keeps its audience while pushing policies that benefit billionaires. The highly educated urban audiences of left-wing parties are timidly changing again with the rebirth of working-class movements like the Democratic Socialists of America, Jeremy Corbyn's Labour Party and Jean-Luc Mélenchon's *La France Insoumise* party, but none of these have so far gained a foothold in the halls of power. Until less educated blue collars feel they can participate in progressive politics without risking the opprobrium of degree-wielding urbanites, and until the educated middle classes take pains to understand and value the contributions of working-class people, social justice movements are unlikely to succeed.

Third, progressive performance doesn't just slow action and undermine class solidarity, it also drags social justice movements towards implosion. In the aftermath of the racial reckoning that followed the murder of George Floyd in the United States in 2020, *The New York Times* sounded the alarm on the toxic culture within social justice organizations in America.[38] The quest for perfection isn't merely being used to defer action and perform moral one-upmanship, it also breeds suspicion and hair-breadth trigger sensitivity within social justice movements. Incremental progress, stopgap solutions and trial-and-error are under fire from within progressive groups, where younger activists demand immediate, large-scale systemic change and are unprepared to compromise towards smaller but more achievable goals. As a result of the infighting, *The New York Times* reported that a significant number of left-wing groups are imploding and closing down. The winners of this struggle are right-wing groups.

Trauma, again

I think the quest for moral perfection and hostility towards those who operate from imperfect solidarities comes from what Pam Armitage termed 'social justice fixation', which is a fight reflex.[39] This reflex doesn't seek rational solutions to injustice but vindication by force. This is why some social justice activists primarily direct their anger and bile towards well-meaning people who make mistakes rather than people who fundamentally disagree with their views. They know people with good intentions are much more susceptible to moral chastising than people who don't care, and the point of these attacks isn't to achieve concrete progress but to cause as much hurt as possible to release pain. In psychoanalytic terms, perpetrators of these kinds of attacks sublime a subconscious sadistic drive triggered by trauma into a moral crusade that operates within the tolerable bounds of their conscious superego. When I read news reports of professors suspended from American colleges for doing what I would consider to be their job, despite taking ample precautions to prevent offence, I can't help but think that professors are merely easy targets for ineffable traumatic rage that yearns to burn the world down as retribution for hurt.[40]

While I don't think this response is very productive, I can understand where the rage comes from among marginalized groups. I find the zeal with which some White middle-class students join public pile-ons against their professors more puzzling. Perhaps White students feel that, as a privileged demographic, they have to put in extra effort to give a convincing performance of allyship. This leads to a paradoxical situation, which I have encountered in my classroom, where the oxygen in the room is expended on placating White middle-class social justice fundamentalism,[41] at the expense of students of colour, who may not feel represented in identity politics but stay quiet to avoid the drama. At the extreme end of this behaviour, I've witnessed White activists claiming that African and Asian people who don't subscribe to the 'everything is racism' mantra suffer from false consciousness. White saviourism comes full circle when White activists claim that people of colour who disagree with them are too oppressed by whiteness to express their own opinions cogently.

Progressive politics are so toxic that I seriously hesitated before writing this chapter. Luckily, European universities still have a semblance of academic freedom, but things are changing fast in the wrong direction, so I'm aware of the risky nature of this endeavour. In the end, I decided to go ahead because I want social justice to succeed, and would like to offer a constructive alternative to perfection performance that could steer social justice movements towards progress: imperfect solidarities.

Webs of love that bind us

The success of pedagogies of collapse hinges upon building and committing to imperfect solidarities. By solidarities, I mean the kind of generous love expressed by Simone de Beauvoir in *The Ethics of Ambiguity* and Paolo Freire in *The Pedagogy of the Oppressed*: a movement towards the liberation of all humankind from oppression, and the meaningful embrace of each others' humanity from a place of free and fair love.[42] How does one go about building imperfect solidarities?

Pain binds us

The first item on the agenda of imperfect solidarities is ending the trauma olympics of identity politics that subdivide marginalized groups into incommensurable tribes whose interests cannot align. We need to move away from the politics of validation and reinstate material change in the living conditions of all oppressed people as the centrepiece of progressive politics: we must unite towards broader progress. In order to do this, we need to recognize that beyond race, gender, religion, ethnicity, class and other demographic characteristics, experiences of oppression bind us in solidarity. Identity politics have entrapped us in isolated experience bubbles, chipping away at the number of people qualified to understand us and act with us until all that's left is a small, homogenous circle of peers who look and sound alike. Newly re-segregated college campuses may feel like safe spaces, but they are hardly brave or revolutionary.[43] They cannot be the birthplaces of radical change. Imperfect solidarity cannot exist when understanding, empathy and common cause require a convincing trauma-CV before dialogue can begin. So long as the conversation focuses on whether a White working-class transgender child from Mississippi is more oppressed than a girl from the slums of Delhi, we remain in the realm of verbiage. We must embrace instead the universal human capacity for love, bonding, caring, but also suffering, mourning and raging, and revolt together in our incomplete humaneness.

After a decade of working with communities in Zambia, Zimbabwe and India, I have come to the following conclusion: there is more that binds us than separates us. This does not amount to denying the evils of colonization or the persistence of White privilege. It does not obfuscate the material power differential that comes from the very different state of bank account balances.

Rather, I believe that the pain that binds us is a spawning pool of kinship. I passionately reject the assumption that the Other is forever unknowable to us because we do not share the exact barcode of their intersectional oppression. I refuse to see the world as an eternal exercise in phenomenology – there's a time to examine and understand, but at some point, we have to go with what we know, imperfect as it is, and jump into the fray. Mistakes will be make, but if they are addressed from the perspective that what binds us is stronger than what separates us, they can be overcome.

With this foundational trust in place, I recommend treating privilege and power in whatever form as currencies to spend where required to further our common agenda. I recently followed Ajay Patel, a tireless education activist, to the squats of Untouchable communities in Uttar Pradesh. The Untouchables are reduced to begging on land that is rightfully theirs by an enduringly oppressive caste system that dictates their position at the bottom of the social rung. Ajay has been fighting his own caste for two decades to have the land rights of the Untouchables restored so they can build water pumps, brick houses and send their children to school. Despite some remarkable successes in the areas surrounding Varanasi, he had been struggling to get a foot in the door of official buildings to have his cause heard by magistrates with the power to expedite land dispute settlements. So I was happy to lend him my European name and academic titles to get him through the door. The magistrate in question was annoyed when he realized our ruse, but at the end of the day, Ajay got his message through to the people who needed to hear it. I have performed this combination many times under different circumstances, and by and large, it works. I trust my fellow activists to tell me when they need me, and I know exactly what my job is when I'm there: wave around business cards, smile politely on photos, and let them do their thing. Should it work? No. It's a legacy of a colonial system that grants certain people access merely on the basis of skin colour, perceived wealth and power. But let's be honest, am I going to overthrow this system? No. Leastwise, not yet, and not on my own. So rather than wait for the perfect system-ending revolution (which may or may not come during my lifetime), we use the tools we have to get things done. Is this a perfect solution? No. But it keeps us moving forwards.

Rage binds us

Having open conversations about trauma is a welcome change from the dominant mental health discourse of my parents' generation, which could best be summarized as 'suck it up buttercup', and left a trail of dysfunctional adults in its wake, including both my parents. Creating spaces to talk about trauma, to commune and cry together about the lasting damages it leaves imprinted in us is wonderful progress. But what I'm seeing now is a pathologizing of trauma, turning what should be triggers for revolutionary change into psychopathological conditions and symptoms. The logical conclusion of this approach is the medication of vast swathes of the population to alleviate the symptoms of trauma rather than almighty revolt to change the causes, with legal drugs for those who can afford it, and illegal drugs and alcohol for those who can't. In *The Body Keeps the Score*, Bessel van de Kolk highlighted the dire consequences of the psychological profession's unwillingness to contend with causes.[44] The lasting symptoms of trauma get repackaged with different names as static things we 'have' rather than a dynamic product of individual and shared life histories of oppression. The pathologizing of pain discourages us from seeking out deeper explanations. When our experiences of oppression are labelled as depression, bipolar disorder, anxiety, fibromyalgia and so forth, the social justice space becomes a giant group therapy room where broken individuals shout their clinical history into a moshpit of pain. Validating people's pain is important. As philosophers from Hegel to Simone de Beauvoir noted, our humanity is born from being recognized as fully human by others. But, as a colleague once beautifully put it, at some point we have to get off the floor, stop crying and start doing something! We have the power to give coherence to our pain by hinging it to action.

In the quest to articulate rage into a coherent plan for progress, I would caution against two unproductive action pathways: allowing rage to be hijacked by corporate interests, and getting caught up in perfect processes at the expense of tangible results.

The corporate trap

A rainbow flag flies atop the headquarters of the oil giant Shell in Rotterdam. There is something pathetic and frightening about the desperate lengths this corporation, whose business model depends on annihilating life on Earth, will go to buy its social license to operate. Shell is a particularly grotesque example, but the past decade offers abundant evidence of the corporate sleights of hand by which environmental and social harms are washed over with promises of virtue. I need not dwell on the false promises of industrial giants; it stands to reason that so long as the incentive structure of economic behaviour is determined by shareholder interest and executive bonuses, any claims by multinational corporations to participate in social justice will be purely instrumental. Critics will point to the outdoor apparel firm Patagonia, whose owner placed his shares into a trust fund for the planet and whose advertisements actively discourage customers from buying their products, as proof positive that companies can be a force for good.[45] I have no doubt that they could be, if the incentive structure were radically changed. Until it is, it's a risky bet to rely on benevolent billionaires to see the light before collapse comes for us. For every Yvon Chouinard, there are dozens of jet-flying, offshore account-owning, tax-avoiding, absurdly over-consuming billionaires who won't give up an inch of their wealth until they are forced to, and we have to admit that our efforts at holding corporations and their owners to account on social and environmental justice have been rather meek. Worse still: we tolerate absurd levels of corporate bullshit, produced by slick advertising agencies to convince us that companies are taking their justice commitments *very* seriously, so we can keep consuming consequence-free while the big boys work on technological solutions to save the planet.[46]

Volumes have been written about the failure of carbon offsets, cap and trade plans and other industrial-scale greenwashing tactics: chopping down native forests and displacing indigenous people to plant eucalyptus for carbon capture, entire groves of saplings dying or burning down before they remove one ton of carbon from the atmosphere, the list would be laughable if it weren't tragic.[47] By and large, the public tends to be quite alert to these strategies – I don't think many people seriously believes that clicking the box for carbon compensation on the side of an airfare purchase will magically make the flight's environmental footprint disappear. Lawsuits for false advertising are coming in hard and fast now, and companies are beginning to be more wary of lying about their environmental credentials. Of course, the more alert the public is, the more sophisticated the greenwashing tactics become. But I, for one, take pleasure in systematically reporting Shell ads in my social media feeds as false advertisements, and judging by the angry comments flooding their posts, I'm not the only one.

However, I'm not seeing the same level of savvy when it comes to corporate diversity and inclusion initiatives. Companies with otherwise atrocious human rights records, whose supply chains include, at best, underpaid and exploited workers from countries with lax labour laws (e.g. in the textile industry), and at worst, child labour and modern slavery (e.g. in the mining industry); companies that financially support homophobic, transphobic and misogynist politicians, who underpay their blue-collar workers, engage in union busting and don't pay their fair share of taxes, are seemingly given a free rein to showcase their diversity credentials on social media. I am flummoxed by the number of people from underprivileged groups who buy into these tactics with barely a whiff of criticism. Seeing female, Black, Brown and LGBTQ+ faces on corporate campaigns makes people feel seen, and in a social justice space that prizes validation above all else, such validating campaigns are bound to succeed. Under late-modern capitalism, companies live or die by their ability to read the public space, and they have cottoned onto the fact that they can coax marginalized groups with the warm glow of recognition while keeping meaningful progress at bay. So instead of Queer liberation and Black Lives Matter, we are served rainbow coffee cups and sport apparel advertisements, while the system continues its steady march towards collapse. Unfortunately, so long as we let our rage be placated by vacuous promises of corporate validation, there can be no meaningful progress, no matter how many Black, Brown and LGBTQ+ faces grace our social media feeds.

Perfect processes

The second action trap I'd like to caution against is the quest for perfect processes at the expense of measurable results. Many environmental and social justice student groups love the idea of doing away with formal hierarchies, rigid decision-making processes and division of labour. From the environmental movement to the early days of my own foundation, I've been in organizations where nothing could be decided without having long discussions with absolutely everybody about it. I appreciate the appeal of decentralized organizations and consensus model decision-making for people who have lost faith in representative, top-down procedures. However, in practice, such modes of working tend to be slow and inefficient, prone to pushing infighting and activist burnout, and only suited to punctual actions like protest rather than the daily grind of managing social justice projects. I witnessed the damaging impact of focusing on process at the expense of outcomes when my university was occupied by a student climate protest group.[48] Many university staff members supported the students' cause, even if they had some reservations about the method of action. The staff were the first to stand up against the university board when they called the riot police to clear what was a very gentle protest without bothering to show up to speak with the students. Under pressure from all sides, the board were quick to realize the extent of their error. Backed into a corner, they were ready to offer more climate concessions than any university management team in the history of our institution. The students had a wide opening to request real, concrete change. However, due to their insistence on decentralized sociocracy, they were not able / willing to make decisions in time to seize the opportunity. Seeing the momentum slipping away, a small group of staff, including me, jumped into the arena to take over the process and get things moving within the institution, culminating in the organization of eleven sustainability dialogues and a climate emergency declaration from the board.[49] By the time the second student occupation rolled around, the board was much better prepared: they came to the protest ready to meet and speak with the students as soon as it started and even allowed them to stay overnight in the university hallways. However, the decentralized nature of the movement meant that no student was able or willing to act as a representative, and therefore, the students refused to engage with the board to negotiate concrete measures. The protest was cleared by the police again after two days of occupation, but by this point, the students had largely lost the support of the university community, and excluded themselves from action.

When it comes to overemphasizing the process, in my experience, some action groups seem more interested in tending to their internal culture than producing measurable markers of progress. When being part of a group becomes about action for its own sake, it's difficult to keep the agenda focused. One day it's about reproductive justice, the next it's about cutting fossil fuel ties, and then it's about freeing Palestine – these are all worthy causes, to be sure, but it gives critics an easy shot to argue that activists are more interested in following trends than fighting with passion and commitment. This makes it difficult to generate the required broad momentum and support for large-scale change on issues. Proponents of this approach argue that everything is intersectionally connected, and the very suggestion that one should focus on one problem at a time perpetuates intersectional oppression. I understand the academic argument for linking all justice issues together, but as we found out during the recent parliamentary elections in The Netherlands, in which the far-right surged ahead and the intersectional left was left in the dust, that kind of thinking doesn't win seats in the halls of power or move national politics forward. I fear that the clumsy (sometimes frankly condescending) way intersectional messaging has been relayed into the public sphere inadvertently leans currency to right-wing fearmongering about environmental issues being a trojan horse for 'the woke agenda'. Deeply committed intersectional colleagues might disagree with me on this, but I think it matters who wins elections. Left-wing academics and social justice activists alone are never going to form a majority voting block, so some strategizing is necessary to avoid repeatedly handing the keys of parliament to racist, sexist climate deniers with a penchant for authoritarian governance. Unfortunately, politics and perfect solidarity make poor bedfellows, so if we want working-class voters on board and out of the clutches of the far-right, we'll have to make space for imperfect action and processes.

Love binds us

How do we build this space for imperfection? What constitutes imperfect solidarities? I will etch some basic guidelines.

A foundation of self-love

I'm going to follow bell hooks in claiming that self-love is the necessary foundation for any kind of love towards others.[50] This raises a serious challenge: the alienation of neoliberal capitalism sapped our ability to love ourselves, for the reasons I mentioned earlier. Struggling with the aftermath of childhood alienation makes it difficult to build a healthy, nurturing self-concept. A poor sense of self makes it difficult to relate to others, and a lack of healthy, balanced relationships with others threatens the self in a vicious cycle of alienation. This perpetuates the unhealthy flight and fight responses explored in this chapter. Maté reminds his audience that the root of the word 'healing' comes from 'wholeness' – healing from trauma is learning to be whole again.[51]

This sounds like an arduous task – the work of healing is an ongoing process, and most of us will not find perfect wholeness within our lifetimes. But perfect self-love isn't required for imperfect solidarities. What is required is a willingness to engage earnestly with the process, to develop enough belief in our value as loving and lovable humans to weather the storms of human relationships without falling into destructive flight-or-fight trauma reflexes the moment things get complicated. This breeds two foundational abilities; the capacity to engage emotionally and to draw appropriate boundaries when the response to our own engagement is hostile, toxic or unhealthy. Having the capacity to love doesn't mean we owe engagement to every person who calls upon us. Recognizing the point at which others encroach on us to escape their own trauma protects our healing. Drawing boundaries isn't an easy process: there isn't a hard and fast rule about where they should be drawn, depending on one's own resilience, capacity and willingness to give. This may fluctuate over time and vary depending on the nature of our relationship with others. But as Maté noted, the ability to say 'no', especially when demands only go one way, is critical to maintaining a healthy sense of self, and leaves us with enough giving capability to say 'yes' to things that really matter. The ability to hold fast and draw lines is the ultimate act of self-love from which imperfect solidarities can spring. Finding the imperfect balance between engagement and self-care is the starting point for generous love.

Loving, generously

Generous love, according to De Beauvoir, is willing others to be as free as we will ourselves to be, and committing moral and material means towards that liberation.[52] There's an impersonal interpretation, which consists in a kind of arms-length solidarity that erects walls of dispassion between donor and receiver. Arms-length solidarity is emotionally comfortable for the giver – from keyboard social justice warriors to so-called effective altruists and billionaire philanthropists, people seek the high of solidarity without the pain of human passions. This interpretation portrays generosity as a kind of moral largesse and love as a non-committal, impersonal generality, the kind preached by New Age gurus who beseech us to seek spiritual unity with humanity. It's undeniable that impersonal philanthropy generates a positive impact, on balance – there are hundreds of community organizations that depend on it for survival. But it ensnares the giver in moral solipsism and stoic distance from the world. And while, in the best cases, it may materially help the receiver, it fails to make the humanizing contact that whispers, 'I see you, you are fully human'. Dispassionate, arm's-length solidarity cannot change the world because it maintains givers and receivers in the very nodes of the system that created power imbalances in the first place.

De Beauvoir herself indicated that she had an engaged vision of generous love.[53] It was visible in her actions, as a committed activist for socialist, feminist and decolonial causes, in reprisal for which her apartment was bombed twice. It was visible in her relationships, where she sought out the messy entanglements of human love, sometimes enmeshed with physical passion, sometimes as platonic lifelong appreciation. It was visible in her work, in *The Ethics of Ambiguity*,[54] as well as in her novel *Les Mandarins*,[55] where she deliberately blurred lines between political solidarity and human passions.

Ultimately, imperfect solidarities are connections of love, opening an ambiguous space where beings can shape each others' humanity. This gets messy because relating to people on a human level makes the outcomes difficult to predict. Sharing ourselves with passion driven towards justice can birth all manner of strange interactions. Positive feelings can emerge, like sisterly or brotherly love, deeply nurturing, mentoring relationships, distant respect, an understated understanding and deep appreciation, including the capacity to disagree with integrity. But a lot of the time, it's also plain hard work, with frustration, overwhelming feelings, disappointment, anger, sadness, betrayal or destructive physical desire as plausible emotional outcomes. That's because people, on the whole, are complex beings with drives, egos and traumas that get in the way of open communication. Successful relating eschews attempts at classification, shape-shifting without settling on a final form. We are called upon to abandon our obsession with fitting people into neat boxes, to cease seeing them as projects, as means to ends, and to work with the messy, uncomfortable process of making common cause. Pain and rage bind us towards revolutionary progress; this is true. But the march forward is slow and arduous. We will spend much time on the journey, so we had best get comfortable with the idea that we will want to pull our hair out and push our companions off the cliff at some point along the way. Breathe, joke about it and let it out, it's part of the process.

Resisting the temptation to essentialize people, to elevate them onto pedestals only to tear them down when they say or do something that conflicts with their assigned essence, is an existential condition of generous love. People are not totems, and yet we often treat them as such – but that is obsessive love. Teachers, leaders and public figures are particularly vulnerable to totemization because it's comfortable to alienate ourselves in them, to project into them our hopes and fears, and to turn them into objects of love/hate worship. All hell breaks loose if the statue dares to move! But we are not statues; we are humans, and move we will. In the day-to-day business of living, between the revolutionary projects and the grand flow of history, there is the ebb and flow of humanity, with the buoyant energy of days of triumph, the sadness of loss, the frustration of miscommunication, the cyclical fluctuations in physical capacities to respond, including illness and well-being, fatigue and pain, anxiety and euphoria. Before essence can ever crystallize, there's all this existence curdling in the folds of time. There's the early morning trip to the clinic in Varanasi to get a bout of dysentery under control so we can be back on the karate mat in the afternoon, the epic hangover because we've been celebrating a major project milestone in the nightclubs of Lusaka until 3:00 am, the awkward silence in the 1991-model Mazda with barely functioning lights when we realize that it's pitch black and we're lost in a township with no acceleration power, and all the arguing and making up in between. Those human moments are the cement between the bricks of our solidarity projects.

So, I learned to accept the ambiguity of my relationships with my travel companions. I'm not bent on definitions and am happy to go with the flow. As a result, I often change my mind about people, and some of my strongest relationships of solidarity have been with people that I disliked at first approach. Conversely, I have found it necessary to excise people who enthralled me at first glance but were too toxic to be tolerable road companions. In between the two extremes, I try to make space for people as they come, and the moments where we find ourselves together. This helps me to keep a healthy, depressive position of ambivalence towards people, appreciating that no one is wholly good or wholly evil. I have met Black men oppressed by racism and poverty whose drug-fuelled rage turned to bloody violence against vulnerable women, as I have met arrogant, conceited wealthy people who were occasionally prone to wild acts of generosity. I support the emancipation of the working classes, but I also know the frustrating limits of working-class solidarity – alcoholism, violence, particularly domestic and sexual violence, racism, crassness, the propensity to believe conspiracy theories, the absence of class consciousness . . . I grew up around many of these things. People are flawed, but are owed a chance to develop their fullest humanity, and they're not getting it under the current conditions of production. This understanding has kept me out of the paranoid-schizoid position embraced by much present-day social justice discourse, and focused on painstakingly carving a path forward.

To be human is to err

The definition of imperfection is that which contains flaws. Imperfect solidarities invite us to work with the flaws inherent in human behaviour, treating our fellow journeymen and women as people-in-learning rather than essences and archetypes. Whereas the social justice sphere veers towards calling out flaws in unproductive ways, I prefer Loretta J. Ross' concept of calling people in.[56] Calling in invites joint reflection on why what was said or done was hurtful to one of the parties to the conversation. It's a mindset steeped in kindness that aims to produce productive collaboration down the line. The ultimate goal of imperfect solidarities is to be able to keep working together towards our shared goals, and we can't do that if we jump at each other's throats the minute someone says something that displeases the other.

Because of my martial arts background, I like to think of the social justice space as a tatami where we all train together. We bow before we get on the mat, showing courtesy and pre-emptive empathy in case something goes wrong. When someone inevitably gets punched in the nose or thrown a bit too hard, we immediately pause, apologize, work out what went wrong and learn from our mistakes to calibrate our joint efforts better, then we start again. The tatami has physical boundaries, and there are specific rules karateka are expected to play by: respect and empathy only work if they are shared by all. Those with an overtly aggressive, uncollaborative or predatory attitude are a danger to themselves and others, and (should) soon find themselves forcefully encouraged to leave the mat.

Accepting mistakes and creating a learning space only works if it goes both ways. Leaving the space open for toxic people spells trouble for everyone involved. So while I always try calling in first, if I see that I get nothing but violent hostility on the other side, I draw boundaries – not just for myself but to protect those around me who are prepared to be vulnerable and learn together. That's not to say that the door, once closed, is shut forever – everyone deserves a chance to work on themselves, see their own mistakes and grow until they can offer solidarity. Setting boundaries to protect yourself and those around you is healthy. Hatefully holding onto grudges serves no beneficial purpose for solidarity (or for your mental health). As always, finding the balance between the two is an imperfect process of trial-and-error.

Commitment

Imperfect solidarities are built on long-term commitment to the causes we fight for and the people we fight with. Trust, love and solidarity need time to flourish. It takes time to work through errors and learn from our mistakes. Progress is a slow-burn. Yet commitment seems to be something people find increasingly challenging, especially young people. They struggle to commit to small things – meeting times, student clubs, essay topic choices, diets – and big things – friendships, studies, career choices and solidarity causes. My research showed that for cosmopolitan middle-class youths, sustainability and social justice were two among an overwhelming array of lifestyle choices within their *habitus*.[57] These were means to an end of personal growth and positive moral identities, and therefore, susceptible to change when something more appealing came along. In interviews, students casually admitted to abandoning environmentally conscious behaviours after a couple of months, when the lure of novel experiences and the comfort of old ways overrode the dissonance experienced after studying climate collapse. Likewise, despite increasing criticism of the practice, students still partake in voluntourism, treating social justice work in the Global South as a fun holiday with CV benefits, with little regard for the long-term consequences of the fleeting presence of unskilled White youths in poor communities.

I think that our struggle to commit is a product of years of neoliberal socialization that has primed us to prioritize the gratification of immediate desires over all else. In the age of Instagram and TikTok, social media pushes the buttons of our insecurities to make those desires as fleeting as possible, with the promise that the next big thing will change our life for good (if we buy a new subscription or product). This fosters a generation of insecure people who calm their existential anxieties through a flight reflex of hopping from one interest to the next. They make far better consumers than secure, self-reflexive, committed people do, but poor allies for imperfect solidarities. What can be done about this? I do think that education can rebuild the capacity to commit, but this requires classroom practices that address trauma and quell the anxiety.

Teaching through trauma

Though I've talked about trauma in more general terms in this chapter, I'd like to close with a reflection on the specific impact of student trauma reflexes on teaching practices in the climate classroom. The aftermath of the pandemic, the re-emergence of large-scale war and the devastating impact of climate meltdown have left teachers and students contending with trauma the scale of which most teachers have not encountered before. To be clear, none of what follows should be read as an indictment of student behaviour: they didn't choose to be confined to their homes for the best part of two years, or to have their futures torched by climate disaster. Considering the circumstances, I'd say the kids are reacting more appropriately than many of the adults in the room. However, we need to name trauma reflexes and how they show up in our classrooms to address them in our teaching practice.

In my experience, the most noticeable reaction is flight. It appears literally, when we discuss collapse in class, as a consistent number of students step out of the classroom each year, overwhelmed by emotion. This is an obvious example of flight, but as Walker noted, flight shows up in other ways than literal escape.[58] Especially during and after Covid, students anxiously overloaded their social and academic agendas, giving themselves no space to pause and think about the moment they were living through. Students I interviewed during the first lockdown drew up ambitious personal productivity plans including yoga, music, reading and online classes to upskill while confined to their bedrooms.[59] The perverse effect of this flight was that instead of abating their anxiety, intense focus on filling their timetables to the brim seemed to make it worse. When the lockdowns lifted, these students jumped on the opportunity to book the first airline tickets they could find and make up in a matter of weeks what they had missed over two years, throwing environmental considerations out the window.

Covid also exacerbated fight reactions to trauma. Within progressive social sciences and liberal arts programmes, I noticed an increase in the virulence of the social justice fixation problem. It feels like a whole group of (mostly middle class) kids spent their high school years locked at home on a social media doom-loop, forming vicarious opinions of the world divorced from personal experience, then brought those opinions to their university classrooms as truth, prepared to battle anyone who disagrees. The fight reflex also manifests in other ways: my colleagues and I noticed the increasing assertiveness with which some students now request to be protected from uncomfortable learning materials. As a teacher, I've dealt with unhappy students here and there in the past; it goes with the territory. However, since Covid, the nature of student discontent has become more emotional, aggressive and personal. Fortunately, this still concerns a small minority of students, but it creates an uncomfortable environment for students and teachers alike, akin to treading on eggshells.

Teaching collapse also often induces a freeze reaction. For most students who experience this, the shock of discovering what lies ahead for their future on this planet lasts a couple of days. But I have seen students who did not open their mouth for weeks, then came to see me towards the end of the course saying something like: 'I'm normally a talkative person, this isn't me, but it just hit me so hard I found it difficult to process.' This seems to me like a perfectly legitimate reaction to having the rug pulled from under your life plans, but some students are frozen in shock to the extent that they fail to hand in coursework assignments, and it feels wrong to penalize them for what is a valid psychological reaction.

Given all of this, what are teachers supposed to do? To me, this is about teaching with compassion and care, without crossing the boundaries of the teaching profession.

There is a growing body of literature on trauma-informed teaching practices in and around ecological and social justice education.[60] At its core, trauma-informed teaching is about managing stressful information or situations that might trigger underlying trauma, while keeping the space of learning open for students. It is important to note, as Gabor Maté does, that unpleasant learning materials, uncomfortable as they may be, are not per se traumatizing.[61] They may be stressful, but stress only induces a trauma reaction if it triggers pre-existing trauma. We should therefore be wary of the overuse of the word 'trauma' relating to classroom contents; the answer is not to shield students from stress. This would do them a great disservice, in no way preparing them to face a world in crisis with resilience and courage. But we can create space for channelling trauma reactions, giving them a contained space to evolve and work themselves out so that learning can begin.

To address the flight reflex, I keep a simple rule in my classroom, inspired by trauma-informed teaching practices in martial arts: the door is always open (even when I have to physically close it to cancel out the corridor noise). Just like air hostesses point to the nearest exit before take-off, I make sure that students know that they may leave and come back, and no questions will be asked when they do. I do ask that students let me know if they won't be coming to class at all, as this is important for the configuration of the problem or jigsaw, but beyond this, I do not require explanations, within the range of absences authorized by the academic regulations.

The fight reflex is a tougher nut to crack. I have found it most useful to let students decide on the rules of engagement at the start of the course, setting the scene for respectful discord in the classroom. I emphasize that there will be no moral or material punishment (in the form of grade points) on my part for sharing unpopular opinions in the classroom, but that we shall put opinions to the test of scientific scrutiny, together. I cannot control what goes on after they leave the classroom, but I hope that they take with them the kind of courteous dissent that should be the hallmark of academic freedom. I will take students who persistently overstep the boundary between disagreement and aggression aside and try to talk them through the source of their anger. More often than not, it boils down to feeling that their identity and way of life is under attack. Being able to voice that without being immediately silenced offers a space to process, perhaps even grieve. I have seen this happen in real time: a student once fought me for the best part of an hour, protesting virulently at the suggestion that they might need to rethink their life plans in line with the constraints of planetary boundaries. I accepted the anger with compassion, deflecting it away from me personally, and onto the situation. While making space for their rage, I invited them to look the truth in the face, then choose to prepare for it, or not. Providing them with a choice of what to do with this information gave them a sense of agency and control. Judgement-free compassion allowed them to connect with the fear that was really driving their anger, which rapidly turned to sorrow. Over the next couple of weeks, they found their stride in the class, and became an engaged student in various sustainability initiatives on campus.

Addressing the freeze reflex also requires flexibility and compassion. Students should not feel like they will be punished for sitting in stunned silence for a couple of sessions. If the institution requires participation grades, teachers should come up with measures of participation that don't penalize students who are too busy battling their emotions to engage. I personally tick the participation box from the moment a student is present in the room, whether they engage or not. However, I will check up on a student's emotional state after class if I notice that they do not speak for two or more sessions. I am also as generous as I can be with deadline extensions. I have received student medical reports, and essay-like emails detailing students' emotional meltdowns in order to obtain an extension. Nobody comes out in good form from this policing exercise, neither the students who have just disclosed uncomfortable personal information nor the teachers who have to process this information. Within what is allowed by the academic regulations and reasonable good will, I generally grant extensions. Ultimately, this is not just about compassion for students but also maintaining all those important boundaries: just because institutions are cutting back on costs by foisting triage responsibilities for extensions onto course coordinators rather than students counsellors doesn't mean we should accept the role of therapists. I know this is hard for teachers to hear and act upon because our nature is to care for the young people in our classrooms when we feel like no one else will. But think of it this way: by overstepping boundaries, we're hurting ourselves while giving our institutions the green light to keep cutting costs. Why should they invest in student counselling when we're willing to step in? Ultimately, the most revolutionary act of love is sometimes simply to say no.

Thus, our journey through the four dialogues of the *Pedagogies of Collapse* comes to an end. We spoke the truth together in Chapter 1, engaged in reflective practice to make space for grief in Chapter 3, assembled a framework for taking appropriate actions now in our classrooms in Chapter 4 and developed the principle of imperfect solidarities in Chapter 5. I could leave it at that, but I feel I like owe it to you to recognize that educating in times of collapse is a taxing endeavour, and we're only humans. Though teachers worldwide seem to run permanently on empty, especially since Covid, in the long run, we can only give as much as we are able to nurture within ourselves. The most revolutionary acts of love teachers can bring into this world are to care enough about themselves to keep themselves in the fight. Though I feel I'm hardly one to share advice on self-care, given my patchy track record in the matter, it is perhaps *because* I have struggled with myself, my body, my mind and my illness and find myself still standing, ready to fight, that I would like to end this book with reflections on loving, learning and living in times of collapse, in the final chapter.

6

Learning, Loving, Living in Times of Collapse

If the cliché regarding putting one's own oxygen mask on before helping others is overused, it nonetheless holds an essential truth: nobody can be of assistance while incapacitated. Yet teachers are among the worst offenders when it comes to systematically placing other people's needs and concerns above their own. Almost all of us have a story about teachers who went above and beyond to steer us away from bad choices and situations, towards the beginnings of something better, sometimes simply by caring and listening when nobody else would. As students, we take those life-changing moments with us into futures that might never have been birthed without them. As teachers, we don't often see the results of our endeavours once students have left us; we do because it touches our humanity, the reason most of us became teachers in the first place.

As I discussed throughout this book, teachers are on the frontline of collapse. Under neoliberal rule, the teaching profession was already under sustained attack from conservatives desperate to sell off the public education system for profit while maintaining the lucrative pipelines from childhood into the productive apparatus. Now, around the world, the edifice rattles under pressure from harbingers of collapse: disease, extreme weather, failed harvests, war. Faced with this, I am hardly surprised by the volume of teachers throwing their hands up, slamming their books shut and leaving the profession.[1] The remaining teachers can only hold the weight of the world on their shoulders for so long before the whole system comes crumbling down. The problem is that, unlike aircrafts, the teaching profession does not come with a safety manual: nobody knows where the oxygen masks are!

It's been four years since the low point of my environmental reckoning, during the first COVID lockdown. Students, parents and people at public events often ask me how I manage to keep going with everything I know, and I can't say that I've figured it all out. I don't have a silver bullet for the emotional toll of teaching through planetary collapse. But I went from being on medical leave with depression and burn-out symptoms, overwhelmed by chronic pain, fatigue and cognitive impairment, to working as a full-time educator, advocate and activist, passionately invested in the fight for a future worth living. All I can do is share with you my journey though learning, loving and living in times of collapse, and send this book off with a message of hope.

Learning

I always thought of myself as a learned individual, with two master's degrees, a PhD and a compulsive reading habit. However, confronting collapse, I realized that despite all this theoretical knowledge, I knew almost nothing about two things upon which my life depends: the living world, and my own body.

Learning from nature

Before 2019, I had never grown anything in my life. Any plant gifted to me was almost certain to die within days from one ailment or another. I could not tell an oak from a hazel, and though I was vaguely aware that having drinks outdoors in a t-shirt in November in The Netherlands was not how I remembered my childhood, I was too uneducated about the living world to notice the impact of these changing weather patterns on plants and animals.

My dissociation from nature was a product of its time. As a child, I marvelled at my grandmother's garden and the wonderful things that grew in it. Yet it was not by choice that 'Mamie' had come to tend to living things: she was born in 1920 to an impoverished working-class family in Northern France, and workers at the time depended upon their allotments to feed their families. Though my grandparents' generation caught the social elevator of the post-war period of fossil-fuelled abundance, my mother still grew up in an environment where money was tight. Producing food, rearing pigeons, rabbits, chickens for meat and bees for honey, was important to providing a complete diet to the family. My mother has no qualms about killing animals because she watched her father wield a shotgun and skin rabbits in their backyard. But I grew up in the suburbs of Paris in the 1980s and then in the urban polders of The Netherlands in the 1990s. Even though we always had a garden of some sort, I feel my mother was relieved to be among the first generation to buy food entirely from the grocery store. She loved nature, there's no question – enough to study biology for a couple of years after high school and spend her summers collecting bugs in the Vosges mountains. But to the generations that came before, nature wasn't only about communing with crickets and watching sunsets. It was also a fickle and cruel thing that stole children with disease, injury and starvation, and breaking out of this anxious dependency to find shelves stocked with unimaginable abundance was like walking into a dream. We now know that it was a dream fuelled by fossil energy, and I wonder what my grandmother would have thought, had she known the price her great-grandchildren would pay for this cornucopia. Having survived life as a teenage cotton mill worker, the occupation of her home by German soldiers and the death of her firstborn son, would she have said no to progress? I never got a chance to ask, as Mamie got her dearest wish to die peacefully in her sleep after a day's gardening among her beloved plants, at the age of eighty-five.

As I was going through the early days of my environmental depression about six years ago, I felt an inner sense that something had been lost, and wanted to be found again. My father-in-law, a Székely blacksmith who reminds me very much of my grandmother in situation and spirit, helped us build the first raised bed in our 10m x 10m garden, and I purchased an assortment of seeds to fill it. Considering that I knew nothing whatsoever and we started in June, I'd say our first harvest was decent! But the benefit went far beyond a few radishes and kale plants: it birthed within me a deep desire to regenerate and watch things blossom. So I bought a dozen books on permaculture and began experimenting with compost, crop rotation and mulching techniques. We're now on our sixth harvest, with five raised beds, a greenhouse, a composter, two water collectors, three fruit trees, three vines, and an assortment of pots and tables. Restoring soil is one of my favourite things about this whole process. I love to see worms and woodlice doing their thing, and there's something healing about turning barren ground abused by construction and tiling into fertile soil ready to grow food. Permaculture taught me that almost nothing is so damaged that it can't be healed: soils can be replenished, sick plants can often be saved, and from death comes a new cycle of life. Even though, I must say, we're doing our best to make it hard for ourselves, with a number of places in the Randstad unsuitable for food gardening due to PFAS and chemical contamination from industrial activity.

Given the size of our garden, I doubt we would be able to produce enough to feed ourselves even if that were our goal. But growing food broke something in the consumerist thought patterns for me. I began questioning how it was possible that supermarket carrots looked so straight or that their cabbages had no holes in them. Whereas I was previously oblivious to growing seasons, I started wondering why there were beans in the shops in winter, only to find from the labels that they were from Zimbabwe. My daughter, who had previously been somewhat averse to vegetables, began plucking carrots, cucumbers and tomatoes from the beds and eating them. In the summer evenings, she often takes a stool to sit and read 'bedtime' stories to the plants (well, they are planted in vegetable 'beds'!). We observe the different kinds of bees, butterflies, ladybirds and hoverflies that buzz around the borage, chamomile, mallows and other flowers I've interplanted between the vegetables. She knows when things are in season or not.

As our garden blossomed, I began taking an interest in the life hidden away in the Randstad. Living in one of the most densely populated areas of Europe, where every square inch feels like it's covered in concrete, it's easy to forget that nature abhors a vacuum and dandelions and horsetail will find their way between the stone slabs. I took a foraging course in what passes for forests (but are more like managed tree plantations) around here, and learned to recognize trees like medlars, elders, hazels, herbs like ramsons, garlic mustard and wild rocket, and berries like aronia, blackberries and sloes. I even tip-toed into mushroom hunting, plucking boletes from the woods behind my parents' house in France and growing my own oyster mushrooms as companions to my tomato plants at home.

After a couple of years, I began noticing how much sooner berries appeared than the books suggested. I realized the impact of repeated, prolonged droughts on wildflowers, and noted the decline in insect populations as the cityscapes turned yellow and brown. I struggled with my fruit trees that were disturbed by irregular winter patterns and saw my harvest struggle with early and late heatwaves, weeks on end without rain, and downpours that would last for days, if not weeks. Though these losses were annoying for me, I shuddered to think what farmers were going through, and was not shocked to hear that fruit and grain harvests were failing all over the world. What keeps me up at night is wondering what happens when they all fail at once and as I write this, we're not far off that point. But as I cycle past fields of beet or corn, it strikes me just how unnatural and unhealthy these monocultures are: cracked, bare soil between row after row of the same. It's like we're setting ourselves up to fail. My soil never dries out and cracks because it's never bare. There's always either some crop cover or mulch on it. But permaculture requires a lot of manpower, and too few young people are willing to stake their lives in the agricultural sector, especially now that it's become such a volatile and vulnerable profession. So right at the moment where we need to secure our food supply, the means are failing us.

There is no doubt in my mind that by the end of my life, we will be in a situation similar to Cuba after the fall of the Soviet Union, where the only way to stave off starvation will be for everyone to get their hands in the dirt and for every street corner and patch of grass to be turned over to food production.[2] Cubans struggled, and life has been hard on the island, but one thing they did not do was starve. So it feels good to have had the space to make rookie mistakes and not have to pay the consequences of a failed crop, such that when our family's diet does depend on it, at least I'll have the basic knowledge to make sure the plants actually grow. There's no guarantee – under conditions of environmental collapse, we're only ever one polar vortex collapse, one hurricane or one fire away from losing the harvest, and it's a matter of luck as much as anything, whether the freak hailstorm hits your crop or the neighbouring village's. But we all, right now, should invest in rebuilding the knowledge that was lost between my parents' and my generation. Whether we like it or not, whether we plan for it or not, collapse means that most of us alive today will be involved in food production at some point. It will only take one catastrophic summer's harvest loss to drive that point home. What we do have is an opportunity, if we act now, to instill the right skills, knowledge and wisdom in ourselves and in the young, to rebuild the agricultural system from the ground up.

We're going to need to enlist the help of farmers, who are currently struggling under a system designed to barely eek a living wage even when climate conditions are optimal. As well as performing a physically demanding, relentless job, farmers are looked down upon (we still bandy about the expression 'peasants' to mean someone who lacks culture and refinement) or romanticized as vestiges of an idyllic rural past. Now that climate conditions are anything but ideal, many are simply throwing their hands up and giving up while they can, or committing suicide when they can't, so we're losing them right as we're about to desperately need them.[3] When all is said and done, the kind of collapse we will experience largely depends on how fast their knowledge can be transmitted to the rest of us to stave off famine, so the more of us can revive and build on that knowledge of flora and fauna right now, the better-off we will all be. But in order to farm, as the age of mechanized mass agriculture comes to an end, we're going to need our bodies to be up for the task.

Learning from the body-mind nexus

It's fair to say that a significant number of people in the industrialized world have an unhealthy relationship with their body. The increasing rates of chronic inflammatory illness, obesity and cancers indicate something has gone very wrong in the ways we live with our bodies. This is not an indictment of individual behaviours but, rather, the product of a toxic system that feeds us junk food, dirty air, polluted water and then attempts to clean up the mess with pills. Working conditions under late capitalism are not conducive to healthy bodily functions: white-collar workers, including teachers, sit for long hours at a time with precious little mobility, while blue-collar workers stand for long hours performing the same strenuous movements over and over. Neither of these options makes for healthy, well-adjusted bodies. On top of unhealthy working and living conditions, our bodies also have to contend with chronic stress and untreated trauma etched into our muscles, joints and organs, linked to a worrying rise in auto-immune illness, dementia and cancer, among other illnesses.

As I stated earlier, like other members of the 'caring professions' (including nurses, social workers, psychologists and so forth), teachers are prone to ignoring their bodies. How many teachers reading this have readily skipped a meal or two because they were running between classes or rushing to finish grading? How many have lost hours of sleep over a problematic student case? How many come home completely exhausted, but instead of putting work away for the rest of the night, log back on after dinner and end up going to bed wired? Between you and I, how many cups of coffee do you need to get you through the day, and then how many glasses of wine do you need to get you through the evenings? How many are on antidepressants, anti-anxiety medication or some other substance just to keep going? I'm not saying this to judge or hold to account, but because I've been there and at times felt like I would never break the cycle.

We can talk about the different ways in which we can take better care of our bodies, but the body forms a single nexus with the mind, as amply demonstrated by van der Kolk and Maté, so one cannot address the one without addressing the other.[4] Both authors described a host of approaches to heal the mind-body nexus, so I refer the reader to their works for a broader picture on fixing our pathological embodied relationships, but I would like to delve specifically into my own healing journey, and the pivotal role psychedelics played therein.

Psychedelics are a group of psychoactive substances, defined in the medical literature as 'serotonin 2A receptor partial agonists', meaning they act on the brain's 'well-being' neurotransmitters.[5] Psychedelics include natural substances like psilocybin, DMT and mescaline, and synthetic substances like MDMA, LSD and ketamine. Therapeutically, they're used in two ways: in high doses, they induce an altered state of consciousness, including visualizations and lucid dreaming, or in low doses, a practice also known as 'microdosing', a sub-psychedelic experience of well-being and reflexivity. Research on psychedelics showed promising results on treatment-resistant mental health issues in the 1960s, but the research stopped when psychedelics were thrown in with crystal meth and crack in the 'War on Drugs' that began in the United States in the 1970s.[6] Today, as we pick up the pieces from the opioid epidemic, psychedelics research is undergoing a revival, looking for safe, non-addictive alternatives to treating pain and addiction. Colleagues in the field tell me a revolution is coming in mental health and chronic illness care, and I believe it: the research on the effect of psychedelics on trauma, post-traumatic stress disorder (PTSD), depression, addiction and even chronic pain is compelling.[7] But I also know it from personal experience. I am a functioning, (more or less) adjusted human being because of psychedelics.

As I mentioned before, I began my teaching career after a disastrous stint in the field of social justice work. I was an idealistic young person dreaming of making a difference in the world and threw myself into poorly run projects with extremely vulnerable populations I was not equipped to help, even with a master's degree in human rights. By the time I sat in front of my first classroom, I was suffering from intense depressive symptoms, hallucinations, flashbacks and nightmares. I could barely function in or out of the classroom, and with the encouragement of one of my managers, I sought medical help and received a diagnosis of PTSD. Unfortunately, everything the doctors threw at me either didn't work or made it worse: most Dutch therapists are not trained to understand trauma and how to treat it. I was given valium at quite high doses for months, which induced the worst depressive episode I ever experienced. It came to a head about six months into my first teaching job, when I crashed my motorcycle on valium. It wasn't so much the injuries that I suffered that worried me, but the ones I did not – as it was, I slid twenty metres across the road at 80 kmp/h and landed in a ditch. Had another vehicle been on the road, I would not be here to tell the story. Now, imagine: I was teaching full time while going through all of this! One evening, after yet another confrontation with my manager about my erratic behaviour, I decided to quit. A friend dropped by as I was packing my bags with no specific plans about where I might go, and suggested

I try MDMA talk-therapy before I make further decisions. So that's what we did: we dosed with a group of knowledgeable peers for about twelve hours, talking and deeply processing through the night. My PTSD and depression were healed, and I have not experienced any related symptoms in the past decade. As you can tell by this book's existence, I decided to stay in the teaching profession.

I didn't think about psychedelics for quite some time after that. After nine years and three different hospital specialists, I finally got a diagnosis of fibromyalgia to speak to my chronic pain, and I followed the doctor's orders: psychotherapy, antidepressants, physiotherapy and painkillers, which disqualified me medically from using psychedelics. The problem was that it just didn't work: I experienced moderate relief for a few days, but the pain, fatigue and cognitive impairment kept coming back. How many classes did I teach on codeine? I would be out of a job if I cancelled teaching every time I was in pain, so I soldiered on, and I don't think anybody noticed. Most colleagues were shocked to learn that I was ill at all: 'but you're so productive and high-performing, you don't *seem* ill'. Yes, most of us who live with these conditions are; that's part of the problem.

As the psychedelics renaissance gathered pace around me, I felt I was missing out, reading impressive scientific research on psychedelics-assisted therapy and watching so many friends go through life-transforming experiences. However, I was too deeply addicted to pain meds to safely use psychedelics, and though I tried to wean myself off a couple of times, I failed and felt condemned to watch from the sidelines. That changed serendipitously when I contracted dysentery during a visit to Varanasi and could not swallow anything for a week, including meds. I was too ill to notice withdrawal symptoms, and just like that, I was off the hook, and managed to stay off the hook long enough for my first psychedelics experience in a decade.

It's been over a year since that experience, and I struggle to adequately verbalize the extent to which my quality of life has improved. Using regular small doses of psilocybin, which can be legally bought in smartshops around the country, interspersed with macro-doses of this and other psychedelics, I no longer require medication to control my fibromyalgia. The fatigue and cognitive impairment have lifted. Whereas before I could often not bring myself to work productively until noon, I am now regularly up at 6:30 am, working on my computer before my daughter gets up. I no longer wake up feeling like I have been encased in concrete during the night, and while I still experience pain, it does not overwhelm me. This remission is not a miracle cure; the effects last up to seven days after a small dose or ten days after a large dose, but symptoms creep back in after that. But ask any fibromyalgia patient, they will tell you that seven days of remission with no side-effects is close enough to miraculous!

Psilocybin doesn't work like a painkiller; I can't just pop some magic truffles and carry on with my day like with codeine. I never know from one dose to the next what the experience will be, so I only take it when I have the space for it. Sometimes it makes me want to curl up and sleep for two hours, or feel deeply creative and crafty, or put music on and be transported by beauty. I think the reason it helps with my illness is because it allows me to have balanced, healthy conversations with myself about what it means to be embodied. Like a lot of people living with trauma, I dissociated and adopted a dualist mind-body relationship to survive, and now it's time to put that to rest and reintegrate with myself so that I may reintegrate with the world. With psilocybin, I realized that I spent my twenties fixated on trauma from the past, and my thirties consumed by anxiety about the future. Now as I near my forties, I feel connected to the present in ways not experienced before, such that even time seems to slow down. I sometimes just sit with feelings for an hour, experiencing the plenitude of living. I can silence the tyranny of my inner monologue, say, 'I think that's good enough' and leave it at that – the slide deck for my next lecture, the synopsis for my next presentation or the review for a journal article. Nobody is going to care about how perfect my slides were when the food chain comes crashing down. They will care about the feelings and learning I inspired in them. We really should apply the principle of imperfect solidarities to ourselves as well. I'm here to teach, to guide, to hold space for the young, and that doesn't require perfection any more than solidarity does.

Although it hadn't been my intention in taking psychedelics, they have also been remarkably helpful in supporting my mental journey out of eco-depression. High-dose trips have allowed me to visualize and connect deeply with my environmental grief in healing ways. I have come to better understand my place in the vastness of time and the connection of all things. I have contemplated the history of life on Earth from the first bacteria to climate apocalypse and realized that the conscious experience we think of as 'life' is but a speck of time dust in an infinite, knotted weave of matter and energy. Whereas I had always found this kind of thinking existentially overwhelming and anxiety-inducing, I now find comfort in it. The difference is that it was previously an abstract thought, whereas it is now, to me, a lived experience. Don't get me wrong: I still find the thought of collapse heartbreaking, heavy and frightening, and shudder before the increasingly likely prospect that many people I love will die of collapse-related causes. However, death seems less final to me now. From now until the end of time on this planet, the stardust currently assembled into the body I call 'me' will continue to make new wondrous shapes, and I'm okay with that. If anything, it spurs me to use what time I have left as 'me' to protect the beautiful place where these molecules will wander until the sun blasts them back into space and the cycle of planetary life and death begins anew.

I'd like to end with a caution: psychedelics are not a panacea, and they're not for everyone. These powerful mind-altering substances should be treated with respect and intention, as part of a healing process that requires support, work and dedication. Medically speaking, people on antidepressants, pain meds or with a history of certain psychiatric conditions should steer clear, and if you're thinking of trying, I heartily recommend getting a medical all-clear first. Even among those with no medical contra-indication, psychedelics should be taken with guidance and caution, preferably with the support of integrative therapy to process the experience. It's unlikely that psychedelics will become as ubiquitous as antidepressants. To many people, mind-altering substances are too frightening. Beyond the poor connotations inherited from the 1960s, people are generally quite scared of facing their ego, reluctant to be confronted with their unconscious. But psychologists, take heed: in anticipation of the tidal wave of trauma induced by collapse, I do think that psychedelics can be included our the arsenal of tools for a more humane, gentler path through chaos.

Loving

I've talked a lot about love in this book, including the revolutionary love of Freire's *Pedagogy of the Oppressed* and the generous love of De Beauvoir's *Ethics of Ambiguity*.[8] I alluded to what love means in practice in previous chapters, but the points I made were rather more general. In the following segment, I'd like to delve into the concrete ways in which love could help us live and learn through collapse.

Loving the self

I mentioned self-love in the previous chapter, but I would like to return to this theme, central as it is to our capacity to move forward in times of collapse. Most of us in the caring professions feel genuine compassion for our fellow humans. It's why we choose to work long hours in service of others, underpaid and undervalued. Be that as it may, I can't help but think that part of what brings us to give without regard for ourselves is deep-seated, barely conscious self-doubt and self-deprecation and the flight reflex that results therefrom. For the reasons I outlined in Chapter 5, I would argue that some of what drives unhealthy selflessness among educators is a flight attempt to get as far away from ourselves as possible. We are effectively saying: 'here, take all I have, so I don't have to think about myself anymore'. As such, the gift will always be something of a poisoned chalice – why should anybody take what we have to give with respect and care if the unconscious message we convey is that it is unwanted and worthless? If resilience is the capacity to maintain the integrity of a system in the face of external shocks, then how much resilience can a person have when they are systematically trying to escape from themselves? It's difficult to maintain the integrity of a system that constantly tries to pull itself apart.

Partly thanks to insights from psychedelics, I came to realize the extent to which, like many educators, I defined myself according to that which I gave away, rather than that which I was comfortable enough to keep. No boundary would remain uncrossed if it meant I could give away just a little bit more of myself. It was a compulsive method to take away the pain and distress of staying with myself.

As a result, I came to be seen primarily as a giver, and since the world's needs are infinite, it was never enough. People would call me at all hours of the day or night asking for my time, money, energy, involvement in projects without pay or recognition. You know you're in a bad place the moment people start to say, 'She won't mind' about you as they're about to abuse your generosity.

So the foundational act of self-love was uttering a convincing, loud 'no'. I still participate in projects, but only if I am given the proper conditions to do so. Shocking as it may sound to teachers who are not only used to working for free, but whose employers *expect* it from them, I now request to be compensated for my time. It's not only about financial compensation: I'll readily do something for the fun, camaraderie and impact; if it's meaningful and engaging enough to me. But the point is that only *I* should determine what I'm willing to give away. Nobody gets to tell me that I should work and expect nothing but a pat on the back because I'm making a positive impact, and that's compensation enough. Holding to those boundaries means I can continue to donate large amounts of my time and money to support women's empowerment through my foundation, on my own terms. I make a conscious decision about what I share, and build the rest of my work around that. Perhaps unsurprisingly, I've met a lot of resistance: colleagues began questioning my motives and threatening to exclude me from projects because I was no longer willing to put in dozens of hours of uncompensated labour. That's when I realized how deeply engrained and pathological the culture of overwork martyrdom is in education. Some colleagues wear their unpaid overtime like a kind of halo, displaying their burn-out symptoms like stigmata. Some people questioned whether I was betraying my core identity as a 'helper', asking if there would be anything left of me if I ceased giving constantly.

Perhaps this makes me sound selfish, but here's the thing, fellow educators, self-abnegation is not only an act of self-harm, it also serves to maintain our collapsing systems. As long as teachers are willing to keep giving, the system will keep taking, until there is nothing left to give. It doesn't matter how hard we try and how much we care, work will never love us back. When we fall apart from stress and exhaustion, we finally realize (a bit too late) just how replaceable and forgettable we were to our institutions. But every teacher burned out is a teacher lost to the coming education revolution: How are we supposed to rebuild education from the ground up if we're too exhausted, drained, overworked and run-down to fully function? Let me be clear: the revolution cannot be led by an army of zombies. We owe the future our self-preservation. Far from being selfish, self-love is perhaps the most altruistic contribution you can offer the world right now.

This brings me to my next point: the same system that disparages self-love as selfish also derides romantic love as superfluous. We're expected to accept that romantic love is a fleeting hormonal process that fades when it has fulfilled its core function, the (re)production of the next generation of labourers to integrate the productive apparatus. In fact, romantic love has the potential to be the most explosive of all revolutionary catalysts, under the condition it remains generous and open.

Loving romantically

What's the point of talking about romantic love in a book addressed to educators in times of collapse? If you think about it, educators aren't usually associated with healthy romantic passion. In children's shows, teachers are often caricatured as asexual, pleasant but passionless creatures. It's almost as if we expect teachers to have consumed their fleeting share of romance before they enter the profession, then wear the equivalent of a monk's outfit the minute they stand in front of a class. In movies that feature teachers implied to be sexually and romantically active, they are generally also portrayed as *bad* educators, with the implication that a teacher with vibrant, libidinous energy is at best incompetent, at worst a threat to their students.[9] Yet I don't see how educators can inspire students to their full humanity unless they are willing to embrace that same humanity for themselves.

George Orwell understood very well the explosive political potential of love, which is why the plot of his dystopian novel *1984* revolves around the system's sadistic efforts to break the loving bond between the two main protagonists, seen as the ultimate threat to totalitarian mind control.[10] The power of the space between two people whose words and bodies can entangle is a menace to everything the system feeds on to function – anxiety, passivity, compliance, and flight and flight reflexes. Genuine love between people is a revolutionary act of creative destruction that can bring everything into question. Slavoj Žižek muses on the term 'falling' in love, implying something both painful and exhilarating, likely to break things along the way.[11] This kind of love bursts through the comfortable numbness of capitalism and shocks us with a range of emotions and bodily presence we didn't know were possible. This is why, Žižek tells us, late capitalism has resorted to a far more insidious method to stamp it out than the crass torture used in *1984*: they have co-opted it, packaged it in app form, and promised the gentle burn of forever without the revolutionary process of falling. Swipe right, and you'll get all the good feelings without the revolutionary rapture.

But what exactly are we talking about when we speak of love in this way? Male critical pedagogues have traditionally shirked the subject of romantic love; when Freire talks of love, he speaks of a universal love for humanity, something akin to the Christian imperative to love thy neighbour.[12] Hooks and De Beauvoir were more explicit on the subject. De Beauvoir, not so much in her philosophy works, but in novels like her prize-winning *Les Mandarins*, described love as an existential affirmation of life, a process of birthing being in the person giving and receiving love.[13] Though she clearly saw the power of love at its most generous, she also warned of the dangers of falling into possession, obsession and self-abnegation, a theme fully developed in her rather depressing take on the aftermath of failed love, *The Woman Destroyed*.[14] According to De Beauvoir, love fails when self-love is absent, when the love of the other becomes essentialized and the loved object totemized; existential freedom is a precondition of generous love. This is epitomized by the character of Paule in *Les Mandarins*, who vows to respect her lover's existential freedom at the price of her own self-love and liberty, and winds up in a mental institution.

Hooks discussed erotic love in, among others, *Teaching Community* and *All About Love*.[15] I strongly disagree with hooks on certain points, particularly her contention that erotic love could be explored between (former) students and teachers. I don't think I need much space to convey why I think the mutual respect and equality required in romantic relationships cannot exist between a guiding figure and their pupil, no matter how progressive the teacher. Hooks' argument does nothing to assuage fears that libidinously energized teachers represent a threat to their students. I consider this more of an attempt at self-justification of her part than a genuine argument (De Beauvoir was also known to commit indiscretions with female students, but contrarily to hooks, never attempted to pass this off as justified).[16] With these reservations in mind, there is also much to learn from the way in which these women speak to the nature of love at its most powerful, what hooks termed 'true love':

> When it happens, individuals usually feel in touch with each others' core identity. Embarking on such a relationship is frightening precisely because we feel there is no place to hide. We are known. All the ecstasy that we feel emerges as this love nurtures us and challenges us to grow and transform.[17]

I didn't really believe the revolutionary power of love until I experienced it myself. As I explained in Chapter 3, I generally thought of love as a kind of abstraction, something that felt good, but remote, synonymous with solidarity. Romantic love was, to me, either a destructive and futile quest to fulfil childhood wants that manifests as pathological possessiveness, or a slow and steady arrangement that emerges from shared experiences, a compromise accommodation that makes life a little easier as we navigate the challenges of raising a nuclear family under capitalism, but never reaches the kind of plenitude described by hooks.

And yet, despite my skepticism, it happened to me much as it did for hooks: I wasn't looking for it, it hit me out of nowhere, was electrifying for a fleeting moment, and then ended just as abruptly as it had begun, without ever materializing into physical intimacy. We were both in conventional relationships at the time, with all the tragic pretences of ownership and the surrender of bodily and emotional autonomy this implies according to prevailing social norms, and yet, I couldn't have cared less: I didn't want to possess this person. I wasn't interested in who shared their bed or mine. This existed on an entirely different plane - emotions like jealousy and greed felt below it. On the day the connection ended, I felt none of the anger and bitterness that I might have experienced in the past when friendships ended. Instead, I felt transported by a forward push into the world, as if I had just opened my eyes to a whole new potential. Within minutes of our last words, I put pen to paper, and I haven't stopped writing since. This book, written years after the events, lies in the comet's tail of that encounter. The truth is that the fire was always within me - love merely takes away fear and set us free to be authentically ourselves. Far from dimming the lights on other attachments, the experience of being entirely seen and wanted for what I am and what I could become ignited a chain-reaction of deeper love in my other connections and friendships. It gave me the courage to reject the politics of ownership in romantic partnerships and to demand bodily and emotional autonomy. I found the strength to follow De Beauvoir in declaring that I shall not be owned, that my body is mine to do with as I please, and my soul has space for those who seek it out with love. I rejected the overpowering societal message that love is a linear process, repeating multiple times over a lifetime of heterosexual serial monogamy. Love at its best leaves a plenitude, a liberating presence, even after the materials elements of the loving relationships end, and that is politically revolutionary.

However, as De Beauvoir noted, people have been so conditioned to think of love as a possessive investment by what passes as romantic ideation in the public sphere that its liberating potential is hardly ever released.[18] Our culture industry feeds on portraying romantic love either as a unattainable ideal of perfection or as a jealous, obsessive endeavour that often ends in tragedy when the possessive drive takes over the ego. These portrayals of love tap into our deep fears of rejection and loneliness, manifesting as jealousy, resentment and entitlement. But as De Beauvoir forcefully argued, in order to be liberating, love can be neither exclusive, nor possessive. I'm not saying this is easy – as hooks noted, the unfortunate majority of us, consumed by trauma as we are, will never experience the plenitude of true love. So conditioned to think of love in a linear, physically intimate fashion, we may not even recognize it as it passes us with a glancing blow. But as hard as this is, the ability to love someone in all their otherness, respecting their existence as free beings is a great act of hope.

Loving in solidarity

The last manifestation of love I'd like to discuss is that portrayed by Freire, a passionate love for and belief in humanity that manifests as solidarity. I've talked extensively about solidarity, but what does that look like in practice? Despite what self-proclaimed social justice gurus might have you believe (if you buy their books and their courses), there are as many ways to practice imperfect solidarities are there are people on this planet. I've already discussed the theory of imperfect solidarities at length, but would like to close on my own experience, to share what I have learned over the past decade.

The impetus for solidarity

My unfortunate experience in the world of solidarity and development work never quelled my belief that an ethical and meaningful life involves, in one way or another, opening realms of possibilities for others. Particularly those for whom they have been narrowed or closed, by virtue of race, gender, economics, geography or other situational factors. Sometime in late 2012, as I was reaching a point of utter despondency, a couple of months before the 'Malaysian hotel' incident (Chapter 5), I found myself sharing my sorrows with a friend around a bowl of dumpling soup and a bottle of beer in a noodle bar in the South Korean city of Dongtan. With the PTSD taking hold and having lost a coherent sense of purpose and meaning, I questioned what I should do. My perspicacious friend asked me to describe, in a world where anything was possible, what meaningful and important engagement would look like. Strange as it sounds, the first thing that came to my mind was karate. Martial arts was pretty much the one thing that kept me sane during my tumultuous time in Asia. It was a practice that kept me close enough to my body that even though I was using opiates and alcohol more than was healthy, I never fell into an unstoppable cycle of addiction. I knew it could do so much to help people struggling with trauma all over the world, but my heart was especially committed to the fate of women and girls in places plagued by poverty, patriarchy and endemic gendered violence. This conversation in South Korea was the first time I mentioned the idea of opening a school of martial arts for girls. It was more of a thought than a plan, as I didn't have any idea where to start. So in that moment, I left the idea to float in the realm of possibilities.

Two wild years later, in a different bar, this time in The Netherlands, I was sharing a beer with Alex Whitcomb, a Zimbabwean friend. We were relaxing after a hefty boxing session, when I brought up the idea of a martial arts school for girls again. I knew of several martial artists who had gone to economically deprived places around the world to teach children for a month or two, but this wasn't, in my view, a very useful model of engagement. Either these places had no prior martial arts community, and any results achievement in these couple of months would be lost once the guest Sensei left, or they did, and the added value of having a White trainer come over for two months could be queried. Of course, it's always nice to have a guest Sensei; providing and receiving guest teachers is an expected practice in most dojos around the world. But I aimed to build something more durable and impactful than merely sharing technical knowledge and insights from practice. Being only a first dan black belt at the time of writing (having shirked the second dan exam for nine years due to the impact of fibromyalgia), I'm hardly in a position to share insights into karate practice anyways, so I would not even be the right person for that kind of job. What I wanted was to build a long-lasting engagement with a pre-existing martial arts community that has hitherto principally catered to boys, or to the better-off, and provide financial, logistical and technical support for the Senseis in this community to engage girls and women who would not otherwise have had access to martial arts. Alex thought about it, then suggested we try the concept out in his home town in Zimbabwe. It took a lot of convincing and bargaining with university management to acquire the funding and permission to take ten undergraduate students with us, but six months later, we landed in Zimbabwe with 1,500 euros worth of martial arts equipment, met on the other side by the president of the Zimbabwe Karate Union and our first local Sensei. And that's how the FairFight Foundation was born

Principles of imperfect solidarity in action

We are now an international foundation with a core of about fifteen volunteers, supporting over 100 girls in Zimbabwe, Zambia and

India; running karate schools in townships, community and school self-protection programmes that reach several hundreds of women; emotional resilience programmes; high school and university scholarships, and sponsorships for top athletes. For those interested, the story of FairFight has been told in various newspaper articles, blog posts and a documentary.[19] I'd like to dwell here on the principles of solidarity, as I understand them in relation to the work of the foundation – though this should be taken strictly as my personal analysis, not a reflection of the foundation's official policies.

The first application of the principle of imperfect solidarity I see in this case is that our programmes are designed to run in partnership with local charities and martial arts associations, and the partners are the ones making decisions about the martial arts curriculum and the follow-through of that curriculum, including gradings, competitions and other opportunities for the girls. How it works is that we discuss plans on a yearly basis with our local Senseis, approve a compromise budget between what they would ideally like and what we can realistically fundraise, and leave the utilization of that budget for the running of the programmes up to them. They run the karate classes entirely according to the standards of their own federations, with their own grading systems and competition calendar (though we do fund special FairFight tournaments too). We send high ranked martial artists to the programme sites from time to time to verify that the level of teaching and grading corresponds with the technical and pedagogical standards we expect, but otherwise, the local associations have full control over the programme.

As I understand it, our role is primarily to provide the funding, international network, targeted expertise and support these programmes need to function well and improve over time. Since we work in economically deprived areas, it's difficult for our local partners to fundraise for themselves. They do so to the best of their ability, with thriving local collaborations to provide some of the girls' needs such as sanitary pads and school books, but paying dojo rent and competition fees are beyond the means of local sponsors, so the FairFight Foundation provides the bulk of the funding for all our programmes, often in partnership with other national and international Europe-based foundations. Though some might see any kind of financial assistance from the Global North as creating inherently problematic power dynamics, I think it only fair that the funds come from Europe, given the imbalance of wealth between the Global North and the Global South. It is crucial for the operation of imperfect solidarities to bracket ideology, including progressive ideology, and discuss the benefits and drawbacks of intervention, financial or otherwise, with local partners. They may operate from a different ideological framework, perhaps from a more pragmatic standpoint, including cultural and historical factors that escape our understanding. It is especially problematic when the motivations of local partners are read through the lens of American social justice discourses that bear little resemblance to the social dynamics of the local culture. I see this happen too often, with deleterious consequences for collaboration and solidarity.

The fact is that pragmatic, imperfect decision-making is not popular among the ideologically motivated. Pragmatists can easily be criticized for not working hard enough to challenge colonialism and global capitalism. Some might suggest that an organization that lacks an explicit mandate to dismantle these structures would be de facto be colluding with the system. In dealing with this issue, I am reminded of Freire's words:

> When a word is deprived of its dimension of action, reflection automatically suffers as well; and the word is changed into idle chatter, into verbalism, into an alienated and alienating 'blah'.[20]

I fear that in seeking theoretical perfection, progressive advocates surrender the very possibility of solidarity, which requires action. Practitioners of imperfect solidarities need to stand firm in this belief, for the proponents of perfection have great mastery of words and wield them to scupper faith in the messy process of working together. And messy it is: since the beginning of our foundation's operations, we have come across numerous cultural misunderstandings, disappointing outcomes and disagreements. On occasions, these issues have taken on sufficiently daunting proportions that we have had to end some collaborations entirely. But on the whole, we've overcome most of the challenges we've encountered and built more resilient programmes as a result. I think we've been able to keep things afloat, first and foremost, by talking to each other to resolve issues. In such dialogues, it helps all parties to not take things personally, give the benefit of doubt, look for opportunities to grow from problems and search for a way forward that works, even if it feels like fumbling and the end result is less than perfect. The American critical pedagogue Paul Gorski said that 'good intentions are not enough', which is true; they must indeed be followed by action.[21] But when we start to believe that good intentions that do not translate into perfect actions count for nothing, we've already lost the momentum for change, frozen into theoretical discourse by an insurmountable fear of failure.

It's going to be a continuous learning process, and there will always be some tensions, difficulties and disappointments, especially as collapse tightens its hold on the communities we work with. Ultimately, I would say that the biggest success factor in what our foundation has achieved so far is the people we work with. First, their commitment to the process – we have been working with the same Senseis from inception in each of the programmes we run, and we have volunteers so dedicated that they return to the programme sites year in and year out. Second, their intuitive understanding of imperfect solidarities, which requires accepting good will, incremental progress and compromise as foundational values. I'm proud of our team and the incredible things we've built over the years, just as I'm proud of the girls and what they have achieved – certainly, I'm enchanted with every new coloured belt, medal and successful school exam, but beyond that, I'm just proud of the women they're becoming. No matter what choices they make later in life, I wish for them to take with them the confidence, community and self-respect they nurtured with us. It's hard, knowing that they face a collapse; they did absolutely nothing to engineer it, and what we teach them will only go so far in helping them when famine and floods strike. But this is absolutely no reason to give up on them, and perhaps all the more reason to commit.

Living

I'd like to close this book with some thoughts on what it will take to live with the knowledge of collapse. Learning and loving are two core ingredients to living meaningfully under the circumstances, but I will dwell now on the existential implications of what we're going through.

Living lightly

In his most famous book, the Czech author Milan Kundera announced the existential 'lightness' of being to be unbearable.[22] In the midst of the political turmoil that followed the Prague Spring in 1968, where the book is set, the protagonist finds himself struggling with existential freedom, juxtaposed against a context of political oppression and distinct unfreedom. The book asks: love, sex, relationships – do the choices we make matter, since there are no do-overs in life, and the end is all the same regardless? Kundera implies that we should seek heaviness, not as a depressive dark force to drag us down, but because commitment is the source of meaningful lives. I agree with Kundera on the desirability of meaningful, committed love, care and passionate beliefs that ground us. However, in times of collapse, I think it's worth revisiting the lightness of being.

I grew up with the notion that our actions would chase us into an elusive afterlife, that every act was counted by powers beyond my understanding. In theory, God can forgive all, but could you ever be sure that you had done enough to deserve that forgiveness? Losing my religion was a great relief, but also rather anxiety-inducing: Now what? I found myself confronted with the same question that has haunted existentialists since Nietzsche: If 'God' (in the biblical sense) is dead, then what?[23] We already saw (Chapter 3) that Ernst Becker identified 'immortality projects' as our secular solution to the fear of death, a way to restore some ballast to life and keep our feet on the ground. But as I stated in response, collapse threatens to take away our delusions of immortality and confronts us with the fact that in a near-enough future, there may be nothing but ashes left of our time on Earth. During the years of my environmental depression, I found that thought terrifying. What is the point of anything, if it's all to be burned to the ground? But then I gained a new appreciation for living lightly.

I personally find something incredibly liberating in the notion that the world will be engulfed in such chaos that our passing will go largely unnoticed, the sum total of our actions carried away with the storm. Christianity made the dubious promise that all our sins would be forgiven. Collapse makes the definitive promise that all our sins will be forgotten. By that, I don't mean that we should forget the criminals who led us here; if there is a hell on Earth, its chief punishment should be being remembered forever as the incarnation of evil in a world that has forgotten everything else. But for those of us who didn't finance climate denial or vote through planet-destroying legislation, collapse promises the sweet balm of amnesia. Perhaps this is a very personal take on it, but I feel like this liberates me to take more risks, to be wrong, to fail and to try again. Because even if I should be cursed and ostracized for poor decisions and outcomes which I incorrectly judged or make a fool of myself and experience ridicule and shame, this too shall pass, and this too will be buried in the ashes. This is, by no means, an invitation to selfish or nihilistic behaviour. As De Beauvoir noted in *The Ethics of Ambiguity*, no person can fulfil their human potential on that basis; they would not be lifted by lightness, but consumed by emptiness.[24] But the incredible lightness of being in times of collapse blesses our imperfection and frees us to let go.

When my grandmother died, it took about six months for my mother to clear out her house. I remember the smell of that old worker's house in the suburbs of Lille. It smelled of clutter – must gathered over years and years of accumulation, a sure sign of poverty-trauma. A couple of years ago, my parents moved into a smaller house for their retirement, and I saw my mother go through the same process with her own things; only she was still alive to witness it, and downsizing and decluttering were traumatic for her. She clung to knick-knacks, as if the fabric of existence itself were hidden in forty-year-old school textbooks and boxes of old baby clothes. This horrifies me. I recoil at the idea of leaving behind an overflowing collection of worthless junk. Cut me loose, please! For neither material possessions nor money will serve me when the flicker of consciousness dies among this collection of stardust from which I formed. I regularly go around my house with a bag and shed anything that is no longer of use to me, usually in a good enough state that it can be of use to someone else (as opposed to things left in cellars for decades, which are no longer of use to anyone). My sentimental items are in a small chest, such that if we were to evacuate in a flood or fire, I could take that one box with me and with it my most precious incarnated memories. I am by no means a minimalist; you need only walk through my front door to ascertain that. But like trauma reflexes and toxic people, objects that no longer serve us can be bid adieu.

In the age of collapse, living lightly is also a moral imperative, for the heaviness of our footprint sinks us into an ethically unsustainable position. We cannot live lightly, even with a mere suitcase and a laptop, if the moral weight of our air travel and dietary footprint pulls us down. This is a difficult and contentious point to make, as my research has shown that people find carnivorous diets and air travel particularly difficult to relinquish.[25] I don't have ready-made solutions for this, other than to be inspired by two-wheeled adventurers like Martijn Doolaard, who cycled from Amsterdam to Singapore, then from Vancouver to Patagonia over a three-year period.[26] Under our current societal model, this is a highly gendered and class-dependent pursuit – as a woman, I would never cross some of the places he went to by bike on my own out of sheer fear of assault. The capacity to earn a freelance living solely from a laptop and a Wi-fi connection anywhere in the world is also restricted to people with a certain kind of (usually expensive) education. Nonetheless, even with these caveats in mind, we could imagine a world in which all young people are given a year off, paid for by the state, to travel the world lightly, by rail, on their feet, bikes, horses, sail boats of whatever other forms of low-footprint transport they might find. Utopian, perhaps, but this is only limited by our social imaginations, not the boundaries of physics.

So here's to the lightness of being, may it make a world in collapse more bearable. It might also help to connect us more meaningfully with the present.

Living in the present

I think one of the reasons the mindfulness industry has done so well is that it promises a break from our persistent entanglement with trauma from the past and fears about the future. Of course, being inextricably enmeshed with capitalism, the mindfulness industry and its wellness industry twin can only offer a veneer of solutions in the form of slickly packaged, steeply priced relief. The fact remains that there is neither an app nor a supplement that can save you the hard work of acceptance necessary to living in the moment in times of collapse. What I mean by this is that our capacity to truly stay with this moment, fleeting as it is and as foreboding as the dark clouds on the horizon may be, depends on the outcomes of our complicated grieving process. We must first grieve and process the traumas that bind us to the past, then grieve and process the hopes we had for a certain kind of future that will now manifestly not come to pass. This is hard work, and as I showed in Chapter 3, many people will simply never get there, stuck in a paranoid-schizoid position of wishful simplicity and false hopes. I do not begrudge people who need external relief in pill form to escape the weariness of processing and healing, but speaking from experience, antidepressants and opiates draw an opaque veil between us and the full experience of reality, thereby preventing us from experiencing fear, horror, anxiety and sadness, but also joy, beauty meaning and companionship. In fact, following Bessel van der Kolk,[27] I think that the majority of people who require medication to function are not trying to escape the material present, but the imprint that trauma has left all over their perceived present like large ink blotches on a window pane.

The capacity to stay with the present moment has been, for me, the greatest gift along the healing journey. Some people will get there through deep reflexive practice, meditation and personal and collective grieving. I don't think I could have managed it entirely without the help of psychedelics. But the result is that I allow myself to feel the present more deeply, with all my senses. I particularly notice sounds. The blue trickle of piano notes and the black-and-white polka-dots of raindrops falling on my kitchen's skylight resonate more vibrantly. I notice the swaying of the bright orange calendulas, the tiny black wild bees buzzing around them and the particular shade of late summer light that falls upon them. The feelings of hunger and emptiness that plague modern society die down, the moment reveals its plenitude and whispers, 'This is enough.' Cliché as it sounds, I feel momentous gratitude for the gift of being here. As frightening as the future looks, I appreciate that I could literally not have been here at any other time – I should never have made it out of my mother's womb alive without the assistance of modern medicine, nor survived beyond my second birthday had I been born at any other moment in history. And if, by some miracle, I had made it, my daughter and I should both have died in childbirth. So life, with all of its traumas, pain, fears and the immensity and tragedy of collapse, is still a gift to be appreciated for every day that it brings. And if I should die swept away by disease, hunger, war or whatever other consequence of collapse, awful as that would be, every day until that moment has been given to me, a brief self-aware respite between various inert assemblages of molecules. Surely this is worthy of gratitude.

People ask me all the time whether it is wise to speak the truth about collapse, lest the fear of the future paralyse people into catatonic grief. It's hard for me to explain with the vocabulary of scientific rationality how existential wonder and awe have given me the courage to live with the truth. It sounds so esoteric to people hungry for easy fixes. They say: 'Tell me lies! Give me false hope! The truth is too painful'. But I promised real hope in the subtitle of this book, so we shall end this conversation with a reconsideration of what hope means for you, for me and for the young we have in our care.

Living with hope

I feel as though when people ask me for hope, what they're asking me is to tell them that this is all a bad dream, that they will soon wake up and that the prospect of collapse will retreat to the oneiric realm like a moody poltergeist. I think that what we have been passing off as hope in the Global North is actually a form of entitlement, the belief that we have a right to plunder and destroy at the expense of other living things, and a kind of delusion that defeats rationality. We cling to the belief that we can endlessly grow our destructive warfare against the very ground we stand on without harm to ourselves (though we are generally at ease with the notion that this might harm others in lands far away). This will perhaps upset well-meaning progressives who tend to view the Global South with quasi-paternalistic romanticism, but from my decades-long experiences of working with communities in the Global South, hope in those societies at large looks rather like a frantic search to attain the same destructive social and economic outcomes as the North. There are exceptions – indigenous communities, native conservancy groups and places like Bhutan and Costa Rica spring to mind. But ask anyone in the township of Mbare in Zimbabwe, or Chibolya in Zambia, or in the Musahar communities in India, and they will tell you that their wildest hope is to send their children to university so they may become lawyers, doctors or engineers and buy a big house, with a big car and the latest technological products, lifting their entire families into the middle-class living standards expected in the Global North. And surely, fairness dictates that they deserve this as much as anyone living in London or Paris.

But the hard, merciless truth is that nine billion people could not live like Americans *before* we destroyed the biosphere, due to simple resource constraints. As the productive capacity of the biosphere plummets, so will the planet's capacity to absorb American lifestyles. It's hard enough to speak the truth about collapse to people in the Global North, who have had so much for so long already. But there is an especially heartless brutality in taking away the promises of eternal economic growth, endless technological progress and boundless social ascension opportunities for people still struggling with poverty and oppression: it might trigger the existential despair and grief raised in Chapter 3.

If the end of the world as we know it is certain in one way or another, by virtue of the laws of physics, what kind of hope can possibly remain? The obvious answer is that the target of our hope has been misplaced the entire time: who should aspire to live like the Americans, with their gun-crazed, terrifyingly individualistic overconsumption and inequality? American lifestyles have always befuddled Europeans, who live longer, happier lives with an environmental footprint on average *half* of that of Americans.[28] But let us not delude ourselves – firstly, the planet can no more bear the weight of nine billion people living European lifestyles than American ones. With so many people and so few resources, we should all live closer to the average lifestyles of the rural folks of the Global South for the math to work out. This is an argument I raised in Chapter 1 – would we not all be happier and healthier if we returned to the simplicity of subsistence farm labouring? Unfortunately, the kinds of lives we have prepared for ourselves under collapse will not offer a gentle return to idyllic pastoralism. Pining for a return to the simplicity of a bygone past was a historically false hope because the bygone past was replete with death, especially the death of children and mothers, and came at the expense of women in almost every sedentary rural society on the planet. The lives of peasants throughout history have generally been prone to unpredictable curtailment, and that was with a stable climate with more or less reliable seasons. But with the destabilization of the climate, even if progressive dreams come true and we take medical and scientific progress with us back to the countryside in a kind of anarcho-syndicalist back-to-nature utopia, that rural idyl is now challenged by the loss of predictable seasons and monsoons that will threaten harvests. In other words, there will likely be hunger, and where there is hunger, there is also usually disease and death.

What then? I believe the answer is to see hope not as an outcome but as an ethical commitment. Hope is looking horror ahead in the face, and stating boldly that this will not do. Never were more powerful words uttered than the menacing phrase: 'I refuse!' The act of defiance transcends all worlds, possible and impossible, and births a world of meaning unto itself, a world of willful resistance. That meaning echoes through despair and calls us to carry on towards the darkness, as it did for Viktor Frankl in the inhumanity of Auschwitz, as it does for the Ukrainians facing down a madman and his nukes, as it will for us all contending with collapse. In this sense, true hope cannot be born from a vantage point of possession and comfort. There can be no hope that is merely contentment with the status quo. I think about the indigenous peoples of the world, whose cultures were and are still being deliberately erased with brutality that stretches the imagination, and about enslaved Africans who were denied the very existence of an existential for-itself. What monumental acts of defiance carried them into the present, through unspeakable horror and grief, against all odds? What momentous lessons on hope must we learn from their stories?

When I speak of a hopeful education for the end of the world as we know it, I'm not speaking about saving the old world; that ship has sailed. I'm speaking about showing young people how to learn, love and live against all odds, teaching them that there will be no resilience without defiance. And from that defiance, we can survive, and if thriving perhaps feels like a bridge too far for now, then we can pass the seeds of survival on until such time as they may once again sprout and flourish.

Trailing thoughts

It's autumn again, and even though it's still unseasonably warm, rain clouds chase away the last rays of summer sun and the courgette plants stretch out one last time before I put them to bed for the winter. Inside, the first spoils of the pumpkin harvest are roasting in the oven. It's six o'clock in the afternoon, and the air carries with it the lingering scent of new backpacks nonchalantly dumped in the carrier baskets of *oma fietsen*, traditional Dutch bicycles. Around the world, children will be coming home from school now. I think about the girls in Zimbabwe, walking two miles back to their township at dusk. I think about the girls in India, undoing the ties in their neatly plaited hair. Tomorrow, I will meet my new cohort of students, and will find the hallways of the university abuzz with life, the smell of coffee hanging in the air. Next week, I will stand in front of them and tell them the truth, though I suspect after the summer we've had, they already know. And the work will begin again, to carve ways out of despair, to commit to hope against the odds.

An email arrives in my inbox. It's from one of my former students. It reads:

> I hope that your plans whatever they might be for the upcoming academic year, come true and I want to say thank you again for all you have done! You have inspired me to become politically active as a climate activist and changed my life! Thank you so much for having those unpleasant talks and uncomfortable conversations about the climate crisis and our future.

I don't know if my students realize how much it makes me smile to receive these kinds of emails. For all the strangeness and errancy of my life, to know that this at least I did right. Still, I admit, I am sometimes afraid – who am I, a young(ish), female, partially abled, queer pedagogue to stake a claim in starting education revolutions, from my little corner of the planet? But then I remember that the world as we know is ending, and the new world will be brought about by people who look more like me than like the masters of the old world. So I take heart, tread lightly and forge ahead. Now it is with generous love that I release my pedagogies of collapse unto you, fellow educators, wherever you are. After despair and rage, I hope you find joy, fulfilment and hope in them. I hope we find each other, even if we never meet, in the worlds we build in our classrooms. And when the education revolution comes, may those worlds mesh into a future worth fighting for.

Notes

Introduction

1 Francis Fukuyama, *The End of History and the Last Man* (New York: Free Press, 1992).
2 Former French environment minister Yves Cochet is often credited with founding this movement: Yves Cochet, *Devant l'Effondrement, Essai de Collapsologie* (Paris, France: Les Liens Qui Liberent, 2019).
3 Virginie Servant-Miklos and Gera Noordzij, 'Investigating the Impact of Problem-Oriented Sustainability Education on Students' Identity: A Comparative Study of Planning and Liberal Arts Students', *Journal of Cleaner Production* 280, no. 2 (2021): 124846.
4 Luke Kemp, Chi Xu, Joanna Depledge, Kristie L. Ebi, Goodwin Gibbins, Timothy A. Kohler, Johan Rockström et al., 'Climate Endgame: Exploring Catastrophic Climate Change Scenarios', *Proceedings of the National Academy of Sciences* 119, no. 34 (2022): e2108146119.

Chapter 1

1 Jared Diamond, *Collapse, How Societies Choose to Fail or Succeed* (New York: Viking Press, 2011).
2 Cochet, *Devant l'Effondrement: Essai de Collapsologie* [Facing Collapse: a Collapsology Essay] (Paris, France: Broché, 2019).
3 Pablo Servigne and Raphaël Stevens, *Comment tout peut s'Effondrer: Petit Manuel de Collapsologie à l'Usage des Générations Suivantes* [How Everything Could Collapse: A Small Guide to Collapsology for the Use of the Next Generations] (Paris, France: Editions Seuil, 2015).
4 If you want to understand Jancovici's thinking on collapse, the best entry point is his new graphic novel, illustrated by French 'BD'

author Christophe Blain. Jancovici borrows from a graphic novel style very dear to Francophone culture (think Asterix and Tintin) to warn of impending cataclysm. Christophe Blain and Jean-Marc Jancovici, *Le Monde Sans Fin* [The Endless World] (Paris, France: Dargaud, 2022).

5   The term 'Anthropocene' was coined by Paul Crutzen, then used by the community of atmospheric scientists and geologists to describe the impact of humanity on the different planetary systems. Will Steffen, Jacques Grinevald, Paul Crutzen and John McNeill, 'The Anthropocene: Conceptual and Historical Perspectives', *Philosophical Transactions of the Royal Society A: Mathematical, Physical and Engineering Sciences* 369, no. 1938 (2011): 842–67.

6   Johan Rockström, Will Steffen, Kevin Noone, Åsa Persson, F. Stuart Chapin III, Eric Lambin, Timothy M. Lenton et al., 'Planetary Boundaries: Exploring the Safe Operating Space for Humanity', *Ecology and Society* 14, no. 2 (2009): 1–33.

7   Rosamund E. A. Almond, Monique Grooten, D. Juffe Bignoli and Tanya Petersen, *Living Planet Report 2022 – Building a Nature-Positive Society* (Gland: WWF, 2022), last accessed 15 October 2022, https://wwflpr.awsassets.panda.org/downloads/lpr_2022_full_report_1.pdf.

8   David L. Wagner, 'Insect Declines in the Anthropocene', *Annual Review of Entomology* 65 (2020): 457–80.

9   David Tickner, Jeffrey J. Opperman, Robin Abell, Mike Acreman, Angela H. Arthington, Stuart E. Bunn, Steven J. Cooke et al., 'Bending the Curve of Global Freshwater Biodiversity Loss: An Emergency Recovery Plan', *BioScience* 70, no. 4 (2020): 330–42

10 Rosamund E. A. Almond, Monique Grooten, and T. Peterson, *Living Planet Report 2020-Bending the curve of biodiversity loss* (World Wildlife Fund, 2020). https://pure.iiasa.ac.at/id/eprint/16870/1/ENGLISH-FULL.pdf.

11 Yinon M. Bar-On, Rob Phillips and Ron Milo, 'The Biomass Distribution on Earth', *Proceedings of the National Academy of Sciences* 115, no. 25 (2018): 6506–11.

12 Intergovernmental Science-Policy Platform on Biodiversity and Ecosystem Services. 'Global Assessment Report on Biodiversity and Ecosystem Services', *IPBES*, 2019.

13 Emily Elhacham, Liad Ben-Uri, Jonathan Grozovski, Yinon M. Bar-On and Ron Milo, 'Global Human-Made Mass Exceeds All Living Biomass', *Nature* 588, no. 7838 (2020): 442–4.

14 Jonathan Watts, *Concrete: The Most Destructive Material on Earth* (London: The Guardian, 25 February 2019), https://www.theguardian.com/cities/2019/feb/25/concrete-the-most-destructive-material-on-earth.

15 Hannah Ritchie, *Half of the World's Habitable Land Is Used for Agriculture* (Oxford: Our World in Data, 11 November 2019), https://ourworldindata.org/global-land-for-agriculture.

16 Hannah Ritchie and Max Roser, *Meat and Dairy Production* (Oxford: Our World in Data, November 2019). https://ourworldindata.org/meat-production.

17 Our World in Data, 'Share of Cereals Allocated to Food, Animal Feed or Fuel, 2013', https://ourworldindata.org/grapher/cereal-allocation-by-country?time=latest&country=~OWID_WRL.

18 Silva Junior, Celso H. L., Ana Pessoa, Nathalia S. Carvalho, Joao B. C. Reis, Liana O. Anderson and Luiz E. O. C. Aragao, 'The Brazilian Amazon Deforestation Rate in 2020 is the Greatest of the Decade', *Nature Ecology & Evolution* 5, no. 2 (2021): 144–5.

19 Arie Staal, Ingo Fetzer, Lan Wang-Erlandsson, Joyce H. C. Bosmans, Stefan C. Dekker, Egbert H. van Nes, Johan Rockström and Obbe A. Tuinenburg, 'Hysteresis of Tropical Forests in the 21st Century', *Nature communications* 11, no. 1 (2020): 1–8.

20 Most of the data on climate change used in this chapter comes from two sources NASA (https://climate.nasa.gov/evidence/) and the Intergovernmental Panel on Climate Change (https://www.ipcc.ch/). NASA conducts its own research on climate change, but also references serious studies published in peer-reviewed journals like *Nature and Science*, and the IPCC. The IPCC doesn't do its own research on climate, but brings together thousands of renowned scientists to put together a comprehensive overview of the consensus on climate science, published every three years under the aegis of the United Nations. The data on 2023 comes from the World Meteorological Organisation bulletin from 12 January 2024: https://wmo.int/media/news/wmo-confirms-2023-smashes-global-temperature-record.

21 United National Environment Programme, *Emissions Gap Report 2021: The Heat is on* (Nairobi: UNEP, 2021).

22 Make yourself a cup of tea (or a strong whiskey) and place summary of policymakers of the IPCC reports of 2021 and 2022 on your bed-side table for a late-night horror-show: IPCC, 2021: Summary for Policymakers. In: Climate Change 2021: The Physical Science Basis. Contribution of Working Group I to the Sixth Assessment Report of the Intergovernmental Panel on Climate Change [Masson-

Delmotte, V., P. Zhai, A. Pirani, S. L. Connors, C. Péan, S. Berger, N. Caud, Y. Chen, L. Goldfarb, M. I. Gomis, M. Huang, K. Leitzell, E. Lonnoy, J. B. R. Matthews, T. K. Maycock, T. Waterfield, O. Yelekçi, R. Yu and B. Zhou (eds.)]. Cambridge University Press, Cambridge, United Kingdom and New York, USA, 3–32, doi:10.1017/9781009157896.001.IPCC, 2022: Summary for Policymakers [H.-O. Pörtner, D. C. Roberts, E. S. Poloczanska, K. Mintenbeck, M. Tignor, A. Alegría, M. Craig, S. Langsdorf, S. Löschke, V. Möller and A. Okem (eds.)]. In: Climate Change 2022: Impacts, Adaptation and Vulnerability. Contribution of Working Group II to the Sixth Assessment Report of the Intergovernmental Panel on Climate Change [H.-O. Pörtner, D. C. Roberts, M. Tignor, E. S. Poloczanska, K. Mintenbeck, A. Alegría, M. Craig, S. Langsdorf, S. Löschke, V. Möller, A. Okem and B. Rama (eds.)]. Cambridge University Press. In Press.

23 Institute for Economics and Peace, *Over One Billion People at Threat of Being Displaced by 2050 Due to Environmental Change, Conflict and Civil Unrest* (Sydney: IEP, 2020).

24 Trust NASA to explain 'cooking to death' best. I don't know what's worse – the fact that he's explaining how humans will boil in their own skin due to climate change, or the fact that this is literally rocket science (research done at the NASA Jet Propulsion Lab). Alan Bluis, 'Too Hot to Handle: How Climate Change May Make Some Places Too Hot to Live', *NASA Jet Propulsion Laboratory*, 2022, https://climate.nasa.gov/ask-nasa-climate/3151/too-hot-to-handle-how-climate-change-may-make-some-places-too-hot-to-live/.

25 Kim Stanley Robinson, *Ministry for the Future* (London: Orbit, 2020).

26 Will Steffen, Johan Rockström, Katherine Richardson, Timothy M. Lenton, Carl Folke, Diana Liverman, Colin P. Summerhayes et al., 'Trajectories of the Earth System in the Anthropocene', *Proceedings of the National Academy of Sciences* 115, no. 33 (2018): 8252–9.

27 Thomas Chrowder Chamberlin, 'An Attempt to Frame a Working Hypothesis of the Cause of Glacial Periods on an Atmospheric Basis', *The Journal of Geology* 7 (1899): 550.

28 That Shell, Exxon and other large multinational oil conglomerates knew about climate change very early on and did everything in their power to hide the truth is now a well-established fact. I recommend the work of Naomi Oreskes in this regard: Naomi Oreskes and Eric M. Conway, *Merchants of Doubt: How a Handful of Scientists Obscured the Truth from Tobacco Smoke to Global Warming* (New York: Bloomsbury Press, 2010).

29 *A Plastic Ocean* was directed by Craig Leeson and released in 2016: https://aplasticocean.movie/. *Blue* Planet *II* is documentary series produced by the BBC Natural History Unit and released in 2017, narrated by David Attenborough: https://www.bbc.co.uk/programmes/p04tjbtx.

30 Laurent Lebreton, Boyan Slat, Francesco Ferrari, Bruno Sainte-Rose, Jen Aitken, Robert Marthouse, Sara Hajbane et al., 'Evidence that the Great Pacific Garbage Patch is Rapidly Accumulating Plastic', *Scientific Reports* 8, no. 1 (2018): 1–15.

31 Packaging is by far the largest source of industrial plastic waste, accounting for 141 million tonnes in 2015 far ahead of the next largest contributor, textiles, at a mere 42 million tonnes (https://ourworldindata.org/plastic-pollution).

32 Roger Harrabin and Tom Edgington, *Recycling: Where Is the Plastic Waste Mountain?* (London: BBC News, 1 January 2019), https://www.bbc.com/news/science-environment-46566795.

33 Erin McCormick, *Where Does Your Plastic Go? Global Investigation Reveals America's Dirty Secret* (London: The Guardian, 17 July 2019), https://www.theguardian.com/us-news/2019/jun/17/recycled-plastic-america-global-crisis.

34 Roland Geyer, Jenna R. Jambeck and Kara Lavender Law, 'Production, Use, and Fate of All Plastics Ever Made', *Science advances* 3, no. 7 (2017): e1700782.

35 Microplastics particles have in fact been found on top of Mount Everest. Freddie Wilkinson, 'Microplastics Found Near Everest's Peak, Highest Ever Detected in the World', *National Geographic*, 20 November 2020, https://www.nationalgeographic.com/environment/article/microplastics-found-near-everests-peak-highest-ever-detected-world-perpetual-planet. They have also been found at the bottom of the Marina Trench. Rebecca Morelle, *Mariana Trench: Deepest-Ever Sub Dive Finds Plastic Bag* (London: BBC News, 13 May 2019), https://www.bbc.com/news/science-environment-48230157.

36 Antonio Ragusa, Alessandro Svelato, Criselda Santacroce, Piera Catalano, Valentina Notarstefano, Oliana Carnevali, Fabrizio Papa et al., 'Plasticenta: First Evidence of Microplastics in Human Placenta', *Environment International* 146 (2021): 106274.

37 Dunzhu Li, Yunhong Shi, Luming Yang, Liwen Xiao, Daniel K. Kehoe, Yurii K. Gun'ko, John J. Boland and Jing Jing Wang, 'Microplastic Release from the Degradation of Polypropylene Feeding Bottles During Infant Formula Preparation', *Nature Food* 1, no. 11 (2020): 746–54.

38 Stefania D'Angelo and Rosaria Meccariello, 'Microplastics: A Threat for Male Fertility', *International Journal of Environmental Research and Public Health* 18, no. 5 (2021): 2392.

39 Erin McCormick, *It's All on Hold': How Covid-19 Derailed the Fight Against Plastic Waste* (London: The Guardian, 9 July 2020), https://www.theguardian.com/environment/2020/jul/09/covid-19-plastic-bans-california-new-york.

40 Tadele Assefa Aragaw, 'Surgical Face Masks as a Potential Source for Microplastic Pollution in the COVID-19 Scenario', *Marine Pollution Bulletin* 159 (2020): 111517.

41 The Ocean Cleanup is a project founded by Boyan Slat in The Netherlands with the aim of capturing ocean plastic through a complex system of nets. However, nets can only capture visible pieces of plastics: they cannot capture micro and nanoplastics, which make up the vast majority of ocean plastic. https://theoceancleanup.com/.

42 Rachel Salvidge, *'Forever Chemicals': What Are PFAS and What Risk Do they Pose?* (London: The Guardian, 8 February 2022), https://www.theguardian.com/environment/2022/feb/08/what-are-pfas-forever-chemicals-what-risk-toxicity.

43 *Dark Waters* is directed by Todd Haynes and was released in 2019.

44 Juliane Glüge, Martin Scheringer, Ian T. Cousins, Jamie C. DeWitt, Gretta Goldenman, Dorte Herzke, Rainer Lohmann, Carla A. Ng, Xenia Trier and Zhanyun Wang, 'An Overview of the Uses of Per- and Polyfluoroalkyl Substances (PFAS)', *Environmental Science: Processes & Impacts* 22, no. 12 (2020): 2345–73.

45 Agency for Toxic Substances and Disease Registry, *Perfluoroalkyl and Polyfluoroalkyl Substances (PFAS) in the U.S. Population* (Atlanta, GA: ATSDR, 2017), https://www.atsdr.cdc.gov/pfas/docs/PFAS_in_People.pdf.

46 Environmental Working Group, *PCFs: Global Contaminants* (Washington, DC: EWG, 2003), https://www.ewg.org/research/pfcs-global-contaminants.

47 Lauren Richter, Alissa Cordner and Phil Brown, 'Producing Ignorance Through Regulatory Structure: The Case of Per-and Polyfluoroalkyl Substances (PFAS)', *Sociological Perspectives* 64, no. 4 (2021): 631–56.

48 Shafali Garg, Pankaj Kumar, Vandana Mishra, Rosanne Guijt, Prabhjot Singh, Ludovic F. Dumée and Radhey Shyam Sharma, 'A Review on the Sources, Occurrence and Health Risks of Per-/Poly-fluoroalkyl Substances (PFAS) Arising from the Manufacture

and Disposal of Electric and Electronic Products', *Journal of Water Process Engineering* 38 (2020): 101683.
49 National Ocean Service, *What Is a Dead Zone?* (Washington, DC: NOAA), https://oceanservice.noaa.gov/facts/deadzone.html.
50 Vishwambhar Prasad Sati, 'The Environmental Issues in Ganges Basin', in *The Ganges* (Cham: Springer, 2021), 137–48.
51 CNN News, 'Hindus Throng to Ganges for Bathing Festival', *Reuters*, 3 January 2007, https://www.nbcnews.com/id/wbna16447201.
52 Geeta Pandey, *Covid-19: India's Holiest River Is Swollen with Bodies* (London: BBC News, 19 May 2021), https://www.bbc.com/news/world-asia-india-57154564.
53 Mila Luleva, 'Disappearance of the Aral Sea, One of the Biggest Man-made Disasters', *The Green Optimistic*, 18 August 2016, https://www.greenoptimistic.com/aral-sea/.
54 Leon Usigbe, *Drying Lake Chad Basin Gives Rise to Crisis* (New York: United Nations, 24 December 2019), https://www.un.org/africarenewal/magazine/december-2019-march-2020/drying-lake-chad-basin-gives-rise-crisis.
55 Intergovernmental Panel on Climate Change, *Global Warming of 1.5°C, Chapter 3: Impacts of 1.5°C of Global Warming on Natural and Human Systems* (Geneva, Switzerland: IPCC, 2018), https://www.ipcc.ch/site/assets/uploads/sites/2/2019/02/SR15_Chapter3_Low_Res.pdf.
56 Great Barrier Reef Foundation, 'Coral Bleaching', *GBFR*, 2022, https://www.barrierreef.org/the-reef/threats/coral-bleaching.
57 Malin L. Pinsky and Alexa Fredson, 'A Stark Future for Ocean Life', *Science 376*, no. 6592 (2022): 452–3, doi:10.1126/science.abo4259.
58 Food and Agriculture Organization of the United Nations, *The State of World Fisheries and Aquaculture – 2020* (Rome, Italy: FAO, 2020), https://www.fao.org/documents/card/en/c/ca9229en.
59 Dan Collyns, *Chinese Fishing Armada Plundered Waters Around Galápagos, Data Shows* (London: The Guardian, 17 September 2020, https://www.theguardian.com/environment/2020/sep/17/chinese-fishing-armada-plundered-waters-around-galapagos-data-shows.
60 Christopher Pala, 'China's Monster Fishing Fleet', *Foreign Policy*, 30 November 2020, https://foreignpolicy.com/2020/11/30/china-beijing-fishing-africa-north-korea-south-china-sea/.
61 Michael C. Melnychuk, Emily Peterson, Matthew Elliott and Ray Hilborn, 'Fisheries Management Impacts on Target Species Status',

Proceedings of the National Academy of Sciences 114, no. 1 (2017): 178–83, doi:10.1073/pnas.1609915114.

62. Leo Hornak, *Will There Be More Fish or Plastic in the Sea in 2050?* (London: BBC News, 15 February 2016), https://www.bbc.com/news/magazine-35562253.

63. James E. M. Watson, Danielle F. Shanahan, Moreno Di Marco, James Allan, William F. Laurance, Eric W. Sanderson, Brendan Mackey and Oscar Venter, 'Catastrophic Declines in Wilderness Areas Undermine Global Environment Targets', *Current Biology* 26, no. 21 (2016): 2929–34, doi.org/10.1016/j.cub.2016.08.049.

64. Hannah Ritchie and Max Roser, 'Land Use', *Our World in Data*, September 2019, https://ourworldindata.org/land-use.

65. Hannah Ritchie and Max Roser, 'Deforestation and Forest Loss', *Our World in Data*, 2021, https://ourworldindata.org/deforestation.

66. World Health Organisation, *Ebola, West Africa, 2014–2016* (Geneva: WHO, 2022), https://www.who.int/emergencies/situations/ebola-outbreak-2014-2016-West-Africa/.

67. World Health Organization, *Origins on the SARV-Cov-2 Virus* (Geneva: WHO, 30 March 2021), https://www.who.int/emergencies/diseases/novel-coronavirus-2019/origins-of-the-virus.

68. Justine Wise, *Bipartisan lawmakers Call for Global 'Wet Markets' Ban Amid Coronavirus Crisis* (Washington, DC: The Hill, 4 September 2020), https://thehill.com/homenews/senate/491948-bipartisan-lawmakers-call-for-global-ban-of-wet-markets-due-to-coronavirus/.

69. For example, in the case of pigs, see Agnieszka Ludwiczak, Ewa Skrzypczak, Joanna Składanowska-Baryza, Marek Stanisz, Piotr Ślósarz and Przemysław Racewicz, 'How Housing Conditions Determine the Welfare of Pigs', Animals 11, no. 12 (2021): 3484.

70. Thomas Erdbrink and Jasmina Nielsen, *Danish Leader Is Questioned Over 'Minkgate' Cull Driven by Covid Fears* (New York: New York Times, 9 December 2021), https://www.nytimes.com/2021/12/09/world/europe/denmark-mink.html.

71. BBC News, *Russia Anthrax Outbreak Affects Dozens in North Siberia* (London: BBC News, 2 August 2016), https://www.bbc.com/news/world-europe-36951542.

72. Rob Jordan, 'How Does Climate Change Affect Disease?', *Stanford Earth Matters Magazine* (Stanford, CA: Stanford University, 15 March 2019), https://earth.stanford.edu/news/how-does-climate-change-affect-disease#gs.3t1odz.

73 Rob Picheta, 'People in India Can See the Himalayas for the First Time in 'Decades', as the Lockdown Eases Air Pollution', *CNN Travel*, 9 April 2020, https://edition.cnn.com/travel/article/himalayas-visible-lockdown-india-scli-intl/index.html.

74 Travaglio, Marco, Yizhou Yu, Rebeka Popovic, Liza Selley, Nuno Santos Leal and Luis Miguel Martins, 'Links Between Air Pollution and COVID-19 in England', *Environmental Pollution* 268 (2021): 115115859, doi:10.1016/j.envpol.2020. 859.

75 Direction de l'information légale et administrative, 'Peut-on rouler en cas de pic de pollution ? [Is it Allowed to Drive During a Pollution Peak?]', *service-public.fr*, 17 June 2021, https://www.service-public.fr/particuliers/vosdroits/F10332.

76 South China Morning Post, *Singapore Haze Reaches Worst Level in Three Years as Indonesian Forest Fires Rage* (Hong-Kong, China: SCMP, 14 September 2019), https://www.scmp.com/news/asia/southeast-asia/article/3027263/singapore-haze-reaches-worst-level-three-years-indonesian.

77 World Health Organisation, *Health Consequences of Air Pollution on Populations* (Geneva, Switzerland: WHO, 15 November 2019), https://www.who.int/news/item/15-11-2019-what-are-health-consequences-of-air-pollution-on-populations.

78 World Health Organisation, *Ambient Air Pollution* (Geneva, Switzerland: WHO, 13 September 2018), https://www.who.int/teams/environment-climate-change-and-health/air-quality-and-health/ambient-air-pollution.

79 Union of Concerned Scientists, *Does Air Pollution – Specifically Tiny Atmospheric Particles (Aerosols) – Affect Global Warming?* (Cambridge, MA: UCSUSA, 23 August 2016), https://www.ucsusa.org/resources/does-air-pollution-affect-global-warming.

80 Y. T. Lo, Andrew J. Charlton-Perez, Fraser C. Lott and Eleanor J. Highwood, 'Detecting Sulphate Aerosol Geoengineering with Different Methods', *Scientific Reports* 6, no. 1 (2016): 1–9.

81 Naomi Klein, *This Changes Everything: Capitalism vs. the Climate* (New York: Simon & Schuster, 2014).

82 Naomi Klein, *This Changes Everything: Capitalism vs. the Climate* (New York: Simon & Schuster, 2014).

83 Adam Smith, *An Inquiry into the Nature and Causes of the Wealth of Nations* (London: W. Strahan and T. Cadell, 1776).

84 Karl Polanyi, *The Great Transformation* (New York: Farrar & Rinehart, 1944).

85 Max Weber, *The Protestant Ethic and the Spirit of Capitalism*, trans. Stephen Kalberg (Oxford: Oxford University Press, 2010).

86 Joseph A. Schumpeter, *The Theory of Economic Development: An Inquiry into Profits, Capital, Credit, Interest, and the Business Cycle*, trans. Redvers Opie (Cambridge, MA: Harvard University Press, 1934).

87 Jason W. Moore, *Anthropocene or Capitalocene? Nature, History, and the Crisis of Capitalism* (Oakland, CA: PM Press, 2016).

88 bell hooks, *Ain't I a Woman: Black Women and Feminism* (Boston, MA: South End Press, 1981).

89 Thomas Piketty, *Capital et Idéologie* (Paris, France: Seuil, 2019).

90 Lazario Gamio, Constant Méheu, Catherine Porter, Selam Gebrekidan, Allison McCann and Matt Apuzo, *The Ransom: Haiti's Lost Billions* (New York: New York Times, 20 May 2022), https://www.nytimes.com/interactive/2022/05/20/world/americas/enslaved-haiti-debt-timeline.html.

91 Jean-Marc Jancovici and Christophe Blain, *Le Monde Sans Fin* (Paris, France: Dargaud, 2021).

92 Jean-Marc Jancovici, *Dormez tranquille jusqu'en 2100 et autres malentedus sur le climat et l'énergie* [Sleep peacefully until 2100 and other misunderstandings on climate and energy] (Paris, France: Editions Odile Jacob, 2015).

93 This description of humanity was first proposed by Adam Smith in *Wealth of Nations* (1776), but was only adopted as a premise of economics during the Marginalist Revolution. Refer to Dimitris Milonakis and Ben Fine, *From Political Economy to Economics: Method, the Social and the Historical in the Evolution of Economic Theory* (London: Routledge, 2008).

94 Smith, *Wealth of Nations* (1776).

95 Ayn Rand, *Altas Shrugged* (New York: Random House, 1957).

96 Ayn Rand, interviewed by Johnny Carson in August 1967 on *The Tonight Show*. The full interview can be viewed on the video channel of the Ayn Rand Institute, https://www.youtube.com/watch?v=Z8vG8G2nulg&ab_channel=AynRandInstitute.

97 At the university, our reference for an introduction to cognitive psychology was Peter Gray's *Psychology*, 8th Edition (Worth, 2018).

98 Piotr Kropotkin, *Mutual Aid: A Factor of Evolution* (New York: Dover Publications, 2006).

99 Karl Polanyi, *The Great Transformation* (New York: Farrar & Rinehart, 1944).

100 Rutger Bregman, *Humankind: A Hopeful History* (London: Bloomsbury Publishing, 2021).
101 Robin Wall Kimmerer, *Braiding Sweetgrass: Indigenous Wisdom, Scientific Knowledge and the Teachings of Plants* (London: Penguin Books Ltd, 2020).
102 Leanne Betasamosake Simpson, *As We Have Always Done: Indigenous Freedom through Radical Resistance* (Minneapolis, MN: University of Minnesota Press, 2020).
103 The variations on the welfare state were first described by Gøsta Esping-Andersen, *The Three Worlds of Welfare Capitalism* (Princeton, NJ: Princeton University Press, 1990).
104 Jean-Marc Jancovici, *Dormez tranquille jusqu'en 2100 et autres malentedus sur le climat et l'énergie* [Sleep peacefully until 2100 and other misunderstandings on climate and energy] (Paris, France: Editions Odile Jacob, 2015).
105 Adam Curtis, *All Watched Over by Machines of Loving Grace* (London: BBC, 2011).
106 The history of the life and times of nineteenth-century economists can be found in Robert L. Heilbroner's *The Worldly Philosophers, The Lives, Times, and Ideas of the Great Economic Thinkers*, 7th Edition (New York: Simon & Schuster, 1999).
107 John Stuart Mill, *Principles of Political Economy* (New York: D. Appleton and Company, 1885), 480.
108 For the life and times of Karl Marx, refer to Gareth Stedman Jones, *Karl Marx: Greatness and Illusion* (Cambridge, MA: Belknap Press, 2016).
109 This historical anecdote was reported by Heibroner, *The Worldly Philosophers, The Lives, Times, and Ideas of the Great Economic Thinkers*, 7th Edition (New York: Simon & Schuster, 1999).
110 The story of the Marginalist Revolution is best told by Dimitris Milonakis and Ben Fine, *From Political Economy to Economics: Method, the Social and the Historical in the Evolution of Economic Theory* (London: Routledge, 2008).
111 As explained by Gøsta Esping-Andersen, *The Three Worlds of Welfare Capitalism* (Princeton, NJ: Princeton University Press, 1990).
112 Alfred Marshall, 'Principles of Economics, Eight Edition Complete and Unabridged', *Pantianos Classics*, 1920.
113 Jean-Baptiste Say, *Cours Complet d'Economie Politique Pratique* [Complete Course on Practical Political Economy] (Brussels, Belgium: J.P Méline, 1832).

114 Pierre-Yves Gomez, *L'Esprit Malin du Capitalisme* [The malignant spirit of Capitalism] (Paris, France: Desclée De Brouwer, 2019).

115 Alan Rappeport, *U.S. National Debt Tops $30 Trillion as Borrowing Surged Amid Pandemic* (New York: New York Times, 1 February 2022).

116 Jeremy Rifkin, *The Green New Deal: Why the Fossil Fuel Civilization Will Collapse by 2028, and the Bold Economic Plan to Save Life on Earth* (New York: St Martin's Press, 2019).

117 All data in the follow section is extracted from Hannah Ritchie, Max Roser and Pablo Rosado, 'Energy Production and Consumption', *Our World in Data*, 2020, https://ourworldindata.org/energy-production-consumption.

118 Oliver Milman, *Bitcoin Miners Revived a Dying Coal Plant – Then CO_2 Emissions Soared* (New York: The Guardian, 18 February 2022), https://www.theguardian.com/technology/2022/feb/18/bitcoin-miners-revive-fossil-fuel-plant-co2-emissions-soared.

119 Jon Huang, Claire O'Neill and Hiroko Tabuchi, *Bitcoin Uses More Electricity Than Many Countries. How Is That Possible?* (New York: New York Times, 3 September 2021), https://www.nytimes.com/interactive/2021/09/03/climate/bitcoin-carbon-footprint-electricity.html.

120 Javier Blas, Andreas Kluth, Liam Denning and Jonathan Ford, *Why Germany Will Regret Its Nuclear Plant Shutdowns* (Washington, DC: The Washington Post, 25 January 2022), https://www.washingtonpost.com/business/energy/why-germany-will-regret-its-nuclear-plant-shutdowns/2022/01/25/3ab42de8-7dad-11ec-8cc8-b696564ba796_story.html.

121 There is simply too much green growth discourse going round to reference it all, but a few choice examples include the United Nations Sustainable Development Goals (https://sustainabledevelopment.un.org/index.php?menu=1447), the president of the US, who, at the time of writing, is Joe Biden (https://joebiden.com/clean-energy/), the prime minister of the UK, who, at the time of writing, is Boris Johnson (https://www.gov.uk/government/speeches/pm-speech-at-the-un-general-assembly-22-september-2021) and the president of France, currently Emmanuel Macron, who called upon 150 citizens to draft a roadmap for overhauling the economy for climate, and then promptly tossed out the first point of order of said roadmap, which was ending economic growth (https://www.elysee.fr/emmanuel-macron/2020/06/29/le-president-emmanuel-macron-repond-aux-150-citoyens-de-la-convention-citoyenne-pour-le-climat).

122 Sarah Laville, *European Shipping Emissions Undermining International Climate Targets* (London: The Guardian, 9 December 2019), https://www.theguardian.com/environment/2019/dec/09/european-shipping-emissions-in-way-of-nations-meeting-paris-climate-targets.

123 Donella H. Meadows, Dennis L. Meadows, Jørgen Randers and William B. Behrens III, *The Limits to Growth* (Washington, DC: Potomac Associates, 1972).

124 Herman Daly, *Beyond Growth: The Economics of Sustainable Development* (Boston, MA: Beacon Press, 1997).

125 Tim Jackson, *Prosperity without Growth: Foundations for the Economy of Tomorrow*, 2nd edition (London: Routledge, 2016).

126 Full data on how many planet-equivalents we consume per year can be found at the Global Footprint Network (https://www.footprintnetwork.org/).

127 Mark O'Connell, *Why Silicon Valley Billionaires are Prepping for the Apocalypse in New Zealand* (London: The Guardian, 15 February 2018), https://www.theguardian.com/news/2018/feb/15/why-silicon-valley-billionaires-are-prepping-for-the-apocalypse-in-new-zealand.

128 Jayashree Nandi, *Surface Temperature Tops 60°C in Parts of North India, Satellite Images Show* (New Delhi, India: Hindustan Times, 1 May 2022), https://www.hindustantimes.com/india-news/surface-temp-tops-60-c-satellite-images-show-101651343166998.html.

129 David Marchese, *This Eminent Scientist Says Climate Activists Need to Get Real* (New York: New York Times, 22 April 2022), https://www.nytimes.com/interactive/2022/04/25/magazine/vaclav-smil-interview.html.

130 West Virginia et al., v. Environmental Protection Agency et al., No. 20-1530, U.S. (2022), Supreme Court of the United States, decided 30 June 2022.

131 B. D. Zaleha and A. Szasz, 'Why Conservative Christians Don't Believe in Climate Change', *Bulletin of the Atomic Scientists* 71, no. 5 (2015): 19–30.

132 Cynthia Weber, *International Relations Theory, A Critical Introduction*, 5th edition (London: Routledge, 2021).

133 Roy Smith, Imad El-Anis and Christopher Farrands, *International Political Economy in the 21st Century: Contemporary Issues and Analyses* (London: Routledge, 2017).

134 Esteban Ortiz-Ospina and Diana Beltekian, 'Trade and Globalization: Exports and Imports in Real Dollars', *Our World* *in Data*, 2 June 2022, https://ourworldindata.org/trade-and-globalization#exports-and-imports-in-real-dollars.

135 Esteban Ortiz-Ospina and Diana Beltekian, 'Trade and Globalization: South-South Trade is Becoming Increasingly Important', *Our World in Data*, 2016, https://ourworldindata.org/trade-and-globalization#south-south-trade-is-becoming-increasingly-important.

136 Esteban Ortiz-Ospina, 'Does Trade Cause Growth?', *Our World in Data*, 22 October 2018, https://ourworldindata.org/trade-and-econ-growth.

137 Branko Milanovic, *Global Inequality: A New Approach for the Age of Globalization* (Cambridge, MA: Belknap Press, 2018).

138 United Nations Conference on Trade and Development, 'Shipping during COVID-19: Why Container Freight Rates have Surged', *UNCTAD*, 23 April 2021, https://unctad.org/news/shipping-during-covid-19-why-container-freight-rates-have-surged.

139 Jared Diamond, *Collapse, How Societies Choose to Fail or Succeed* (New York: Viking Press, 2011).

Chapter 2

1 The historical account presented in this chapter is sourced from the following works: Lene Rachel Andersen and Tomas Björkman, *The Nordic Secret, a European History of Beauty and Freedom* (Copenhagen, DK: Fri Tanke, 2017); Jeffrey R. Di Leo, *Higher Education Under Late Capitalism* (New York: Palgrave McMillan, 2017); Dennis Lawton and Peter Gordon, *A History of Western Educational Ideas* (London: Woburn Press, 2005); Françoise Mayeur, *Histoire de l'Enseignement et de l'Education III. 1789–1930* (Paris, France: Editions Perrin, 1981); William J. Reese and John L. Rury, *Rethinking the History of American Education* (New York: Palgrave McMillan, 2008).

2 Max Roser and Esteban Ortiz-Ospina, 'Global Education', *Our World in Data*, 2016, last accessed 12 January 2023, https://ourworldindata.org/global-education.

3 Max Roser and Esteban Ortiz-Ospina, 'Global Education', *Our World in Data*, 2016, last accessed 12 January 2023, https://ourworldindata.org/global-education.

4 Tessa Benveniste, Samantha Disbray and John Guenther, *A Brief Review of Literature on Boarding School Education for Indigenous*

Students and Recent Australian Media Coverage of the Issue (The Cooperative Research Centre for Remote Economic Participation: Remote Education Systems, discussion paper, 2014).

5   Universal Declaration of Human Rights, United Nations General Assembly Resolution 217A, 10 December 1948, article 26.
6   John Dewey, *Democracy and Education* (New York: MacMillan, 1916).
7   Universal Declaration of Human Rights, United Nations General Assembly Resolution 217A, 10 December 1948, article 26..
8   Tessa Benveniste, Samantha Disbray and John Guenther, *A Brief Review of Literature on Boarding School Education for Indigenous Students and Recent Australian Media Coverage of the Issue* (The Cooperative Research Centre for Remote Economic Participation: Remote Education Systems, discussion paper, 2014).
9   Brown v. Board of Education, 347 U.S. 483 (1954).
10 Maya Angelou, *I Know Why the Caged Bird Sings* (New York: Ballentine Books, 1969).
11 Bell hooks, *Teaching Community: A Pedagogy of Hope* (New York: Routledge, 2003).
12 Kieth Meatto, 'Still Separate, Still Unequal: Teaching about School Segregation and Educational Inequality', *The New York Times*, 2 May 2019, https://www.nytimes.com/2019/05/02/learning/lesson-plans/still-separate-still-unequal-teaching-about-school-segregation-and-educational-inequality.html.
13 Erin Aubry Kaplan, 'School Choice Is the Enemy of Justice', *The New York Times,* 14 August 2018, https://www.nytimes.com/2018/08/14/opinion/charter-schools-desegregation-los-angeles.html.
14 Ta-Nehisi Coates, *Between the World and Me* (New York: Spiegel & Grau, 2005); Ibram X. Kendi, *How to be and Anti-Racist* (New York: One World, 2019).
15 Charlotte Brontë, *Jane Eyre* (London: Penguin, 2006).
16 Joan Lindsey, *Picnic at Hanging Rock* (Melbourne: F.W. Cheshire, 1967).
17 Michelle Jones and Lori Record, 'Magdalene Laundries: The First Prisons for Women in the United States', *Journal of the Indiana Academy of the Social Sciences* 17, no. 1 (2014): 166–79.
18 Ed O'Loughlin, 'Ireland's Last 'Magdalene Laundry' Will Become a Memorial', *The New York Times*, 21 March 2022, https://www.nytimes.com/2022/03/31/world/europe/ireland-magdalene-laundry-women-abuse.html.

19 UNICEF, 'Education', *UNICEF Data: Monitoring the Situation of Children and Women,* June 2022, last accessed 12 January 2023, https://data.unicef.org/topic/gender/gender-disparities-in-education/.

20 John Self, 'The School that Rules Britain', *BBC Culture*, 14 April 2021, last accessed 12 January 2023, https://www.bbc.com/culture/article/20210413-the-school-that-rules-britain.

21 Amounts vary per country. In the United States the average is 12,350 US dollars (Katherine Hutt Scott, 'How Much Does Private School Cost?', *News*, 14 September 2021, last accessed 13 January 2023, https://www.usnews.com/education/k12/articles/how-much-does-private-school-cost). In The Netherlands, the cost varies between 3,000 euros for part-subsidized schools to 26,000 euros for completely private schools (Young Expat Services, 'Going Local: Dutch Public Schools for Expat Families', *I Amsterdam,* 3 October 2022, last accessed 13 January 2023, https://www.iamsterdam.com/en/live-work-study/living/education-family/dutch-public-schools-for-expat-families). Top boarding schools in Switzerland cost up to 150,000 euros per year (Studying in Switzerland, 'How Much Do Swiss Boarding Schools Cost?', *Study in Switzerland*, 7 March 2022, last accessed 13 January 2023, https://studyinginswitzerland.com/swiss-boarding-schools-cost/), top boarding schools in the US cost up to 60,000 dollars per year (Erin McDowell, 'The 50 Most Expensive Top Boarding Schools in America', *Business Insider*, 11 October 2019, last accessed 13 January 2023, https://www.businessinsider.nl/most-expensive-top-boarding-schools-in-america-2019-10/), while top boarding schools in India charge up to 1,000 euros per month (UniApply, 'Boarding Schools in India', last accessed 13 January 2023, https://www.uniapply.com/schools/boarding-schools-in-india/).

22 The plight of lower-class Dutch children in the public education system was documented in Sarah Sylbing, Ester Gould and Daan Bol's docu-series 'Klassen', released on the Dutch public broadcast channel in 2020 (NPO, 2020). The film-makers reveal shocking statistics, like the fact that 70 per cent of lower-class children are under-evaluated by their teachers, compared with their actual test scores.

23 Oxford Union, 'The Class System is Static/Lisa McKenzie', 21 January 2021, last accessed 13 January 2023, https://www.youtube.com/watch?v=oyL1tu0IiOM&ab_channel=OxfordUnion.

24 Oskar Negt and Alexander Kluge, *Public Sphere and Experience, Analysis of the Bourgeois and Proletarian Public Sphere* (New York: Verso, 2016), 26.

25 Stefan Collini, *What Are Universities for?* (London: Penguin UK, 2012).
26 Friedrich Hayek, *The Road to Serfdom* (Chicago, IL: University of Chicago Press, 1944).
27 David Harvey, *A Brief History of Neoliberalism* (Oxford: Oxford University Press, 2007).
28 J. Barry Riddell, 'Things Fall Apart Again: Structural Adjustment Programmes in SubSaharan Africa', *The Journal of Modern African Studies* 30, no. 1 (1992): 53–68.
29 Christoffer Green-Pedersen, 'New Public Management Reforms of the Danish and Swedish Welfare States: The Role of Different Social Democratic Responses', *Governance* 15, no. 2 (2002): 271–94.
30 The hold of Gary Becker's theories on educational policymaking is analysed in Thomas Piketty, *The Economics of Inequality* (Cambridge, MA: Harvard University Press, 2015).
31 In the US: Melanie Hanson, 'Average Student Loan Debt by Year', *Education Data Initiative*, 19 January 2022, last accessed 13 January 2023, https://educationdata.org/average-student-loan-debt-by-year). In the UK: House of Commons Library, 'Student Loan Statistics', *UK Parliament*, 2 December 2022, last accessed 13 January 2023, https://commonslibrary.parliament.uk/research-briefings/sn01079/). In the Netherlands: Centraal Bureau voor Statistieken, 'Studieschuld blijft toenemen', *CBS,* 15 September 2022, last accessed 13 January 2023, https://www.cbs.nl/nl-nl/nieuws/2022/37/studieschuld-blijft-toenemen).
32 Kenneth J. Saltman, 'The Austerity School: Grit, Character and the Privatization of Public Education', *Symploke* 22 (2014): 41–57.
33 Susan Strange, *The Retreat of the State, the Diffusion of Power in the World Economy* (Cambridge: Cambridge University Press, 1996).
34 Charlie Chaplin, *Modern Times* (U.S.A.: United Artists, 1936).
35 Jack Jenning and Diane Stark Rentner, 'Ten Big Effects of the No Child Left Behind Act on Public Schools', *Phi Delta Kappan* 88, no. 2 (2006): 110–113.
36 Colin Richard, 'More Outstanding Nonsense: a critique of Ofsted criteria', *Forum* 57, vol 2 (2015): 233–238.
37 Katherine Sellgren, 'Ofsted Admits Adding to "teach-to-the-Test" Mentality', *BBC News,* 18 September 2018, last accessed 13 January 2023, https://www.bbc.com/news/education-45560165; Richard Adams, 'Ofsted Plans Overhaul of Inspections to Look Beyond Exam Results', *The Guardian,* 16 January 2019, last accessed 13 January

2023, https://www.theguardian.com/education/2019/jan/16/ofsted-to-reform-school-inspections-in-bid-to-tackle-off-rolling.

38 Maruša Hauptman Komotar, 'Discourses on Quality and Quality Assurance in Higher Education from the Perspective of Global University Rankings', *Quality Assurance in Education* 28, no. 1 (2020): 78–88.

39 European Commission, 'The Bologna Process and the European Higher Education Area', *European Education Area*, last accessed 13 January 2023, https://education.ec.europa.eu/education-levels/higher-education/inclusive-and-connected-higher-education/bologna-process.

40 In the US: Agnes Walton and Nic Pollock, 'Empty Classrooms, Abandoned Kids: Inside America's Great Teacher Resignation', *The New York Times*, 18 November 2022, last accessed 12 January 2023, https://www.nytimes.com/2022/11/18/opinion/teachers-quitting-education-crisis.html; In the UK: PA Media, '44% of Teachers in England Plan to Quit Within Five Years', *The Guardian*, 11 April 2022, last accessed 13 January 2023, https://www.theguardian.com/education/2022/apr/11/teachers-england-plan-to-quit-workloads-stress-trust; in the Netherlands, Joëlle Poortvliet, 'No Region Without a Teacher Shortage', *AOB*, 11 February 2022, last accessed 13 January 2023, https://www.aob.nl/en/nieuws/geen-regio-meer-zonder-lerarentekort/.

41 Lene Rachel Andersen and Tomas Björkman, *The Nordic Secret, a European History of Beauty and Freedom* (Copenhagen, DK: Fri Tanke, 2017).

42 Statistics Denmark, 'Population', last accessed 16 September 2023, https://www.dst.dk/en/Statistik/emner/borgere/befolkning.

43 Paulo Freire, *The Pedagogy of the Oppressed*, 50th Anniversary Edition, trans. Donaldo Macedo (London: Bloomsbury, 2018).

44 I have written extensively about Oskar Negt and the German Critical Pedagogy movement in Virginie Servant, *Revolutions and Re-iterations, an Intellectual History of Problem-Based Learning* (Rotterdam, NL: Erasmus University Rotterdam, 2016).

45 Paulo Freire, *The Pedagogy of the Oppressed*, 50th Anniversary Edition, trans. Donaldo Macedo (London: Bloomsbury, 2018).

46 Oskar Negt and Alexander Kluge, *Public Sphere and Experience, Analysis of the Bourgeois and Proletarian Public Sphere* (New York: Verso, 2016).

47 Oskar Negt, *Soziologische Phantasie und Exemplarisches Lernen: zur Theorie und Praxis der Arbeiterbildung* (Frankfurt am Main, Germany: Europäische Verlagsanstalt, 1971).

48 C. Wright Mills, *The Sociological Imagination* (Oxford: Oxford University Press, 1959).

49 I have told the history of Roskilde University with extensive details in Virginie Servant, *Revolutions and Re-iterations, an Intellectual History of Problem-Based Learning* (Rotterdam, NL: Erasmus University Rotterdam, 2016).

50 Anders Siig Andersen and Simon B. Heilesen, *The Roskilde Model: Problem-Oriented Learning and Project Work* (New York: Springer, 2015).

51 Critical Edge Alliance: An Alliance of Critical Alternative and Innovative Universities Across the World, last accessed 13 January 2023, https://www.criticaledgealliance.com/.

52 Paulo Freire, *The Pedagogy of the Oppressed*, 50th Anniversary Edition, trans. Donaldo Macedo (London: Bloomsbury, 2018).

53 Ashlee Cunsolo and Neville R. Ellis, 'Ecological Grief as a Mental Health Response to Climate Change-Related Loss', *Nature Climate Change* 8, no. 4 (2018): 275–81.

54 Elisabeth Kübler-Ross, *On Death and Dying* (New York: Scribner, 1969).

55 For academic critique of Kübler-Ross' work, refer to Charles A. Corr, 'Should We Incorporate the Work of Elisabeth Kübler-Ross in Our Current Teaching and Practice and, If So, How?', *Journal of Death and Dying* 83, no. 4 (2021), doi: 10.1177/0030222819865397.

56 World Health Organisation, *Pandemic Influenza Preparedness in WHO Member States* (Geneva: World Health Organisation, 2019).

Chapter 3

1 Virginie Servant-Miklos and Gera Noordzij, 'Investigating the Impact of Problem-Oriented Sustainability Education on Students' Identity: A Comparative Study of Planning and Liberal Arts Students', *Journal of Cleaner Production* 280 (2021): 124846.

2 Virginie Servant-Miklos, 'Environmental Education and Socio-Ecological Resilience in the COVID-19 Pandemic: Lessons from Educational Action Research', *Environmental Education Research* 28, no. 1 (2022): 18–39.

3 The images from the James Webb telescope are available on the NASA website, last accessed 7 October 2022, https://www.nasa.gov/webbfirstimages.

4 Simone de Beauvoir, *Pour une Morale de l'Ambiguïté* (Paris, France: Gallimard, 1947).

5 Paulo Freire, *The Pedagogy of the Oppressed*, 50th Anniversary Edition, trans. Donaldo Macedo (London: Bloomsbury, 2018).

6 *Don't Look Up* is an American apocalyptic political satire of the climate crisis released in 2021, directed by Adam McKay, starring Leonardo Di Caprio and Jennifer Lawrence.

7 Eddie Harmon-Jones and Judson Mills, 'An Introduction to Cognitive Dissonance Theory and an Overview of Current Perspectives on the Theory', in *Cognitive Dissonance: Reexamining a Pivotal Theory in Psychology*, ed. Eddie Harmon-Jones (American Psychological Association), 3–24, https://doi.org/10.1037/0000135-001.

8 Referring to renowned Japanese tidying expert, Marie Kondo, *The Life-Changing Magic of Tidying up* (London: Vermilion, 2014).

9 Susanne Stoll-Kleemann, Tim O'Riordan and Carlo C. Jaeger, 'The Psychology of Denial Concerning Climate Mitigation Measures: Evidence from Swiss Focus Groups', *Global Environmental Change* 11, no. 2 (2001): 107–17.

10 *The Game Changers* is a documentary on veganism and sports released in 2018, directed by Louie Psihoyos, and produced by vegan celebrities including director James Cameron, actor and former governor of California Arnold Schwarzenegger, tennis star Novak Djokovic, and Formula 1 driver Lewis Hamilton, among others.

11 Yotam Ottolenghi is an Israeli-British chef renowned for bringing middle-eastern flavours to western tables. In 2020, he published a vegetarian cook-book with Ixta Belfridge that finally converted me to vegetarian cooking. Yotam Ottolenghi and Ixta Belfridge, *Flavour* (London: Ebury Press, 2020).

12 For an overview of heuristics and biases, refer to Peter O. Gray, *Psychology*, 8th Edition (New York: McMillan Learning, 2018).

13 Daniel Friedman, Kai Pommerenke, Rajan Lukose, Garrett Milam and Bernardo A. Huberman, 'Searching for the Sunk Cost Fallacy', *Experimental Economics* 10, no. 1 (2007): 79–104.

14 The original studies on functional fixedness in problem-solving were run out of Stanford University in the 1950s: Robert E. Adamson, 'Functional Fixedness as Related to Problem Solving: A Repetition of Three Experiments', *Journal of Experimental Psychology* 44, no. 4 (1952): 288.

15 The four biases described in this section all come from this study: Dominic Johnson and Simon Levin, 'The Tragedy of Cognition:

Psychological Biases and Environmental Inaction', *Current Science* 97, no. 11 (2009): 1593–603.

16 During the pandemic, the government handed KLM, the Dutch national airline, a 1-billion-euro support package. As the national carrier, KLM is partly owned by the Dutch government, last accessed 6 October 2022, https://www.rijksoverheid.nl/onderwerpen/staatsdeelnemingen/vraag-en-antwoord/financiele-steun-aan-klm; during the first three months of the Ukraine War which began in February 2022, the Dutch oil giant Shell made three times the amount of profit compared with the previous year – Tom Wilson, 'Shell Makes Record Profits as Ukraine War Shakes Energy Markets', *Financial Times*, 5 May 2022, last accessed 6 October 2022, https://www.ft.com/content/b2713bd1-afa5-4638-ab2d-be0c4e8a7ab7.

17 Marilynn B. Brewer, 'In-group Bias in the Minimal Intergroup Situation: A Cognitive-Motivational Analysis', *Psychological Bulletin* 86, no. 2 (1979): 307–24.

18 Slavoj Žižek, *Living in the End Times* (London: Verso, 2011).

19 Alex Miller, 'Superstar Communist Slavoj Zizek Is The Most Dangerous Philosopher in the West', *Vice*, last accessed 7 October 2022, https://www.youtube.com/watch?v=XS_Lzo4S8IA&ab_channel=VICE.

20 Jerome Neu (ed.), *The Cambridge Companion to Freud* (Cambridge: Cambridge University Press, 2006).

21 Žižek's psychoanalysis owes more to Jacques Lacan than Sigmund Freud, but the distinction is not relevant for the sake of the arguments made in this chapter.

22 Slavoj Žižek, *Living in the End Times* (London: Verso, 2011), xi–xii.

23 Donella H. Meadows, Dennis L. Meadows, Jørgen Randers and William W. Behrens III, *The Limits to Growth* (Falls Church, VA: Potomac Associates, 1972).

24 Thomas Piketty, *Capital et Idéologie* (Paris, France: Seuil, 2019), 780.

25 Slavoj Žižek, *Living in the End Times* (London: Verso, 2011), 119.

26 Rutger Bregman, *Utopia for Realists and How We Can Get There* (London: Bloomsbury Publishing, 2018).

27 Thomas Kaplan, 'Bernie Sanders Proposes a Wealth Tax: "I Don't Think That Billionaires Should Exist"', *The New York Times*, 24 September 2019, last accessed 8 October 2022, https://www.nytimes.com/2019/09/24/us/politics/bernie-sanders-wealth-tax.html.

28. My initiation into the work of Melanie Klein and Object Relations Theory came from Robert Caper, *A Mind of One's Own: A Kleinian View of Self and Object* (London and New York: Routledge, 1999).
29. Melanie Klein, *The Collected Works of Melanie Klein, Vol. 2. The Psychoanalysis of Children* (London: Routledge, 2017).
30. Bruno Latour, *Facing Gaia, Eight Lectures on the New Climatic Regime* (Cambridge: Polity Press, 2017).
31. Renée Lertzman, *Environmental Melancholia, Psychoanalytic Dimensions of Engagement* (Hove: Routledge, 2015).
32. Robert Caper, *A Mind of One's Own: A Kleinian View of Self and Object* (London and New York: Routledge, 1999), 101.
33. Sigmund Freud, 'Mourning and Melancholia', *The Journal of Nervous and Mental Disease* 56, no. 5 (1922): 543–5.
34. Pierre Bourdieu, *Language and Symbolic Power* (Cambridge, MA: Harvard University Press, 1991).
35. Pierre Bourdieu, *Other Words: An Essay Towards a Reflexive Sociology* (Stanford, CA: Stanford University Press, 1990).
36. Anthony Giddens, *Modernity and Self-identity: Self and Society in the Late Modern Age* (Stanford, CA: Stanford University Press, 1991).
37. Martin Heidegger, *Being and Time*, trans. John Macquarrie and Edward Robinson (New York: Harper Collins, 2008).
38. Friedrich Nietzsche, *Thus Spoke Zarathustra, a Book for Everyone and No One* (London: Penguin Classics, 1961).
39. For a history of the development of individualism during the 'German Spring' and the Romantic counter-revolution, refer to Lene Rachel Andersen and Tomas Björkman, *The Nordic Secret, a European Story of Beauty and Freedom* (Copenhagen, DK: Det Andersenske Forlag, 2017).
40. United Nations General Assembly, *Universal Declaration of Human Rights* (Paris, France: 217 [III] A, 1948).
41. John Naughton, 'China is Taking Digital Control of its People to Chilling Lengths', *The Guardian*, 27 May 2018, last accessed 8 October 2022, https://www.theguardian.com/commentisfree/2018/may/27/china-taking-digital-control-of-its-people-to-unprecedented-and-chilling-lengths.
42. The Times of India, *Honour Killings: More than 300 Cases in Last Three Years* (Delhi, India: The Times of India, 22 September 2018), last accessed 8 October 2022, https://timesofindia.indiatimes.com/india/honour-killings-more-than-300-cases-in-last-three-years/articleshow/65908947.cms.

43 Virginie Servant-Miklos and Gera Noordzij, 'Investigating the Impact of Problem-Oriented Sustainability Education on Students' Identity: A Comparative Study of Planning and Liberal Arts Students', *Journal of Cleaner Production* 280 (2021): 124124846, doi: 10.1016/j.jclepro.2020. 846.

44 Jonathan Riley, 'Mill's Political Economy: Ricardian Science and Liberal Utilitarian Art', in *The Cambridge Companion to* Mill, ed. John Skorupski (Cambridge: Cambridge University Press, 2006), 293–337.

45 Dimitris Milonakis and Ben Fine, 'Marginalism and the Metodensreit', in *From Political Economy to Economics: Method, the Social and the Historical in the Evolution of Economic Theory* (London: Routledge, 2009), 91–118.

46 Ernest Becker, *The Denial of Death* (New York: Free Press, 1973).

47 Rachel E. Greenspan, 'On Facebook, the Dead Will Eventually Outnumber the Living. What Does That Mean for Our Histories?', *Time*, 30 April 2019, last accessed 9 October 2022, https://time.com/5579737/facebook-dead-living/.

48 Martin Heidegger, *Being and Time*, trans. John Macquarrie and Edward Robinson (New York: Harper Collins, 2008).

49 Isabelle Stengers, *Au temps des Catastrophes* (Paris, France: La Découverte, 2009).

50 Donna Haraway, *Staying with the Trouble: Making Kin in the Chthulucene* (Durham, NC: Duke University Press, 2016).

51 Ursula K. Le Guin, *The Dispossessed* (New York: Harper Collins, 1974).

52 Robin Wall Kimmerer, *Braining Sweetgrass* (Minneapolis, MN: Milkweed Editions, 2013).

53 Leanne Betasamosake Simpson, *As We Have Always Done: Indigenous Freedom through Radical Resistance* (Minneapolis, MN: University of Minneapolis Press, 2021).

54 Donna Haraway, *Staying with the Trouble: Making Kin in the Chthulucene* (Durham, NC: Duke University Press, 2016). Also refer to Donna Haraway, *The Companion Species Manifesto: Dogs, People and Significant Otherness* (Chicago, IL: Prickly Paradigm Press, 2003).

55 Virginie Servant-Miklos, 'The Love at the End of the World', in *International Yearbook for Philosophical Anthropology: Ecology 2.0 – The Contribution of Philosophical Anthropology to Mapping the Ecological Crisis*, ed. Katharina Block and Julien Kloeg (Berlin, Germany: De Gruyter, 2020), 149–76.

56 Ramachandra Guha and Joan Martinez Alier, *Varieties of Environmentalism: Essays North and South* (London: Routledge, 1997).

57 Alexander Koch, Chris Brierley, Mark M. Maslin and Simon L. Lewis, 'Earth System Impacts of the European Arrival and Great Dying in the Americas after 1492', *Quaternary Science Reviews* 207 (2019): 13–36.

58 Holly Honderich, 'Why Canada Is Mourning the Deaths of Hundreds of Children', *BBC News*, 15 July 2021, last accessed 9 October 2022, https://www.bbc.com/news/world-us-canada-57325653.

59 Susan Clayton, 'Environmental Identity: A Conceptual and an Operational Definition', in *Identity and the Natural Environment: The Psychological Significance of Nature*, ed. Susan Clayton and Susan Opotow (Cambridge, MA: MIT Press, 2003), 45–65.

60 Anne-Caroline Prévot, Susan Clayton and Raphael Mathevet, 'The Relationship of Childhood Upbringing and University Degree Program to Environmental Identity: Experience in Nature Matters', *Environmental Education Research* 24, no. 2 (2018): 263–79.

61 James Lovelock argued that the human population should be reduced to 500,000 individuals to preserve the Earth-system's balance, as quoted in Isabelle Stengers, *Au temps des Catastrophes* (Paris, France: La Découverte, 2009), 56. The Gaïa hypothesis was first put to paper in 1974 by Lovelock and his colleague Lynn Margulis: James Lovelock and Lynn Margulis, 'Atmospheric Homeostasis by and for the Biosphere: The Gaia Hypothesis', *Tellus* 26, no. 1 (1974): 2–10.

62 These numbers are based on the calculations of the Ecological Footprint Network (EFN). According to the EFN, in 2017, the average Dutch person was consuming seven times the available biocapacity available in The Netherlands per person, while the average Angolan citizen consume less than six times the biocapacity available per person in Angola. Accordingly, if every country consumed at the rate of The Netherlands, the Earth could only carry 15 per cent of its current population before reaching biosphere limits. The country-by-country footprint of the EFN can be accessed here, last accessed 10 October 2022, https://data.footprintnetwork.org/?_ga=2.200199274.554847846.1665385915-1702947661.1665385915#/.

63 I have written at length about deep ecology and its problematic relationship with nature in Virginie Servant-Miklos, 'The Love at the End of the World', in *International Yearbook for Philosophical Anthropology: Ecology 2.0 – The Contribution of Philosophical Anthropology to Mapping the Ecological Crisis*, ed. Katharina Block and Julien Kloeg (Berlin, Germany: De Gruyter, 2020), 153–8.

NOTES

64 Jainism is an Indian belief system, with a dedication to non-violence as its core pillar. Refer to National Geographic, *Jainism*, last accessed 10 October 2022, https://education.nationalgeographic.org/resource/jainism.

65 Kate Kirkpatrick, *Becoming Beauvoir: A Life* (London: Bloomsbury, 2019).

66 'L'existence précède l'essence' is at the heart of Jean-Paul Sartre's magnum opus, *l'Etre et le Néant: Essai d'ontologie phénoménologique* (Paris, France: Gallimard, 1943), 613.

67 Viktor E. Frankl, *Trotzdem ja zum Leben sagen: Ein Psychologe erlebt das Konzentrationslager* (Vienna, Austria: Verlag für Jugend und Volk, 1946).

68 De Beauvoir argued in a short essay titled *Œil pour Œil* (an eye for an eye) that hanging Nazis was necessary to remedy the inhumanity of their crimes. The essay can be found in Simone de Beauvoir, *Idéalisme moral et réalisme politique* (Paris, France: Gallimard, 2017), 109–39. An account of her commitment to the cause of Algeria can be found in Kate Kirkpatrick, *Becoming Beauvoir: A Life* (London: Bloomsbury, 2019), 297–312.

Chapter 4

1 Virginie F. C. Servant, 'Revolutions & Re-iterations: An Intellectual History of Problem-Based Learning' (PhD dissertation, Erasmus School of Social and Behavioural Sciences, 2016), http://hdl.handle.net/1765/94113.

2 Knud Illeris, *Problemorientering og Deltagerstyring: Oplæg til en Alternativ Didaktik* (Copenhagen: Munksgaard, 1974).

3 Virginie F. C. Servant-Miklos and Claus M. Spliid, 'The Construction of Teaching Roles at Aalborg University Centre, 1970–1980', *History of Education* 46, no. 6 (2017): 788–809.

4 This critique is prominent in hooks' work: bell hooks, *Teaching Community: A Pedagogy of Hope* (New York: Routledge, 2003) and bell hooks, *Teaching to Transgress* (New York: Routledge, 1994).

5 Gert J. J. Biesta, 'Say You Want a Revolution . . . Suggestions for the Impossible Future of Critical Pedagogy', *Educational Theory* 48, no. 4 (1998).

6 Gert J. J. Biesta, 'Say You Want a Revolution . . . Suggestions for the Impossible Future of Critical Pedagogy', *Educational Theory* 48 (1998): 508.

7. bell hooks, *Teaching Community: A Pedagogy of Hope* (New York: Routledge, 2003).
8. bell hooks, *Teaching to Transgress* (New York: Routledge, 1994).
9. Sara Carpenter and Shahrzad Mojab, *Revolutionary Learning: Marxism, Feminism and Knowledge* (London: Pluto Press, 2017).
10. Tim Urban, *What's Our Problem?* (Wait But Why, 2023). When I challenged him on this, Tim Urban admitted to me that he had not read Paulo Freire. Personal communication 06/07/2023.
11. Lev S. Vygotsky, 'Thinking and Speech', trans. Kozulin, Alex in *The Collected Works of Lev Vygotsky*, Vol. 1, ed. R. Rieber and A. Carton, trans. N. Minick (New York: Plenum, 1987), v 285, *Applied Psycholinguistics* 11, no. 1 (1990).
12. Jerome Bruner, *Toward a Theory of Instruction* (Cambridge, MA: Belknap Press of Harvard University, 1966).
13. For instance: Richard C. Anderson, Rand, J. Spiro and Mark C. Anderson, 'Schemata as Scaffolding for the Representation of Information in Connected Discourse', *American Educational Research Journal* 15, no. 3 (1978): 433.
14. These are listed and explained in: Henk G. Schmidt, 'Foundations of Problem-Based Learning: Some Explanatory Notes', *Medical Education* 27, no. 5 (1993): 422–432.
15. Lev S. Vygotsky, 'Thinking and Speech', trans. Kozulin, Alex in *The Collected Works of Lev Vygotsky*, Vol. 1, ed. R. Rieber and A. Carton, trans. N. Minick (New York: Plenum, 1987).
16. Richard C. Anderson, 'The Notion of Schemata and the Educational Enterprise: General Discussion of the Conference', in *Schooling and the Acquisition of Knowledge*, ed. Richard Anderson, Rand Spiro and William Montague (Hillsdale, NJ: Lawrence Erlbaum Associates, 1977).
17. For more on this, see Stellan Ohlsson, 'The Problems with Problem Solving: Reflections on the Rise, Current Status, and Possible Future of a Cognitive Research Paradigm', *The Journal of Problem Solving* 5, no. 1 (2012), http://dx.doi.org/10.7771/1932-6246.1144.
18. Richard M. Ryan and Edward L. Deci, 'Intrinsic and Extrinsic Motivation from a Self-Determination Theory Perspective: Definitions, Theory, Practices, and Future Directions', *Contemporary Education Psychology* 61 (2020): 101860.
19. For alternative interpretations of the name 'problem-based learning', refer here: Virginie Servant-Miklos, 'Problem-Oriented Project Work and Problem-Based Learning', *UIScholarWorks Journal* 14, no. 1 (2020).

20 Virginie Servant-Miklos, 'The Harvard Connection: How the Case Method Spawned Problem-Based Learning at McMaster University', *Health Professions Education* 5, no. 3 (2019), doi:10.14434/ijpbl.v14i1.28596.

21 Lisette Wijnia and Virginie F. C. Servant-Miklos, 'Behind the Times: A Brief History of Motivation Discourse in Problem-Based Learning', *Advances in Health Sciences Education* 24, no. 5 (2019): 915–929.

22 Henk Schmidt, Sofie M. M. Loyens, Tamara van Gog and Fred Paas, 'Problem-Based Learning Is Compatible with Human Cognitive Architecture: Commentary on Kirschner, Sweller, and Clark (2006)', *Educational Psychologist* 42, no. 2 (2007): 91–97.

23 Henk G. Schmidt, *Activatie van Voorkennis, Intrinsieke Motivatie en de Verwerking van Tekst* (Apeldoorn: Van Walraven, 1982).

24 Geri W. Beers and Susan Bowden, 'The Effect of Teaching Method on Long-Term Knowledge Retention', *Journal of Nursing Education* 44, no. 11 (2005): 511–514.

25 In a large study performed in Dutch medical school in response to PBL-naysayers, Schmidt et al. noted that the main benefit of PBL seemed to be that students rated the curriculum higher (i.e. they had more fun), and graduated faster, with fewer drop-outs than in the regular medical programme: Henk G. Schmidt, Henk T. van der Molen, Wilco W. R. te Winkel and Wynard H. F. W. Wijnen, 'Constructivist, Problem-Based Learning Does Work: A Meta-Analysis of Curricular Comparisons Involving a Single Medical School', *Educational Psychologist* 44, no. 4 (2009): 227–249.

26 Geoffrey Norman, personal correspondence, 20 July 2023.

27 Henk G. Schmidt, Jerome I. Rotgans and Elaine H. J. Yew, ' Process of Problem-Based Learning: What Works and Why', *Medical Education* 45, no. 8 (2011): 792–806.

28 Jos H. C. Moust, Henk J. M. van Berkel and Henk G. Schmidt, 'Signs of Erosion: Reflections on Three Decades of Problem-Based Learning at Maastricht University', *Higher Education* 50, no. 4 (2005): 665–683.

29 Virginie F. C. Servant-Miklos, 'Problem Solving Skills Versus Knowledge Acquisition: The Historical Dispute That Splits Problem-Based Learning into Two Camps', *Advances in Health Sciences Education* 24 (2019): 619–635.

30 Virginie Servant-Miklos, 'PBL, Change or Risk Irrelevance: A Friendly Warning', *Heath Professions Education* 9, no. 1 (2023): 9–12.

31 Maurice Merleau-Ponty, *Phénoménologie de la Perception* (Paris, France: Gallimard, 1976).

32 Jean-Paul Sartre, *L'être et le Néant* (Paris, France: Gallimard, 1976).
33 Maurice Merleau-Ponty and Claude Lefort, *Le Visible et l'Invisible/ Notes de Travail* (Paris, France: Gallimard, 1979).
34 Hans Rosling, Anna Rosling Rönnlund and Ola Rosling, *Factfulness: Ten Reasons We're Wrong About the World – and Why Things Are Better Than You Think* (New York: Flatiron Books, 2018).
35 Viktor E. Frankl, William J. Winslade and Harold S. Kushner, *Man's Search for Meaning* (Boston, MA: Beacon Press, 2006).
36 Simone de Beauvoir, *Pour une Morale de l'Ambiguïté* (Paris, France: Folio Essais, 2003).
37 Emio Greco and Pieter C. Scholten, 'DS/DM the Method', *ICK Dans Amsterdam*, n.d., https://www.ickamsterdam.com/nl/academy/dansprofessionals/ds-dm-the-method-20.
38 See for instance in: Jos Moust, Peter Bouhuijs and Henk Schmidt, *Introduction to Problem-Based Learning* (London: Routledge, 2021).
39 W. R. Bion, *Experiences in Groups and Other Papers* (New York: Routledge, 1961).
40 Elliot Aronson and Shelley Patnoe, *Cooperation in the Classroom: The Jigsaw Method* (London: Pinter & Martin Ltd., 2011).
41 John Dewey, *Democracy and Education* (Oxford: Benedicton Classics, 2011).
42 Peter Felten and Patti H. Clayton, 'Service Learning', *New Directions for Teaching and Learning* 128 (2011): 75–84.
43 Anders Siig Andersen and Simon B. Heilesen, *The Roskilde Model: Problem-Oriented Learning and Project Work* (Berlin: Springer Cham, 2014).
44 Bruno Latour, *Facing Gaia* (Cambridge: Polity Press, 2017).
45 Donna J. Haraway, *Staying with the Trouble: Making Kin in the Chthulucene* (North Yorkshire: Combined Academic Publ., 2016).
46 Isabelle Stengers, *In Catastrophic Times: Resisting the Coming Barbarism*, trans. Andrew Goffey (London: Open Humanities Press, 2015).
47 Anna Lowenhaupt Tsing, *The Mushroom at the End of the World: On the Possibility of Life in Capitalist Ruins* (Princeton, NJ: Princeton University Press, 2015).
48 Chilled Winston, 'How to Play | Collapse the Board Game', *YouTube*, 15 November 2022, Educational video, 18:26, https://youtu.be/-ttQhImJUTU?si=S1GMg-N6m_p9M3u2.

49 Virginie F. C. Servant-Miklos and Claus M. Spliid, 'The Construction of Teaching Roles at Aalborg University Centre, 1970–1980', *Journal of the History of Education Society* 46, no. 6 (2017): 1–22.

50 Anders Siig Andersen and Simon B. Heilesen, *The Roskilde Model: Problem-Oriented Learning and Project Work* (Berlin: Springer Cham, 2014), 3–17.

51 Virginie Servant-Miklos, Aida Guerra, Examining Exemplarity in Problem-Based Engineering Education for Sustainability (2019), 1022–32, SEFI, 'Varietas Delectat . . . Complexity is the New Normality', in *47th Annual SEFI Conference*, ed. Balázs Vince Nagy, Mike Murphy, Hannu-Matti Järvinen, and Anikó Kálmán (Budapest, SEFI, 2019).

52 Oskar Negt, *Soziologische Phantasie und Exemplarishes Lernen: Zur Theorie und Praxis der Arbeiterbildung* (Frankfurt: Europaïsche Verslagsanstalt, 1971).

53 She expressed this to me in personal communication in 2016 that was reported in: Virginie F. C. Servant-Miklos and Claus M. Spliid, 'The Construction of Teaching Roles at Aalborg University Centre, 1970–1980', *Journal of the History of Education Society* 46, no. 6 (2017): 796.

54 Virginie F. C. Servant, 'Revolutions & Re-iterations: An Intellectual History of Problem-Based Learning' (PhD dissertation, Erasmus School of Social and Behavioural Sciences, 2016), 197–244.

55 Poul Bitsch Olsen, *Problem-Oriented Project Work* (Rosenørns Allé: Samfundslitteratur, 2021).

56 Karin Beyer, 'On the Development of the Idea of Project-Organization at the Natural Science Basic Studies Course, RUC', Conference paper from 1976, RU-History Collection Mag RHS a 104. (Roskilde: Roskilde University Center, 1976).

57 While this paper cites seven steps, I think these can be effectively summarized as five: Jette Egelund Holgaard, Aida Guerra, Anette Kolmos and Lone Stub Peterson, 'Getting a Hold on the Problem in a Problem-Based Learning Environment', *The International Journal of Engineering Education* 33, no. 3 (2017): 1070–1085.

58 Russell R. Rogers, 'Reflection in Higher Education: A Concept Analysis', *Innovative Higher Education* 26 (2001): 37–57.

59 James E. Stice, 'Using Kolb's Learning Cycle to Improve Student Learning', *Engineering Education* 77, no. 5 (1987): 291–6.

60 Derek Cavilla, 'The Effects of Student Reflection on Academic Performance and Motivation', *SAGE Open* 7, no. 3 (2017): 215824401773379.

61 David Emerald, *The Power of TED: The Empowerment Dynamic* (Bainbridge Island, WA: Polaris Publishing, 2009).

62 W. R. Bion, *Experiences in Groups and Other Papers* (New York: Routledge, 1961), 141–191.

63 W. R. Bion, *Experiences in Groups and Other Papers* (New York: Routledge, 1961), 141–191.

64 C. Wright Mills, *The Sociological Imagination* (Oxford: Oxford University Press, 2000).

65 Oskar Negt, *Soziologische Phantasie und Exemplarishes Lernen: Zur Theorie und Praxis der Arbeiterbildung* (Frankfurt: Europaïsche Verslagsanstalt, 1971).

66 Lorenzo Duchi, Virginie Servant-Miklos, Loïs Kooij and Liesbeth Noordegraaf-Eelens, 'The "Sweet Spot" for Reflection in Problem-Oriented Education: Insights from Phenomenographic Action-Research', *Journal of Problem Based Learning in Higher Education* 11, no. 1 (2023): 1–35.

67 Virginie F. C. Servant-Miklos and Gera Noordzij, 'Investigating the Impact of Problem-Oriented Sustainability Education of Students' Identity: A Comparative Study of Planning and Liberal Arts Students', *Journal of Cleaner Production* 280, no. 2 (2021): 124846.

68 Virginie Servant-Miklos and Irene van Oorschot, 'Collaboration, Reflection and Imagination: Re-Thinking Assessment in PBL Education for Sustainability', in *8th International Research Symposium on Problem-Based Learning, IRSPBL 2020*, ed. Aida Guerra, Enette Kolmos, Juebei Chen and Maiken Winther (Aalborg: Aalborg University Press, 2020).

69 Joseph Dumit, 'Writing the Implosion: Teaching the World One Thing at a Time', *Cultural Anthropology* 29, no. 2 (2014): 344–62.

70 Justin Jin, 'Children Collapse from Hunger after Poor Harvests in Zimbabwe – in Pictures', *The Guardian*, 23 December 2016, https://www.theguardian.com/global-development/gallery/2016/dec/23/children-collapse-from-hunger-after-zimbabwe-poor-harvests-in-pictures and N. A., '10 Million Additional Girls at Risk of Child Marriage Due to COVID-19 – UNICEF', Unicef, 8 March 2021, https://www.unicef.org/eap/press-releases/10-million-additional-girls-risk-child-marriage-due-covid-19-unicef#.

71 Paulo Freire, *The Pedagogy of the Oppressed*, 50th Anniversary Edition, trans. Donaldo Macedo (London: Bloomsbury, 2018).

72 William H. Kilpatrick, 'The Project Method: The Use of the Purposeful Act in the Educative Process', *Teachers College Record* 19, no. 4 (1918): 7.

73 John Dewey, *How We Think* (Lexington, KY: D.C. Heath and Company, 1933).
74 John Dewey, *How We Think* (Lexington, KY: D.C. Heath and Company, 1933), 273.
75 Elaine H. J. Yew and Janice J. Y. Yong, 'Student Perceptions of Facilitators' Social Congruence, Use of Expertise and Cognitive Congruence in Problem-Based Learning', *Instructional Science* 42 (2014): 795–815.
76 Paulo Freire, *The Pedagogy of the Oppressed*, 50th Anniversary Edition, trans. Donaldo Macedo (London: Bloomsbury, 2018).
77 The Lancet, 'An Age of Uncertainty: Mental Health in Young People', *The Lancet* 400, no. 10352 (2022): 539.
78 E.g.: Lisa R. Fortuna, Isabella C. Brown, Gesean G. Lewis Woods and Michelle V. Porche, 'The Impact of COVID-19 on Anxiety Disorders in Youth', *Child and Adolescent Psychiatric Clinics of North America* 32, no. 3 (2023): 531–42; and N.A., 'COVID-19 Pandemic Triggers 25% Increase in Prevalence of Anxiety and Depression Worldwide: Wake-up Call to All Countries to Step Up Mental Health Services and Support', *World Health Organisation*, 2 March 2022, https://www.who.int/news/item/02-03-2022-covid-19-pandemic-triggers-25-increase-in-prevalence-of-anxiety-and-depression-worldwide.
79 Tim Urban, *What's Our Problem?* (Wait But Why, 2023).
80 Tessa Hofland, 'Students and Staff About Diversity: From "Fear of Cancellation" to "Toxic Climate"', *Erasmus Magazine*, 12 December 2022, https://www.erasmusmagazine.nl/en/2022/12/12/students-and-staff-about-diversity-from-fear-of-cancellation-to-toxic-climate/.

Chapter 5

1 Rutger Bregman, 'Poverty Isn't a Lack of Character; It's a Lack of Cash', TEDxAmsterdam, November 2014, video, last accessed 15 April 2023, https://www.ted.com/talks/rutger_bregman_poverty_isn_t_a_lack_of_character_it_s_a_lack_of_cash.
2 For an evolutionary history of the cooperative traits in humankind, refer to Peter Kropotkin, *Mutual Aid: A Factor of Evolution* (London: Freedom Press, 1902), and more recently, Rutger Bregman, *Humankind: A Hopeful History* (London: Bloomsbury Publishing, 2020).

3 Social cohesion is defined by three characteristics: social relations, identification and orientation towards the common good by David Schiefer and Jolanda Van der Noll, 'The Essentials of Social Cohesion: A Literature Review', *Social Indicators Research 132* (2017): 579–603. The OECD has been warning since 2012 that unbridled economic growth was putting social cohesion at risk in rapidly developing countries: OECD, *Perspectives on Global Development 2012: Social Cohesion in a Shifting World* (Paris, France: OECD Publishing, 2011), https://doi.org/10.1787/persp_glob_dev-2012-en.

4 For those interested in a vivid description of what late-stage Communist Romania was like, I refer you to Patrick McGuinness, *The Last Hundred Days* (London: Serpent's Tail, 2011).

5 George Orwell, *Animal Farm* (New York: Harcourt, Brace and Company, 1946).

6 Milan Kundera, *The Unbearable Lightness of Being* (New York: Harper & Row, 1984).

7 Karl Polanyi, *The Great Transformation: The Political and Economic Origins of Our Time* (Boston: Beacon Press, 2001).

8 Thomas Piketty, *Capital et Idéologie* (Paris, France: Éditions du Seuil, 2019).

9 Gary Becker, 'Human Capital', in *The Columbia Encyclopedia*, 6th edition, ed. Paul Lagasse et al. (New York: Columbia University Press, 2008).

10 Thomas Piketty, *The Economics of Inequality* (Cambridge, MA: Harvard University Press, 2015).

11 Thomas Piketty, *The Economics of Inequality* (Cambridge, MA: Harvard University Press, 2015), 828.

12 For an explanation of moral identities and their prominence in the formation of the self, see StNina Strohminger and Shaun Nichols, 'The Essential Moral Self', *Cognition* 131, no. 1 (2014): 159–71.

13 Paul Piff, 'Does Money Make You Mean?', *TEDxMarin*, June 2013, video, last accessed 15 April 2023, https://www.youtube.com/watch?v=rvskMHn0sqQ.

14 This dishonest intellectual position has a name: deficit thinking. Deficit thinking has been perpetuated by conservative scholars such as James Q. Wilson and Charles Murray. Murray went as far as to argue that the deficiencies of the poor were caused by genetics. Charles Murray and Richard Herrnstein, *The Bell Curve: Intelligence and Class Structure in American Life* (New York: Free Press, 1994).

15 Choice entertainment in this regard includes 'Bling Empire', *Netflix*, 15 January 2021, and 'Young, Famous and African', *Netflix*, 25 September 2021.

16 Virginie Servant-Miklos, Eleanor Dewar and Pia Bøgelund, "I Started This, and I Will End This': A Phenomenological Investigation of Blue Collar Men Undertaking Engineering Education as Mature Students', *European Journal of Engineering Education* 46, no. 2 (2021): 287–301.

17 See, for instance, Josh Hayes, *The Invisible Class*, film (San Francisco: Visual Anarchy, 2020).

18 582,500 homeless people in 2023, to be precise, according to Francis Torres, 'Housing Supply and the Drivers of Homelessness', *Bipartisan Policy Center,* 7 February 2023, https://bipartisanpolicy.org/report/housing-supply-and-homelessness/.

19 Sixty-four per cent of the US population was living paycheck to paycheck in 2022, which amounts to roughly 217 million people, according to Jessica Dickler, '64% of Americans are Living Paycheck to Paycheck – Here's How to Keep Your Budget in Check', *CNBC*, 31 January 2023, last accessed 7 May 2023, https://www.cnbc.com/2023/01/31/share-of-americans-living-paycheck-to-paycheck-jumped-in-2022.html.

20 Gabor Maté, *When the Body Says No: The Cost of Hidden Stress* (Hoboken, NJ: John Wiley & Sons, 2003).

21 Bessel van der Kolk, *The Body Keeps the Score: Brain, Mind, and Body in the Healing of Trauma* (New York: Penguin Books, 2015).

22 Pete Walker, *Complex PTSD: From Surviving to Thriving* (Berkeley, CA: Azure Coyote, 2013).

23 Gabor Maté, *The Myth of Normal, Trauma, Illness, & Healing in a Toxic Culture* (London: Vermillion, 2022), 53.

24 Hans Rosling, *Factfulness: Ten Reasons We're Wrong About the World--And Why Things Are Better Than You Think* (New York: Flatiron Books, 2018).

25 Referring here to Maslow's pyramid of needs. Abraham H. Maslow, 'A Theory of Human Motivation', *Psychological Review* 50, no. 4 (1943): 370–96.

26 Gabor Maté, *The Myth of Normal, Trauma, Illness, & Healing in a Toxic Culture* (London: Vermillion, 2022), 53.

27 Mary Trump, *Too Much and Never Enough: How My Family Created the World's Most Dangerous Man* (New York: Simon & Schuster Ltd, 2021).

28 Virginie Servant-Miklos, 'Environmental Education and Socio-Ecological Resilience in the COVID-19 Pandemic: Lessons from

Educational Action Research', *Environmental Education Research* 28, no. 1 (2022): 18–39.

29 Pete Walker, *Complex PTSD: From Surviving to Thriving* (Berkeley, CA: Azure Coyote, 2013), 108.

30 bell hooks, *Teaching Community: A Pedagogy of Hope* (New York: Routledge, 2003), 31.

31 Social psychologist Jonathan Haidt situated the shift around 2013, with the generation that grew up post 1995. Jonathan Haidt and Greg Lukianoff, *The Coddling of the American Mind: How Good Intentions and Bad Ideas Are Setting Up a Generation for Failure* (New York: Penguin Press, 2018).

32 This development was chronicled with humour by Tim Urban, *What's Our Problem: A Self-Help Book for Societies* (Wait but Why, 2023).

33 Robin DiAngelo, *White Fragility: Why It's So Hard for White People to Talk About Racism* (Boston: Beacon Press, 2018); William Watson, *Twelve Steps for White America: For a United States of America* (San Diego: Cognella Press, 2022).

34 Tim Urban also noted the religious connotation of current social justice discourse in Tim Urban, *What's Our Problem: A Self-Help Book for Societies* (Wait but Why, 2023).

35 I'm not going to cite this specific paper so as not to single out one particular author, but just type 'queer futurities' into Google Scholar and see for yourself.

36 Thomas Piketty, *Capital et Idéologie* (Paris, France: Éditions du Seuil, 2019).

37 Referring to the tirade of the then-Lord Chancellor of the UK Michael Gove, who declared on national television: 'I think the people of this country have had enough of experts'. As reported by Richard Portes, 'I Think the People of this Country have had Enough of Experts', *London Business School*, 9 May 2017, last accessed 21 April 2023, https://www.london.edu/think/who-needs-experts.

38 Michelle Goldberg, 'The Left's Fever Is Breaking', *The New York Times*, 16 December 2022, last accessed 21 April 2023, https://www.nytimes.com/2022/12/16/opinion/left-activism.html?.

39 Pamela Armitage, 'An Uncomfortable Reality: Trauma Is at the Core of Violence Prevention and Self Defense Education', *Your Self Defense Experts*, last accessed 16 September 2023, https://www.yourselfdefenseexperts.com/post/the-topic-of-trauma-is-at-the-core-of-self-defense-training-uncomfortable-good.

40 Two recent examples: Vimal Patel, 'A Lecturer Showed a Painting of the Prophet Muhammad. She Lost Her Job', *The New York Times*, 10 January 2023, last accessed 21 April 2023, https://www.nytimes.com/2023/01/08/us/hamline-university-islam-prophet-muhammad.html and Conor Friedersdorf, 'The Educators Who Decided That Context Doesn't Matter', *The Altantic*, 7 February 2022, last accessed 21 April 2023, https://www.theatlantic.com/ideas/archive/2022/02/logical-end-language-policing/621500/.

41 Borrowing here again a term from Tim Urban, *What's Our Problem: A Self-Help Book for Societies* (Wait but Why, 2023).

42 Simone de Beauvoir, *Pour une Morale de l'ambiguïté* (Paris, France: Éditions Gallimard, 1947); Paulo Freire, *Pedagogy of the Oppressed* (London: Bloomsbury, 2018).

43 Richard Vedder, 'Racial Segregation on American Campuses: A Widespread Phenomenon', *Forbes*, 15 November 2018, last accessed 21 April 2023, https://www.forbes.com/sites/richardvedder/2018/11/15/racial-segregation-on-american-campuses-a-widespread-phenomenon/?sh=45384c334455.

44 Bessel van der Kolk, *The Body Keeps the Score: Brain, Mind, and Body in the Healing of Trauma* (New York: Penguin Books, 2015).

45 Erin McCormick, 'Patagonia's Billionaire Owner Gives Away Company to Fight Climate Crisis', *The Guardian*, 15 September 2022, last accessed 21 April 2023, https://www.theguardian.com/us-news/2022/sep/14/patagonias-billionaire-owner-gives-away-company-to-fight-climate-crisis-yvon-chouinard.

46 Case in point, the latest Apple campaign: Gregory Barber, 'Your New Apple Watch Won't Be Carbon Neutral', *Wired*, published 7 September 2023, https://www.wired.com/story/new-apple-watch-series-9-wont-be-carbon-neutral/.

47 See, for instance, Nafeez Ahmed, 'World Bank and UN Carbon Offset Scheme 'Complicit' in Genocidal Land Grabs – NGOs', *The Guardian*, 3 July 2014, last accessed 21 April 2023; Camilla Hodgson, 'Wildfires Destroy Almost All Forest Carbon Offsets in 100-Year Reserve, Study Says', *Financial Times*, 5 August 2022, last accessed 21 April 2023, https://www.ft.com/content/d54d5526-6f56-4c01-8207-7fa7e532fa09.

48 Erasmus Magazine Special, 'Protest at the Sanders Building', *Erasmus Magazine*, 7 February 2023, last accessed 21 April 2023. https://www.erasmusmagazine.nl/en/specials/protest-at-sanders-building/.

49 'EUR Organises 14 University-Wide Dialogues on Sustainability', Erasmus University Rotterdam, published 24 April 2023, https://www.eur.nl/en/news/eur-organises-14-university-wide-dialogues-sustainability. 'Erasmus University Rotterdam Declares Climate and Ecological Emergency', Erasmus University Rotterdam, published 6 February 2023, https://www.eur.nl/en/news/erasmus-university-rotterdam-declares-climate-and-ecological-emergency.

50 bell hooks, *All About Love: New Visions* (New York: William Morrow, 2000).

51 Gabor Maté, *When the Body Says No: The Cost of Hidden Stress* (Hoboken, NJ: John Wiley & Sons, 2003), 8.

52 Simone de Beauvoir, *Pour une Morale de l'ambiguité* (Paris, France: Éditions Gallimard, 1947).

53 Kate Kirkpatrick, *Becoming Beauvoir: A Life* (London: Bloomsbury, 2019).

54 Simone de Beauvoir, *Pour une Morale de l'ambiguité* (Paris, France: Éditions Gallimard, 1947).

55 Simone de Beauvoir, *Les Mandarins* (Paris, France: Gallimard, 1954).

56 Loretta J. Ross, 'Calling In: A Less Disposable Way of Holding Each Other Accountable', TEDx Talks, 30 October 2017, last accessed 23 April 2023, https://www.youtube.com/watch?v=1yB0lZFV3Fk.

57 Virginie Servant-Miklos and Gera Noordzij, 'Investigating the Impact of Problem-Oriented Sustainability Education on Students' Identity: A Comparative Study of Planning and Liberal Arts Students', *Journal of Cleaner Production* 280 (2021): 124846.

58 Pete Walker, *Complex PTSD: From Surviving to Thriving* (Scotts Valley, CA: INGP, 2013).

59 Virginie Servant-Miklos, 'Environmental Education and Socio-Ecological Resilience in the COVID-19 Pandemic: Lessons from Educational Action Research', *Environmental Education Research* 28, no. 1 (2022): 18–39.

60 E.g. Shantel D. Crosby, Penny Howell and Shelley Thomas, 'Social Justice Education Through Trauma-Informed Teaching', *Middle School Journal* 29, no. 4 (2018): 15–23 and Shantel D. Crosby, 'An Ecological Perspective on Emerging Trauma-Informed Teaching Practices', *Children & Schools* 37, no. 4 (2015): 223–30.

61 Gabor Maté, *The Myth of Normal, Trauma, Illness, & Healing in a Toxic Culture* (London: Vermillion, 2022).

Chapter 6

1. For instance, in the UK: Richard Adams, 'Record Numbers of Teachers in England Quitting Profession, Figures Show', *The Guardian*, 8 June 2023, https://www.theguardian.com/education/2023/jun/08/teachers-england-schools-figures-department-education-survey in the USA: Matt Barnum, '"I Just Found Myself Struggling to Keep Up': Number of Teachers Quitting Hits New High', *USA News Today*, n.d., https://eu.usatoday.com/story/news/education/2023/03/06/more-teachers-quitting-than-usual-driven-stress-politics-data-shows/11390639002/ and The Netherlands: NLTimes, 'Half of Dutch Schools Short 1 to 6 Teachers for Next Academic Year', *NL Times*, 20 July 2023, https://nltimes.nl/2023/07/20/half-dutch-schools-short-1-6-teachers-next-academic-year.

2. A. Bryan Endres and Jody M. Endres, 'Homeland Security Planning: What Victory Gardens and Fidel Castro Can Teach Us in Preparing for Food Crises in the United States', *Food Drug Law Journal* 64, no. 2 (2009), https://pubmed.ncbi.nlm.nih.gov/19999291/.

3. The farmer suicide issue is particularly dire in India: Nanda Kishore Kannuri and Sushrut Jadhav, 'Cultivating Distress: Cotton, Caste and Farmer Suicides in India', *Anthropology and Medicine* 28, no. 4 (2021), https://www.ncbi.nlm.nih.gov/pmc/articles/PMC8734467/.

4. Bessel van der Kolk, *The Body Keeps the Score: Brain, Mind and Body in the Healing of Trauma* (London: Penguin Books Ltd., 2015).

5. Kwonmok Ko, Emma I. Kopra, Anthony J. Cleare and James J. Rucker, 'Psychedelic Therapy for Depressive Symptoms: A Systematic Review and Meta Analysis', *Journal of Affective Disorders* 322 (2023): 194–204.

6. The history of psychedelics and the War on Drugs is explained in Michael Pollan, *How to Change Your Mind* (London: Penguin Press, 2018).

7. For instance, for MDMA: Sarah Tedesco et al., 'The Efficacy of MDMA (3,4-Methylenedioxymethamphetamine) for Post-traumatic Stress Disorder in Humans: A Systematic Review and Meta-Analysis', *Cureus* 13, no. 5 (2021): e15070, Simon B. Goldberg et al., 'The Experimental Effects of Psilocybin on Symptoms of Anxiety and Depression: A Meta-Analysis', *Psychiatry Research* 284 (2020): 112749, and for ketamine: John H. Krystal et al., 'Ketamine: A Paradigm Shift for Depression Research and Treatment', *Neuron* 101 (2019): 774–8.

8. Paulo Freire, *Pedagogy of the Oppressed* (New York: Bloomsbury, 1968/2000). Simone de Beauvoir, *Pour une Morale de l'Ambiguité* (Paris, France: Folio Essais, 2003).

9. For instance: Bad Teacher, directed by Jake Kasdan (Columbia Pictures, and Mosaic Media Group, 2011), 92 minutes.

10. George Orwell, *1984* (London: Penguin Books Ltd., 2008).

11. Slavoj Zizek, 'Žižek – Our Fear of Falling in Love', *YouTube*, 15 March 2017, 4:10, https://youtu.be/rrxk2WzrE14?si=IreHVEIBAHgCSk-U.

12. Paulo Freire, *Pedagogy of the Oppressed* (New York: Bloomsbury, 1968/2000).

13. Simone de Beauvoir, *Les Mandarins* (Paris, France: Gallimard, 1973) and Simone de Beauvoir, *Les Mandarins 2* (Paris, France: Gallimard, 1973).

14. Simone de Beauvoir, *Le Femme Rompue* (Paris, France: Gallimard, 2000).

15. bell hooks, *Teaching Community: A Pedagogy of Hope* (New York: Routledge, 2003), chapter 12; bell hooks, *All About Love* (New York: Avon A, 2016).

16. Kate Kirkpatrick, *Becoming Beauvoir: A Life* (London: Bloomsbury Academic, 2019).

17. bell hooks, *All About Love* (New York: Avon A, 2016), 184.

18. Simone de Beauvoir, *Pour une Morale de l'Ambiguité* (Paris, France: Folio Essais, 2003).

19. A few samples: N.A., '#KarateValues: Alton Brown Strives to Give Girls in India a Fighting Chance', *WKF.net*, 7 May 2020, https://www.wkf.net/news-center-new/karatevalues-alton-brown-strives-to-give-girls-in-india-fighting-chance/1296; Lorraine Hoffman, 'Dr. Ginie Servant-Miklos', *Fighteress Tales*, 2021, https://fighteresstales.wordpress.com/europe-5/; Bess Browning, 'Karate Champion Mark Caddy to Travel to Zimbabwe with Fair Fight to Teach Women Martial Arts', *Kent Online*, 10 November 2015, https://www.kentonline.co.uk/faversham/news/karate-champion-fundraising-for-charity-46114/

20. Paulo Freire, *Pedagogy of the Oppressed* (New York: Bloomsbury, 1968/2000), 87.

21. Paul C. Gorski, 'Good Intentions Are Not Enough: A Decolonizing Intercultural Education', *Intercultural Education* 19, no. 6 (2019): 515–25.

22. Milan Kundera and Michael Henry Heim, *The Unbearable Lightness of Being* (New York: Harper Perennial, 2009).

23 Friedrich Nietzsche, *Thus Spake Zarathustra: A Book for All and None* (The Project Gutenberg).

24 Simone de Beauvoir, *Pour une Morale de l'Ambiguïté* (Paris, France: Folio Essais, 2003), 121–43.

25 Virginie Servant-Miklos, Jette E. Holgaard and Anette Kolmos, 'Sustainability Matters', *Problem Based Learning* 11, no. 1 (2023): 124–54 and Virginie F. C. Servant-Miklos, and Gera Noordzij, 'Investigating the Impact of Problem-Oriented Sustainability Education of Students' Identity: A Comparative Study of Planning and Liberal Arts Students', *Journal of Cleaner Production* 280, no. 2 (2021): 124846.

26 Martijn Doolaard, *One Year on a Bike: From Amsterdam to Singapore* (Berlin: Gestalten, 2017) and Martijn Doolaard, *Two Years on a Bike: From Vancouver to Patagonia* (Berlin: Die Gestalten Verlag, 2021).

27 Bessel van der Kolk, *The Body Keeps the Score: Brain, Mind and Body in the Healing of Trauma* (London: Penguin Books Ltd., 2015).

28 Alexandre Bourgeois et al., 'One Third of the European Union's Carbon Footprint Is Due to Its Imports', *Insee Analyses* 71 (2022): 1–8.

Index

Note: Page locators followed by 'n' refer to notes.

Aaronson, Elliot 138
abundance-seeking 117
Academic Ranking of World Universities 66
academic research 95
addiction 24, 41, 204
ADHD 155
Adorno, Theodor 73
agricultural runoff in rivers 19
Ain't I a Woman (bell hooks) 27
air quality 23–4
alcoholism 49–50, 188
All Watched over by Machines of Loving Grace (Curtis) 32
Altas Shrugged (Ayn Rand) 30
Amazon basin 14
American identity-politics 129
Andersen, Hanne Leth 77
Andersen, Lene Rachel 69, 130
Angelou, Maya 53–4
Animal Farm (Orwell) 163
Anthrax 23
Anthropocene 12, 19, 109, 230 n.5
anti-depressants 205, 222
anti-war movement 61
anxiety 88, 92–3, 107, 109, 115–16, 153, 155, 180, 187, 190–1, 203, 206–7, 211, 219, 222
Apartheid 53
Aral Sea in Russia 20
Armitage, Pamela 169, 176
arms-length solidarity 185–6

As We Have Always Done (Simpson) 30
atmospheric aerosol loading 12–13
attachment 93–4, 111, 122, 213
Austen, Jane 53
availability biases 100

Bad Mother, manifestation of 109–11
bargaining 4, 67–8, 80, 104, 106, 118, 122, 215
Barrau, Aurélien 11
basic-assumption dependency group 111, 137–8
Becker, Ernest 118, 219
Becker, Gary 63, 118, 164
bell hooks 27, 54, 73, 77, 130, 173, 184
Bentham, Jeremy 35
Bezos, Jeff 110
Biesta, Gert 129
'big-T' trauma 170
Bildung 69–72, 83, 130, 139, 145–6
  aesthetics and practice-oriented activities 72
  education for the masses 70
  evolution of 70
  folk-bildung 71
biocapacity 39
biochemical flows 13
biodiversity
  hotspots 13–14, 21, 38, 45
  loss 38, 78
Bion, Wilfred 111, 137, 147

INDEX

biosphere 5, 12, 14, 24–5, 44, 64, 113, 224
Bismark, Otto von 34
Bitcoin 37
Black Death 41
Black Lives Matter 182
Blair, Tony 62
body-consciousness relationship 146
The Body Keeps the Score (van der Kolk) 169, 180
Bologna Process 66, 77, 246 n.39
Bourdieu, Pierre 114
Braiding Sweetgrass (Kimmerer) 30
Branson, Richard 110
Bregman, Rutger 30, 106, 160
A Brief History of Neoliberalism (Harvey) 62
Brontë, Charlotte 54
Brown vs. Board of Education, 1954 53
Bruner, Jerome 132
Byron, Lord 116

Callaghan, James 62
calling in invites, concept of 188
Capital and Ideology (Piketty) 164, 175
capitalism 25, 39–42, 51–2, 61, 67, 69, 72, 83, 110, 112–13, 130, 162–4, 202, 211–12
  and associated oppressions 83
  building 27
  description 25
  doctrinal tenets of capitalism 29
  and endless growth 32–5
  fossil fuel 135, 161
  global 43, 48, 64, 120, 152, 170, 217
  impact 171
  and individualism 29–32
  industrial 49
  late-modern capitalism 170, 182
  material components/dimension 26, 28–9
  neoliberal 8, 106, 117, 184
  resources and energy 26–9
  social 106
  social conditions for 25
  'superstructure' of 25
  technological innovation and entrepreneurship 26
carbon emissions 14
Carter, Jimmy 62
Catholic (Church) 123, 174
Ceausescu regime 2
Chamberlin, T. C. 16
Chapelle, Gauthier 11
Chaplin, Charlie 65
cheap nature 27
chemical contamination 200
chemical pollution 17–20, 38
Chibolya in Zambia 24
Chikungunya 23
children
  as cheap labour and mass exploitation 48–9
  religious conversion of Indigenous children 51
  vocational secondary schools 57
Chinese fishing fleets 21
chronic pain 82, 198, 204–5
CITO test 56–8
classical political economy 35
Classroom Experiments 128, 131
Clayton, Susan 121–2
climate change 12, 14, 19–23, 78, 86–7, 117, 119, 173, 231 n.20, 232 n.24, 232 n.28

INDEX

The Climate Crisis (course) 2–3, 17, 89, 149–51, 226
　XP Matrix for Course Coordinators Adapted for 151
climate education, impact on learners 85
climate grief 79, 120
Clinton, Bill 62
Clinton, Hillary 87
coal-fuelled electricity 37
Coates, Ta-Nehisi 54
Cochet, Yves 11
CO_2 emissions 37–9
cognition 97, 99, 123, 136, 182, 209
cognitive bias(es) 30, 97, 102
　cognitive dissonance 97–9
　heuristics and biases 99–102
cognitive dimension 131–4
　cognitive load theory 133
　long-term memory storage 132
　problem-based learning (PBL) 133–4
cognitive load theory 133
cognitive psychology 30, 100, 129, 155
cognitive reflection 146, 148
cognitivism 96–7, 102–3, 113
Cold War 112
COLLAPSE! (game) 142, 149, 151–2
Collapsology 2, 11
collective denial, state of 104
collective depression, state of 107
collectivism 163
Collini, Stefan 60
commitment 5–6, 69, 93, 122, 135, 181, 184, 189–90, 218–19, 225
Commonwealth 53
Communism 34, 107, 162–3

The Communist Manifesto (Marx) 33
Communist Romania 2, 112, 161, 260 n.4
Complex PTSD (Walker) 169
confirmation bias 30
consumerism, impact of 105
Cooper, Anthony Ashley 69
Cooperation and reciprocity 31
corals 20–1, 78
Corbyn, Jeremy 175
corporate trap 180–2
corruption 163
cost of education 156
COVID-19 1, 3, 5–6, 20, 22–3, 31, 39–40, 43, 55, 59, 81, 89, 94, 100, 106, 118, 128, 131, 135, 140, 148, 153, 155–6, 161, 171, 191, 194, 198
　vaccines 140
Cowboy billionaires 108, 110, 112
Critical Edge Alliance of universities 77
critical pedagogues 77, 129–30, 140, 211
critical pedagogy 61, 69, 72–3, 75–6, 83, 127, 129–30, 139, 141–3, 146–7, 157, 246 n.44, *see also* Freire, Paulo; Negt, Oskar
　reflection in 147–8
Cuba 201
cultural capital 7, 115
'culture wars' 159, 172
Cunsolo, Ashlee 79

Daly, Herman 39
Danish Association of Folk High Schools 71
Danish Student Union (DSU) 75, 143

INDEX

Dark Waters (2019) 19
de Beauvoir, Simone 92, 97, 123–5, 134–5, 146, 148, 177, 180, 185–6, 208, 210–13, 220
Deci, Edward 132
Declaration of Human Rights 52, 116.
deep ecologists 123
deep ecology 122–3, 252 n.63
Democracy and Education (Dewey) 140
dengue fever 23
The Denial of Death (Becker) 118
dependency groups 137
depression 5, 68, 79–80, 104, 107, 155, 168, 180, 198–9, 204–6, 219
depressive position 109, 111–12, 161, 188
Dewey, John 52, 63, 140, 146, 154–5
Diamond, Jared 11, 45
DiAngelo, Robin 174
Di Caprio, Leonardo 96
Dickens, Charles 53
Dion, Cyril 11
(cognitive) dissonance 87, 97–100, 166, 248 n.7
DODGE space missions 109
Don't Look Up (film) 96, 248 n.6
Doolaard, Martijn 221
double-skin-double-mind (DS-DM) 136
droughts 20, 43, 78, 105, 201
dualist mind-body relationship 135, 206
Duchi, Lorenzo 149
Dumit, Joseph 152
Dutch educational system 58-9
dystopian theocracy 90

Earth Summit in Rio in 1992 37
ebola, outbreaks 22
eco-depression 2, 206
eco-feminism 92, 120–1
The Economics of Inequality (Piketty) 165
education(al), *see also* Bildung
  banking education 73, 154
  bridge-programme 145
  (Socio-economic) class 55–66
  climate 85
  Danish higher education 75-7
  design 134
  Dutch educational system 58–9
  ecological and social justice 192
  emancipatory 72
  experiential citizen-education 140
  free elementary 52
  funding 52
  gender 54–5
  impact of neoliberalism on 60
  imperialism 53
  liberal 83
  mass education 48, 50, 74–5
  meta-philosophy 131
  moral 33, 70
  movements of 1970s 128
  neoliberal 61–4
  place-based 122
  primary 51–2, 55
  problem-posing education 73, 75
  progressive education movement 154
  progressive theory 141
  psychology 92
  public 55, 63, 197, 244 n.22

revolutions 72, 128, 210, 227
school as a factory 50–1
secondary 55–6, 65
standardization and reporting 64–6
state-funded system of mass education 48
sustainability 2, 88
system 4, 8–9, 45, 47, 53, 56, 61, 68, 122, 154, 157, 197
transformative 129–30, 144
Education and Inspections Act in 2006 65
Education Innovation 128
ego 103–4, 207, 213
emancipatory courses 149
enclosing of the commons 48
energy
  fossil fuel 37, 49, 116, 162, 199
  global 37–8
  mechanical 28
  renewable 37
  shortage 12, 37
  solar 28
  systems, role of 12, 67
Engels, Friedrich 33
environmental activists 40
environmental awakening 87
environmental degradation 13
environmental depression 199, 219
environmental identities 121–3
environmentalism for the rich 121
environmental loss 111
environmentally destructive behaviours 118
Environmental Protection Agency 42
The Ethics of Ambiguity (Beauvoir) 92–3, 136, 177, 186, 208, 220

'everything is racism' mantra 177
existential abyss 120
existential environmental ethics 123–5
existential fear 118–19
existentialism 96, 113–15, 123, 135, 151
experiential citizen-education 140
Experimental Pedagogics (XP) 5, 9, 83, 127, 131, 148–9
  cognitive dimension 131–4
  experimental practices 142–8
  global level 141–2
  group level 137–9
  individual dimension 134–6
  matrix
    for course coordinators adapted for the climate crisis 151
    retrofitting 150
  problem-based education 127–8
  retrofitting 152–3
  scene, settings 128–31
  societal level 139–40
experimental practices
  concept of exemplarity 143
  critical pedagogy 142
  Danish problem-oriented project method 142
  K-12 142
  participant-directed learning 143
  PPL 142–6
  problem-orientation 143
  reflection 146–8
  vocational skills 144
  XP course 144
  XP Project Matrix 145

factory system 48–9
FairFight Foundation 6, 215–16

false advertisements 181–2
farming
  basic skills 82
  experimental 70
  industrial 23
  innovation management 70
  mass farming 23
  mechanized 28
  regenerative 145
Fetischistic disavowal 104
fibromyalgia 5, 169, 180, 205–6, 215
fight reflex 157, 176, 191, 193
flight-or-fight trauma reflex 185
flight reflex 172, 190, 192, 208, 211
folk high school(s) 70–2, 83–4, 130
fossil fuels 16, 24–5, 28, 37–8, 43, 50, 64, 82, 135, 152, 161–3, 170, 184, 199
  capitalism 43, 135, 161, 170
  consumption 37
  industry 16
Frankfurt School of critical pedagogy 60
Frankl, Viktor 124, 135, 184, 225
freeze trauma reflex 193
Freire, Paulo 61, 73–5, 79, 92–3, 139, 154–5, 177, 208, 211, 214, 217
  hinge-thematics for learners 155
  humanizing education with dialogue 74–5
  literacy programmes for the Brazilian peasantry 75
  love 92, 211, 214
  Marxist class analysis 73
  relationships between people 74
French Revolution 165

freshwater
  contamination 38
  ecosystems 20
  species populations 13
  use 13
Freud, Sigmund 103–4, 108, 113, 125, 137
Fukuyama, Francis 2
fundamental attribution error 30, 100
fusion technology 141

Gaïa hypothesis 122, 252 n.61
The Game Changers (2018) 99, 248 n.10
Ganges 20
garbage ships, re-routed 16
GCSEs 65
gender 54–5, 116, 178, 214
  equality 29
  gendered dynamics. 93
  oppressive gender roles 61
  primary education gender gap 55
  and race 55, 93
  studies 81, 83
  violence 214
generous love 93–4, 177, 185–7, 208, 211, 227
genocide 121
geopolitical collapse 42–4
George Floyd murder 176
German Critical Theory 73
Giddens, Anthony 115–16
gilets jaunes 105
Giroux, Henry 60, 73
global banking crisis of 2008 62
global Bildung community 130
Global Bildung Network 69
global capitalism 43, 48, 64–6, 120, 152, 217
global energy, *see also* energy
  consumption since 1800 38
  demand 37

global heating 7, 15, 24
global industrial system 43
Global North phenomenon 1, 116
Goethe, Johann Wolfgang 70, 116
Gomez, Pierre-Yves 36
Grandes Ecoles 86
grandiose narcissistic delusions 110
Great Dying 21
Great Pacific Garbage Patch 18
Great Recession of 2008 12, 62
The Great Transformation (Polanyi) 25, 30, 163
Green Deal in the European Union 106
green growth 38, 141, 240 n.121
Green Left parties 4, 159
Green New Deal 106
The Green New Deal (Rifkin) 37
'green' products 105
grief
    associated with future losses 79
    five stages of, Kübler-Ross's 80, 102, 104, 107
    and psychoanalysis 102–8
    Žižek's interpretation of 107
group dynamics 137, 139, 146–7
group level learning 137–9
    pairing groups work 138
    student types 137
Grundtvig, Nikolaj Frederik Severin 70, 72
guiding students through collapse 97–102

habitus 58, 114, 116, 160, 175, 190
    cosmopolitan 116, 160
    formation 175
    identity 114

lifestyle choices 190
    middle-class 175
Hamas terror attack on Israel, 2023 105
Haraway, Donna 120, 141, 150, 152
Harvey, David 62
Hayek, Friedrich 62
healthy growing up 108–9
healthy mourning in psychoanalysis 111
Heidegger, Martin 115, 120
Herder, Johann Gottfried 70
hinge-thematics 155
Holocene 6
home-schooling 8
homo economicus 35, 164
hooks, bell 27, 54, 73, 77, 130, 173, 184
hothouse Earth 15, 41
How Everything Could Collapse (Servigne and Stevens) 11
Hultengren, Eva 143
Human Capital Theory (Becker) 63
human needs 14
    Maslow's perspective on 170

id 102
identitary hostility 159
identity 114
    crises in times of collapse 114–18
    and existentialism environmental ethics 123–5
    environmental identities 121–3
    fear of finitude 118–19
    in habitus 114–15
identity-building programmes 50
    moral 121

INDEX 275

personal identity 116
politics, American 129, 172, 177–8
self-identity 115
immortality projects 118–19, 219
imperfection 84, 96, 184, 188, 220
imperfect solidarity(ies) 6, 8, 84, 129, 158–95, 206, 214, 217–18
  concept of 6
  in education 137
  long-term commitment 189
  principle of 216
India 6, 15, 20, 22, 37, 41, 43–4, 101, 153, 170, 178, 216, 224, 226
indigenous children 51–3, 121
individualism 8, 31, 35, 120, 148, 161–6, 168–72
  and capitalism 29–32
  as ideology 162–8
  and trauma 169–72
Industrial Revolution 25–6, 48, 61, 70, 116
industrial-scale greenwashing 181
infinite growth 32, 35–9, 78, 104
in-group/out-group bias 101
Intergovernmental Science-Policy Platform on Biodiversity and Ecosystems Services (IPBES) 13
International Monetary Fund 42, 62
International Political Economy 64
invisible hand, concept of 29, 164

Jackson, Tim 39
James Webb telescope 91
Jancovici, Jean-Marc 11, 12, 28, 31
Jane Eyre (Brontë) 54

Jevons, Stanley 34
Jigsaw (Classroom) / jigsawing 138–9, 150
  problem-based learning with 150
Johnson, Dominic 100
Journaling 85, 96, 151

Kendi, Ibram X 54
Kilpatrick, William 52
Kimmerer, Robin Wall 30, 120–1
Kirkpatrick, William 154
Klein, Melanie 97, 108
knowledge acquisition 132–3
Kolb cycle 146
Kold, Christen 70–2, 145
Kritische Erziehungswissenschaft 73
Kropotkin, Piotr 30
K-12 school teachers 8
Kübler-Ross, Elisabeth 80, 102, 104
Kundera, Milan 163, 219

Labour Party 175
La France Insoumise party 175
land conversion 13, 38
land-system change 13
Latour, Bruno 109, 141, 150
leadership 83
learning
  from the body-mind nexus 202–7
  in denial 47–8
  in despair 61
  in dialogue
    appropriate action 81–3
    perfection 83–4
    space for grief 79–81
    speaking the truth 78–9
  from nature 198–202
  in revolution 69
Le Guin, Ursula 120
Lertzman, Renée 111–13

INDEX

Les Mandarins (De Beauvoir) 186, 211
Levin, Simon 100
LGBTQ+ 182
liberal meritocracy 4
libertarian/libertarianism 30
lifestyle projects 116, 118, 122
life-transforming experiences 205
living
   with hope 223–6
   lightly 219–21
Living in End Times (Žižek) 102
Living Planet report of 2022 13
long-term memory storage 132
long-term retention 133–4
love
   as a possessive investment 213
   revolutionary power of 211
   romantic 210–13
   self 208–10
   without learning 93
Lovelock, James 122

Macron, Emmanuel 105, 240 n.121
Magdalen Asylums 54–5
malaria 23
Man's Search for Meaning (Frankl) 135–6
marginalism / marginalist revolution 34–5, 62, 117, 140, 164, 239 n.110, 251 n.45
marginalized groups 171, 173, 177–8, 182
Marshall, Alfred 34–5
martial arts 6, 136, 189, 192, 214–16
Marx, Karl 4, 32–4, 76, 93
Marxism 35, 140
Maslow, Abraham H. 170
mass climate migrations 43
mass education 48, 50, 74–5
mass extinctions 12, 21, 91
Maté, Gabor 169–71, 185, 192, 203
Mbare in Zimbabwe 224
McKenzie, Lisa 58
MDMA talk-therapy 203, 205
Meadows Report, 1972 45, 104
mechanized mass agriculture / farming 28, 202
medical education, method of 127
megafauna, decline of 22
melancholia 110–12
Mélenchon, Jean-Luc 175
memory storage, long-term 132
meritocracy 4, 62, 164–5, 168
meritocratic ideology 7, 164
meritocratic mythology 163–5
Merleau-Ponty, Maurice 134–5, 146
meta-philosophy 131
Methane 14–17, 38, 67
microplastics 17–18, 233 n.35
Mill, John Stuart 33–4, 117, 140
Miller, Alex 102
Mills, C. Wright 75, 148
mind-altering substances 207
mind-body fantasies 135
missionary schools 121
modern medicine 8, 223
monogamy 213
Montessori, Maria 52
Moore, Jason 26–7
moral purity 54, 173–6
Mother Earth 109
motivation theory 133
Mugabe, Robert 89
Murdoch empire 175
Musahar communities in India 224
The Mushroom at the End of the World (Tsing) 141
Musk, Elon 4, 100, 110

INDEX 277

mutual aid 30–1
Mutual Aid (Kropotkin) 30
The Myth of Normal (Maté) 170

Napoleon 51
narcissism/narcissist 93, 110, 171
national identity-building programmes 50
Nationalism 50, 70, 107
Negt, Oskar 60–1, 73–5, 139, 142–3, 148
   concept of exemplarity 75
   German Critical Pedagogy movement 73
   speech barriers' problem 74
neoliberal(ism) 60, 62–3, 65, 161
   capitalism 8, 106, 117, 184
   education 60–1
   governance 155
   government 105
   socialization 148, 190
New Deal in 1930 62
New Labour 62
New Public Management 63, 66, 156
Nietzsche, Friedrich 115, 120, 219
NIMBYism 40
No Child Left Behind Act of 2001 64
Noordegraaf-Eelens, Liesbeth 149
The Nordic Secret: a European Story of Beauty and Freedom (Andersen and Bjorkman) 69
Norman, Geoffrey 133
novel entities 12–13
nuclear Armageddon 90
nuclear family 164, 171, 212
nuclear/nuclear-armed 6, 38, 44, 88, 90

Obama, Barrack 87
object relations theory 108
Ocean Cleanup (non-profit) 18
Office for Standards in Education (Ofsted) 65, 245 n.37
oil crises of 1970s 12
Olesen, Salling 73, 143
Omicron 5
On Death and Dying (Kübler-Ross) 80
oppression, race and gender 1, 73, 75, 83, 92–3, 104, 130, 177–8, 180, 184, 219, 224
Orwell, George 163, 210

Pala, Christopher 51
paranoid-schizoid position 109–12, 123, 138, 188, 222
Paris Climate Accord 15, 87
Paris Commune of 1871 34
Paris 8 University 77
Parkhurst, Helen 52
Patel, Ajay 179
patriarchy 4, 8, 130, 173, 214
peasants 48, 70, 75, 119, 202, 225
pedagogy
   critical (*see* critical pedagogy)
   pedagogical/assessment elements 150
   revolutionary 85
Pedagogy of the Oppressed (Freire) 73, 92, 155, 177, 208
peer-review 94
perfect processes 180, 182–3
performative perfection 173–6
permaculture 3, 82, 200
personal mental breakdowns 156
phallic techno-magic 111
phantasy 109–11
   sociological 147

phenomenology, existential 134–6, 146, 178
phthalates 18
Picnic at Hanging Rock (1967) 54
Piketty, Thomas 27, 105, 164–5, 175
place-based education 122
planetary boundaries 12–13, 87–8, 117, 130, 144, 151, 193
A Plastic Ocean and *Blue Planet II* (documentary) 17
plastics 19, 26, 36
   microplastics 17–18
   pollution 17
   recycling 17–18
Polanyi, Karl 25, 30–1, 163
polarization 159
political economy 2, 12, 33–5, 60, 64, 83, 150, 151
Polyfluoroalkyl Substances (PFAS) 17, 19, 200
Populists 175
positive illusion bias 100–10
positive self-identities 166
post-humanism 141, 152
post-traumatic stress disorder (PTSD) 169–70, 204–5
poverty 25, 40–1, 56, 112, 160–1, 170, 188, 214, 220, 224
poverty-trauma 220
power of reflexivity 85
Prague Spring in 1968 219
Praxis 8, 75, 93, 124–5, 127, 130
Principles of Political Economy (Mill) 33
privatization 54, 63
privilege narratives 160
problem-based education 128
problem-based learning (PBL) 72, 125, 127, 128, 133, 150, 254 n.19

problem-oriented projects (PPL) 128–9, 140, 142, 144
progressive education movement 154
progressive education theory 141
property 25, 27, 117
prospect theory 101
proto-superego 108
Prussian-Danish war of 1848–51 70
psilocybin 203, 205–7
psychedelics 203–8, 222
   effect on trauma 204
psychoanalysis 81, 92, 96, 102–4, 108, 111, 113, 151
   of collapse, Žižek's 108
psychoanalytic grief 145
psychology 2, 9, 30, 75, 83, 85, 92, 97, 100–3, 125, 129–30, 132, 150, 152, 155, 166, 169
PTSD, *see* post-traumatic stress disorder (PTSD)
Putin, Vladimir 44, 107, 131

Queer liberation 182
queer(ness) 8, 94, 139, 157, 174, 182, 227, 262 n.35

race and gender oppression, *see* oppression, race and gender
race/racism 8, 27, 40, 52–5, 60, 110, 129, 130, 164, 177, 178, 188, 214
racial discrimination 161, 168
Rand, Ayn 29, 32
(University) rankings 66, 246 n.38
Reagan, Ronald 62
reflection 75, 96–7, 102, 125, 136, 145–9, 152, 188, 190, 195, 216–17
   self 85

INDEX

reparations/repairing 27, 54, 87, 113, 121, 133, 141
reproductive justice 183
reproductive labour of women 27, 164
residential schools 52, 121
The Retreat of the State (Strange) 64
Revolutionary Learning (Carpenter and Mojab) 130
revolutionary movements of the 1960s 61
Ricardo, David 32–3, 35
Rifkin, Jeremy 37
Road to Serfdom (Hayek) 62
Romania 2, 107, 112, 161, 163
romantic love 210–13
Roskilde University 75–8, 142–3
  architecture of the university 76
  Danish Student Union (DSU) 75–6
  disciplinary specializations 76
  problem-oriented, participant-directed project learning (PPL) 76
  social reality 76
Rosling, Hans 170
Ross, Loretta J. 188
Rotterdam Arts and Sciences Lab 136
Ryan, Richard 132

Salling Olesen, Henning 73, 127
Sanders, Bernie 106
Sartre, Jean-Paul 74, 93, 120, 135
Say, Jean-Baptiste 35, 51
Schmidt, Henk 127
school choice 54
Schuman, Lee 133
Schumpeter, Joseph 26
scientific endeavour 28
Second World War 42, 49, 135

segregation 53–4
self-actualization 171
Self-Determination Theory (SDT) 132–3
self-identity 115
self-love 184–5, 208–11
self-preservation 124, 210
service learning 140
Servigne, Pablo 11
sexual violence 116, 188
Simpson, Leanne 30, 120–1
'small-t' trauma 170–1
Smil, Vaclav 41, 119, 179, 226
Smith, Adam 25, 29, 32
smog 23
social awakening 87
socialism 34, 87
social justice
  fixation 176, 191
  literature 174
  movements 77, 159, 173–7
social psychology 101
society of radical freedom, Giddens' 116
socio-economic collapse 24–6, 40
sociological imagination 75, 148, 155
Sociological Imagination (C.Wright) 75, 148
solidarity, loving in
  impetus for solidarity 214–15
  practitioners of 214–15
  principles of imperfect solidarity in action 215–18
  self-protection programmes 216
Sozialepolitik 34
stagflation (stagnation and inflation) 62
standardizing language 50
stationary state/steady state 32–3, 39–40

Steffen, Will   15
Stengers, Isabelle   120, 141
Stevens, Raphaël   11
Stockholm Resilience Centre   12–13
Stoll-Kleemann, Susanne   98
storm   15, 17–18, 41, 62, 78, 109, 136
  Eunice   3
Strange, Susan   64
Stratospheric Aerosol Injections (SAI)   24
stratospheric ozone depletion   12
student debt   63–4
Suez Canal   43
superego   102, 103, 108, 176
surveillance system, China's   116

Tata Institute of Social Sciences in Mumbai   77
Teaching Community (bell hooks)   54, 130, 211
teaching profession   192, 197–8, 205
Teaching to Transgress (bell hooks)   130, 253 n.4, 254 n.8
technological innovation   26, 88
techno-optimism   18
Thatcher, Margaret   62
Theory of Comparative Advantages (Ricardo)   32
Theory of Human Capital (Becker)   164
thermo-industrial civilization   12, 40, 87, 107
This Changes Everything (Klein)   24
3Rs (reading, writing and arithmetic)   50

Times Higher Education Ranking   66
Titanic   16
trauma   176–7
  big-T' trauma   170
  class and racial   161
  of collapse in educational spaces   159
  conversations about   179–80, 185
  cycle of   1
  description   169–70
  education's power to overcome   8
  effect of psychedelics on   204
  of environmental loss   111
  impact of   170
  individualism and   169–72
  intergenerational   171
  neuropsychiatry of   169
  permanent   107
  personal   57, 156
  poverty-   160, 220
  psychoanalytical experience of collapse   110
  rage   176
  responses- fight, flight, freeze and fawn   169
  shock   79
  'small-t' trauma   170
  teaching through   190–5
    fight reflex   193
    flight reactions   191
    freeze reaction   192
    freeze reflex   193–4
    trauma-informed teaching practices   192
  theory   92, 169
trauma-informed teaching practices   68, 192
Trump, Donald   87–8, 171
Tsing, Anna Lowenhaupt   141, 150
Tunca, Suzan   136

INDEX

Ubuntu in rural Zimbabwean communities 162
Ukraine, Russian invasion of 1, 3, 31, 43, 44, 100, 101, 107, 118, 131, 249 n.16
Unbearable Lightness of Being (Kundera) 163
UN Food and Agriculture Organisation 21
United Nations Environment Programme report of 2021 15
Universal Basic Income (UBI) 106
Universal Declaration of Human Rights 52, 116
Untouchables 170, 179
Urban, Tim 130, 157
utilitarianism 117
utility 117
  maximization principle 35

vaccines, COVID-19 140
van der Kolk, Bessel 169, 203, 222
violence 20, 31, 49, 107, 153
  domestic 56, 169
  endemic gendered 214
  political 89
  public 116
  sexual 116, 188
  against women 41, 188
vocational school 57–8
Vygostky, Lev
  work on language 132
  Zone of Proximal Development 132

Walker, Pete 169–70, 172, 191
Walras, Leon 34
Warren, Elizabeth 106
Watson, William 173
The Wealth of Nations (Smith) 25
welfare state 4, 12, 31, 34, 40, 52, 63
wet markets 22
What Are Universities For (Collini) 60
When the Body Says No (Maté) 169
Whitcomb, Alex 215
White privilege 178
White saviourism 177
White-supremacist imperialist capitalist patriarchy 173
White supremacy(ist) 28, 53
Wieland, Christoph Martin 70
wilderness 21–3
The Woman Destroyed (De Beauvoir) 211
working-from-home 5, 89
working-group scenario 147
World Bank 42
World Health Organisation (WHO) 23–4, 81
World Trade Organisation 42
World War
  First 42
  Second 49, 135
  Third 11
World Wildlife Fund 13
Wright, Mills, C. 75, 148

Zambia 178, 215, 224
Zimbabwe 6–7, 53, 56, 59, 81, 89, 153, 161–2, 200, 215, 224, 226, 258 n.70
Zimbabwe Karate Union 215
Žižek, Slavoj 102–8, 210, 211
zoonotic diseases 23